Józef Baniak

The Image of the Priest in the Awareness of Polish Youth

Development in Humanities

edited by

Zbigniew Drozdowicz
(General Editor)

and Sławomir Sztajer

Volume 11

LIT

Józef Baniak

The Image of the Priest in the Awareness of Polish Youth

A Sociological Study

LIT

NARODOWY PROGRAM
ROZWOJU HUMANISTYKI

The present thesis has been financed as a part of a programme of the Ministry of Science and Higher Education, which is called: the National Programme for the Development of Humanities (NPRH)

Typesetting by Michał Staniszewski

This book is printed on acid-free paper.

Bibliographic information published by the Deutsche Nationalbibliothek
The Deutsche Nationalbibliothek lists this publication in the Deutsche Nationalbibliografie; detailed bibliographic data are available in the Internet at http://dnb.d-nb.de.

ISBN 978-3-643-90380-8

A catalogue record for this book is available from the British Library

Klosbachstr. 107
CH-8032 Zürich
Tel. +41 (0) 44-251 75 05
Fax +41 (0) 44-251 75 06
E-Mail: zuerich@lit-verlag.ch
http://www.lit-verlag.ch

LIT VERLAG Dr. W. Hopf
Berlin 2013
Fresnostr. 2
D-48159 Münster
Tel. +49 (0) 2 51-62 03 20
Fax +49 (0) 2 51-23 19 72
E-Mail: lit@lit-verlag.de
http://www.lit-verlag.de

Distribution:
In Germany: LIT Verlag Fresnostr. 2, D-48159 Münster
Tel. +49 (0) 2 51-620 32 22, Fax +49 (0) 2 51-922 60 99, E-mail: vertrieb@lit-verlag.de
In Austria: Medienlogistik Pichler-ÖBZ, e-mail: mlo@medien-logistik.at
In the UK: Global Book Marketing, e-mail: mo@centralbooks.com
In North America: International Specialized Book Services, e-mail: orders@isbs.com
e-books are available at www.litwebshop.de

Contents

Introduction

Representatives of various branches of the humanities and social sciences, including sociologists of religion and the Church, deal theoretically and empirically with institutional priesthood as a specific vocation and profession of a religious profile. Literature on the subject in question indicates that more often, theoretical and analytical studies are devoted to the phenomenon of the priesthood,[1] rather than in-depth empirical research studies of a sociological and psychological profile on the subject. These include the social determinants and dynamics of priestly and religious vocations in different time intervals,[2] or the social perception of the hierarchical nature of the priesthood,[3] or indicate a discrepancy between the official and environmental models of the priest.[4] However, most often there is interest in the priesthood fragmentarily

---

[1] Cf. H. Carrier, *Sociologie du Christianisme. Bibliographie Internationale*, Roma 1975; J. Baniak, *Socjologia religii i religijności. Bibliografia prac polskich i przekładów obcych za lata 1929–1979* [Sociology of Religion and Religiosity. Bibliography of Polish Works and Foreign Translations from 1929–1979], Warsaw 1981; idem, "Bibliografia ważniejszych prac w języku polskim na temat powołań duchownych, kapłaństwa i życia zakonnego w latach 1945–1994" [Bibliography of Important Works in Polish on the Topic of Clerical Vocations, Priesthood and Religious Life from 1945–1994], in idem, *Dynamika powołań kapłańskich i zakonnych w Kościele rzymskokatolickim w Polsce w latach 1900–1994. Studium socjograficzne* [Dynamics of Priestly and Religious Life Vocations in the Roman Catholic Church in Poland from 1900 to 1994. A Socio-Graphics Study], Cracow 1997, pp. 193–252.

[2] Cf. P. Taras, *Społeczne uwarunkowania i motywy wstąpienia do zakonnego seminarium duchownego* [Social Conditions and Motivations for Entering the Religious Order Seminary], Poznan – Warsaw 1972; J. Baniak, *Dynamika powołań kapłańskich i zakonnych w Kościele rzymskokatolickim w Polsce w latach 1900–1994...* [Dynamics of Priestly and Religious Life Vocations in the Roman Catholic Church in Poland from 1900 to 1994...], op. cit.; K. Pawlina, *Kandydaci do kapłaństwa trzeciego tysiąclecia* [Candidates to the Priesthood in the Third Millenium], Warsaw 2002; A. Postawa, *Powołania kapłańskie w Towarzystwie Salezjańskim w Polsce* [The Priestly Vocation in the Salesian Society in Poland], Cracow 2005.

[3] Cf. J. Majka (ed.), *Osobowość kapłańska* [Priestly Personality], Wroclaw 1976.

[4] Cf. P. Taras, "Problem modelu kapłana w Kościele katolickim" [The Problem with the Model Priest in the Catholic Church], *Znak*, 1968, no. 20, pp. 1110–1127; J. Baniak, "Model

or "additionally" within broader studies on the prestige and development of professions,[5] as well as studies involving the authority[6] and role of the priest in the Church and society.[7] In the late 1980s, sociological studies were performed for the first time in Poland on the image of the priest inherent to the religious and social awareness of adult lay Catholics.

The results of these studies have been published in a compact monograph[8] and several sub-articles.[9] Yet there is still no sociological research on this topic among a representative group of respondents nationwide who would represent the general attitude of Polish Catholics towards the priesthood, parish priests and the religious. Perceptions of high school youth of the institutional priesthood and their personal attitude towards priests were already tested in a narrow range in the eighties of the twentieth century.[10] This topic was undertaken in the wider range of social science research in the years

kapłana diecezjalnego w Kościele katolickim. Analiza socjologiczno-teologiczna" [The Diocesan Priest Model in the Catholic Church. A Sociological and Theological Analysis], *Człowiek i Światopogląd*, 1987, no. 8, pp. 72–86.

[5] Cf. A. Sarapata, "Z badań nad prestiżem zawodów w Polsce" [From Studies on Professional Prestige in Poland], in A. Sarapata (ed.), *Przemiany struktury społecznej w Polsce i w ZSRR* [Change in the Social Structure in Poland and in the USSR], Warsaw 1965, pp. 126–134; E. Ciupak, "Kapłaństwo: powołanie i zawód" [Priesthood: Vocation and Profession], in idem, *Kult religijny i jego społeczne podłoże* [Religious Cult and its Social Foundation], Warsaw 1965, pp. 391–414; J. Baniak, "Aksjologiczny wymiar zawodu księdza" [Axiological Dimension of the Priest's Profession], *Studia Socjologiczne*, 1989, no. 4, pp. 215–232.

[6] Cf. J. Mariański, "Autorytet księdza – aspekty socjologiczne" [Priestly Authority – sociological aspects], *Chrześcijanin w Świecie*, 1977, no. 50, pp. 74–94; J. Baniak, "Autorytet księży parafialnych (cz. 1)" [Authority of Parish Priests (part 1)], *Przegląd Powszechny*, 1998, no. 2, pp. 150–163; idem, "Autorytet księży parafialnych" (cz. 2)," [Authority of Parish Priests (part 2)], *Przegląd Powszechny*, 1998, no. 3, pp. 325–337; W. Piwowarski, "Tradycyjny autorytet księdza w procesie przemian" [Traditional Priestly Authority in Transition], in W. Piwowarski (ed.), *Religijność ludowa – ciągłość i zmiana*, Wroclaw 1983, pp. 129–151.

[7] Cf. W. Goddijn, "Rola kapłana w Kościele i w społeczeństwie" [Role of the Priest in Church and Society], *Znak*, 1966, no. 139–140, pp. 6–21; J. Baniak, "Kapłan jako typ roli społecznej" [Priest as a Type of Social Role], in I. Borowik, W. Zdaniewicz (ed.), *Od Kościoła ludu do Kościoła wyboru. Religia a przemiany społeczne w Polsce* [From the Church of the People to the Church of Choice. Religion and Social Change in Poland], Cracow 1996, pp. 148–175.

[8] Cf. J. Baniak, *Obraz kapłana w świadomości katolików świeckich (na przykładzie Kalisza, Kotłowa i Przedborowa). Studium socjologiczne* [The Image of the Priest in the Awareness of Lay Catholics based on Kalisz, Kotłowa and Przedborowa. Sociological Studies], Poznan 1994.

[9] Cf. J. Baniak, "Obraz kapłana w świadomości współczesnych katolików polskich" [The Image of a Priest in the Awareness of Contemporary Catholics in Poland], *Colloquium Salutis. Wrocławskie Studia Teologiczne*, 1988, vol. 20, pp. 221–251; J. Baniak, *Obraz kapłana w świadomości świeckich* [The Image of a Priest in the Awareness of the Laity], Poznan 1990, pp. 84–92.

[10] Cf. S. Dobrzanowski, "Młodzież o kapłaństwie i kapłanach" [Youth on Priesthood and Priests], *Chrześcijanin w Świecie*, 1977, no. 50, pp. 95–110.

1983–1998–2008, including representative groups of high school and academic students in Kalisz. The results of these studies from the years 1983–1998 were published in a compact monograph[11] and partial dissertation.[12] The results of studies carried out in the years 2007–2008 will be published in full in this study, comparing them with the results of the previous studies from the 80s and 90s of the 20th century. This comparison allows for seeing trends in the change of attitudes and evaluations of Polish youth concerning the institution of the priesthood and priests.

It is worth noting here that in the late 90s of the 20th century, for the first time in Poland, a sociological study was carried out on the crisis of priestly identity in "former" priests, concerning their resignation from the priesthood,[13] and similar research was also carried out in the years 2001–2006 among active priests (working) in the Church, whose goal was to search for the sources and causes of the crisis of priestly and professional identity in this group of Catholic priests.[14]

The results presented in this book show in a broad and objective way the knowledge of young Poles about the priesthood and their attitude towards parish priests – towards their professional role in the Church and society, including the evaluation of the authority of priests, as well as the virtues and vices of the priests they know. The lives of priests in parishes proceed differently – some are able to meet the demands of their specific profession and continue in their priestly vocation, successfully completing the mission of the Church, while others break down under the weight of these requirements, which include

[11] Cf. J. Baniak, *Ksiądz w oczach młodzieży. Obraz kapłana w świadomości młodzieży licealnej i akademickiej na przykładzie Kalisza. Studium socjologiczne* [The Priest from the Viewpoint of the Youth. The Image of the Priest in the Awareness of High School and College Youth in the Example of Kalisz. A Sociological Study], Poznan 1993.

[12] Cf. J. Baniak, "Kapłaństwo hierarchiczne w świadomości licealistów i studentów – analiza socjologiczna" [The Hierarchical Priesthood in the Awareness of High School and College Students – A Sociological Analysis], *Studia Gnesnensia*, 2000, vol. 14, pp. 285–304.

[13] Cf. J. Baniak, *Wierność powołaniu a kryzys tożsamości kapłańskiej. Studium socjologiczne na przykładzie Kościoła w Polsce* [Faithfulness to a Vocation and Priestly Identity Crisis. A Sociological Study Based on the Church in Poland], Poznan 2000; idem, *Rezygnacja z kapłaństwa i wybór życia małżeńsko-rodzinnego przez księży rzymskokatolickich w Polsce. Studium socjologiczne* [Resignation from the Priesthood and Choice of Life in Marriage and Family by Roman Catholic Priests in Poland. A Sociological Study], Cracow 2001.

[14] Cf. J. Baniak, "Czynniki kryzysu tożsamości kapłańskiej wśród księży rzymskokatolickich w Polsce. Studium socjologiczne" [Factors of Priestly Identity Crisis among Roman Catholic Priests in Poland. A Sociological Study], *Teologia Praktyczna*, 2007, vol. 8, pp. 209–264; idem, "Źródła i przyczyny kryzysu tożsamości kapłańskiej księży rzymskokatolickich w Polsce. Studium socjologiczne" [Sources and Reasons for the Identity Crisis of Roman Catholic Priests in Poland. A Sociological Study], in M. Libiszowska-Żółtkowska (ed.), *Tożsamości religijne w społeczeństwie polskim. Socjologiczne studium przypadków* [Religious Identity in Polish Society. A Sociological Case Study], Warsaw 2009, pp. 67–107.

mandatory celibacy and extensive loneliness, resulting in a profound crisis of priestly identity and giving up the practice of priesthood, returning to a secular state, starting their own community in marriage and family, mostly with women they met while working as parish priests or in other aspects of their lives.[15]

This book includes the results of three of my personal sociological research studies in the years 1983–1998–2008, which were carried out in the environment of high school students and academic youth in Kalisz, in order to determine their attitude towards the institutional priesthood. These results provide a comprehensive insight into the attitudes and behaviors of these adolescents with regards to the hierarchical priesthood and priests. Comparing them with each other, one can see if and what type of changes occurred in the religious and social images of the priesthood and the Catholic priest in the consciousness of the high school and university students surveyed, as well as their attitudes towards parish and academic ministry priests. The attitudes and behavior of my respondents towards the hierarchical priesthood and priests will be compared with the attitudes and studies of high school youth and college students, which have already been explored by other sociologists of religion working on the subject. In a narrower sense, I will also take into account the position of junior high school students regarding priesthood and parish priests, based on interviews concerning these issues conducted in the context of independent sociological research studies of their religious, ecclesiastical and moral awareness.[16]

The research topic of this broad academic dissertation, is therefore the institutional priesthood as a religious, cultural and social fact, evident in the profession of the priest, and its perception in the religious and social awareness of Polish youth. Its aim is to introduce and demonstrate the perceptions of institutional priesthood observed during three sociological research studies among high school and university students in Kalisz.[17] The results of these studies will allow me to answer fundamental questions as to whether and to

[15] Cf. J. Baniak, "Katolicki etos małżeńsko-rodzinny w świadomości »byłych« księży" [The Catholic Ethos of Marriage and Family in the Awareness of "Former" Priests], *Problemy Rodziny*, 2000, no. 6, pp. 23–30; idem, "Dlaczego księża w Polsce rezygnują z kapłaństwa?" [Why Do Priests in Poland Resign from the Priesthood?], *Przegląd Powszechny*, 2000, no. 5, pp. 158–176 and no. 6, pp. 317–324.

[16] Cf. J. Baniak, "Duchowieństwo parafialne w ocenach badanych gimnazjalistów" [Parish Clergy in the Evaluation of Surveyed Junior High Schoolers], in idem, *Między buntem a potrzebą akceptacji i zrozumienia. Świadomość religijna i moralna a kryzys tożsamości osobowej młodzieży gimnazjalnej. Studium socjologiczne* [Between Rebellion and the Need for Acceptance and Understanding. Religious and Moral Awareness and the Personality Identity Crisis of Junior High School Youth. A Sociological Study], Cracow 2008, pp. 300–352.

[17] Comp. J. Sztumski, *Wstęp do metod i technik badań społecznych* [Introduction to the Methods and Techniques of Sociological Research Studies], Katowice 1999, pp. 19–23.

what extent recent social, cultural, political and economic changes in Poland and in the transformation of the Roman Catholic Church have influenced the attitude of young Catholics towards the hierarchical priesthood and priests working in parishes and in academic pastoral ministries. From these questions also arise the research hypotheses directly related to this issue.[18] What does this concept mean, which features or elements create it, what does it include within its framework as to the essence of priestly ministry and the life of priests?

The concept of the priesthood creates a group of fundamental characteristics, functions, responsibilities, tasks and rights of the priest, which forms his religious and social role within structures of the Church, especially in the parish as an institution and community of the faithful, as perceived by Catholic youth attending junior high schools, high schools and studying at colleges in Kalisz. These young people belong to the environment as active or passive religious members of the ecclesial community. This concept of the priesthood is also composed of the opinions and evaluations of young people moving away from religion and the institutional Church, or even hostile towards the institution of the priesthood and priests, and in general towards all religious values.

Among contemporary Polish youth, negative attitudes, critical opinions and behavior hostile towards the Roman Catholic Church and parish clergy are clearly growing, and this is also evident in their relation to the institution of the hierarchical priesthood. Although these are still on a moderate scale, we can no longer ignore them, and what is more, their dynamics in youth environments are clearly on the rise and increasing in scope. The Church and the priests themselves often give young people reasons to take on such attitudes, shaping opinions and taking action detrimental to their external image. It is this concept of the priesthood, the institutional model and the image of the priest, which is demonstrated here, based on the results of my own sociological studies, conducted on high school and university students, and indirectly also on urban and rural middle school students.

These studies are based on many theoretical and practical, general and specific questions. In the first chapter of the book, these questions are set out in their entirety. However, at this point, practical questions are more important, since they allow for verification of the accepted research problems included in the design of all three sociological research studies. These questions are: How do the high school and university respondents perceive and interpret the hierarchical nature of the priesthood and its basic characteristics? Does the institutional priesthood, in their opinion, continue to designate the framework

---

[18] Cf. J. Baniak, *Desakralizacja kultu religijnego i świąt religijnych w Polsce. Studium socjologiczne* [The Desacralization of Religious Cult and the Religious World in Poland. A Sociological Study], Cracow 2007.

of a life perspective for young men trying to find their place in society, so that they would be able to resign from other important and valuable existential values to achieve it? Do the high school and university students still evaluate the hierarchical priesthood as an attractive profession, on par with other socially significant secular professions, in the sense that it may be attractive to religious men and encourage them to choose it as a personal way of life?

In the evaluation of the respondents, must the decision to choose the profession of a priest necessarily be justified by a kind of "religious vocation" in the candidate, and how do the respondents themselves understand this calling? Do the high school and university students surveyed believe that mandatory celibacy should be a basic condition for ordination to the priesthood and a precondition for hierarchical priesthood? In their opinion, should the Catholic Church abandon celibacy for its priests because of the significant problems in ecumenical Christianity? Would the high school and university students studied accept married priests with their own families as their parish priests, in academic ministries or as religious educators?

Which model of the parish priest and university chaplain do these respondents prefer, and is this model synchronized with the model of the official priest, who works in the Church currently? Which virtues and vices do the respondents perceive in the parish and academic priests familiar to them, and which virtues should characterize these priests? Do the high school and university students surveyed grant Catholic priests religious and moral authority?

Do they accept the leadership role of the priest in the ecclesial community and in their own religious life? Which professional competencies do they attribute to a parish priest? How do the researched respondents perceive and evaluate the political commitment of parish priests and Polish bishops? How do respondents themselves perceive and understand the relationship of the institutional Church to a secular state and culturally diverse nation and civil society? Do respondents maintain personal contacts and relationships with parish and academic priests and how often do they correspond?

In a more general sense, we may ask which image of the institutional priesthood and the parish priest functions in the religious and social awareness of the high school and university students surveyed, and what has shaped them? Is the noted attitude of respondents during the research towards the priesthood and priests connected with their personal faith in God and religiosity, as well as their age, level and subject of academic knowledge acquired in high school and college? What characterizes the model constructed by the parish priest in the studied high school and university students in Poland? Does this model stem from their religious needs and expectations of the type of the Church which they are looking for?

How, according to the respondents, should parish priests and academic ministers play their role in the Church and in civil society so that they can meet the expectations of the laity as well as ecclesiastical authority requirements? Does the status of a secondary school pupil or university student have an impact on his or her attitude towards the institutional Church and the clergy? These questions will be discussed in detail in the chapter on methodology, and the response to each of them will be presented in the chapters analyzing the results of the empirical research.[19]

This book consists of an introduction, seven thematic chapters, a conclusion and footnotes citing works in the text.

In the first chapter, I discuss the theoretical assumptions and methodology of my own sociological research, which is divided into two parts. In the first part, I present the institutional priesthood as a cultural phenomenon and a social fact, in terms of its sociological, psychological and theological dimensions. I also take into account the nature and purpose of the hierarchical priesthood in light of the doctrine of the Church and the indications of Vatican Council II. The analysis and evaluation of views of the surveyed high school and university students on the priesthood and priests is based on a broad approach to this central issue. In the second part, I present my personal research methodology among these respondents, meaning the central problem and the research issues, empirical hypotheses, organization and execution of environmental studies and statistical characteristics of the high school youth and university students.

In the second chapter, I discuss the young people's statements on the institutional priesthood, taking into account the following specific issues: religious vocation as a necessary criterion for selection to and endurance in the priesthood, the structure of the institutional priesthood, the circumstances conditioning the continuity of the charisma of the priesthood in the priest's daily life, social prestige of the priesthood and priests through the eyes of the interviewed young people, the authority of priests in civil society during the study period, career advancement in the priesthood in Poland during the study period, and declarations of the respondents concerning the desire to have a priest in their family.

The third chapter is devoted to the presentation of the social role of the priest, as seen through the eyes of the young people interviewed. This chapter addresses the following questions and issues: the role of the priest in sociological terms; the ministerial priesthood as the cornerstone and essence of the role

[19] Cf. J. Baniak, *Ksiądz w oczach młodzieży...* [The Priest in the Evaluation of Youth...], op. cit., pp. 9–10.

of the priest in the Church; the features and implementation of this role and conflicts related to its fullfilment by priests; the scope of the role of the priest as perceived by the interviewed youth – his mediation between God and man in matters of religion; the mutual contact between youth in schools and universities and parish priests; the youth's need to have contact and relationships with priests in different life circumstances and situations; the youth's assessment of the social and political roles of priests in Poland during this period in history.

In the fourth chapter, I discuss ideas and evaluate the respondents regarding the authority of Catholic priests in Poland, including the following specific issues: the multidimensionality of authority and its sociological understanding; the nature and source of the authority of priests in the parish community; the scope of the authority of priests in Poland during the study period as perceived by the youth; professional competence of priests in the evaluations of the respondents; the problem Polish youth's trust and confidence in the institutional Church and parish priests, and the role of the moral authority of priests in the formation of the conscience of the interviewed young people.

In the fifth chapter, I discuss the postulates of the high school and university students with regards to the model parish priest, taking into account such issues as: a sociological interpretation of the term "model" and the term "personal role-model;" model and personality model of a priest – its nature, structure and function; the psychosocial image of the priest as perceived by the young people, including his personal and professional virtues and vices; the model parish priest constructed by the respondents – a friendly person with understanding for their problems in life; Pope John Paul II as a personal role-model and the model of the modern priest minister in the evaluations of respondents.

In the sixth chapter, I present and analyze the attitudes of the young people towards compulsory celibacy for Roman Catholic priests – their views and evaluation of celibacy, including: various theoretical approaches including the necessity and universality of clerical celibacy and its criticism; the attitude of young people towards the required form of celibacy for priests; its role in the crisis of priestly vocations and in causing a "double standard" of morality for priests; and the perception of celibacy as a factor inhibiting the process of religious ecumenism in contemporary Christianity.

The seventh chapter presents the socio-religious correlates of attitudes of the young people studied towards the hierarchical priesthood and parish priests, taking into account such criteria as gender, type and degree of education, global religious creeds and religiousness, religious beliefs, religious practices; I also take into account changes in the attitudes of respondents towards institutional priesthood and priests over a period of 25 years.

In conclusion, I present a synthesis of all three sociological research studies, and at the same time point out the basic trends in the views and attitudes of Polish youth towards institutional priesthood and priests. I also postulate the need for sociological research on a nationwide statistical sample of young people, to gain further understanding of this important cognitive issue.

This study could be carried out thanks to the kindness and support of many different individuals and institutions, in particular, my respondents – the students, including middle school students – who have played a personal role in these studies and carefully responded to numerous survey questions. I thank them all most cordially. Many thanks also to the reviewers of this work, who became thoroughly familiar with its original content and wished to improve its overall cognitive quality with their personal insights and critical comments. I am also grateful to the publishers of this book for their effort to compile and publish it in an attractive layout.

This book aims to enrich the scientific knowledge and sociology of the Roman Catholic Church in Poland and its priests serving during the given period of 25 years. The portrayals by academic youth and high school students and, indirectly, junior high school students, serve as study material. However, the contents of this work do not solve the addressed problems, often taken as a whole, but more often present and highlight their many dimensions, while inviting different readers to continue discussions on this religiously important and socially interesting topic. If I have succeeded in this goal, at least to some extent, then the book will also play its proper role as an original message and communiqué on this important cognitive topic in civil society and democratic structures of the Church.

Chapter I

Theoretical and methodological assumptions of the sociological research

1. Institutional priesthood as a religious and cultural phenomenon and social fact

Edward Ciupak, in analyzing the lineage of the institution of the priesthood, rightly wrote 35 years ago that "the institution of the priesthood in cultures where the phenomenon of religious life is massive presents an interesting object of research. Priests are the leaders of religious life, heads of formal institutions and informal groups, educators and moralists. In fulfilling these functions, they influence a number of non-religious matters of public interest. The priesthood is properly the subject of interdisciplinary interests, that is: theology, history of religion and the Church, pedagogy, psychology, social engineering, sociology and others. A group of factors specific to the priest developed from a historical point of view as a result of the social division of labor within the group. Henri Spencer,[1] deriving the institution of the priesthood from the original polytheistic religion, is of the view that it arose as a result of the social division of activities within the group. Originally, the priestly functions were combined in one person with the functions of the wizard, exorcist, prophet, physician, chief of the tribe, etc. Later, as the social hierarchy develops and magical and religious activities are isolated through increasing specialization, a special group of people is created, dedicated to cultic activities. In the social division of labor, priests were excluded from production activities and therefore, in many cultures, they initiated many fields of art and science. For

---

[1] Cf. H. Spencer, *Instytucje religijne* [Religious Institutions], Warsaw 1981.

our purposes, it is important to separate two basic periods in the evolution of the priestly institution – Mosaic and Christian,"[2] Spencer presents the nature and specificity of the Christian priesthood, and notes that "[...] The Christian priesthood, though it differs from the institution of the sacramental nature of the priesthood in the religions of the past [...], was formed similarly in terms of hierarchy and power. [...] In Christianity, especially Catholicism, priesthood is a professional institution which adheres to two basic criteria: activities meant for others and requiring prior preparation."[3]

The hierarchical priesthood falls best into three different aspects or dimensions: theological, psychological and sociological. These aspects together completely and accurately reflect the nature and character of the original institution of the priesthood. Therefore, further analysis will focus on these three aspects of the priesthood. Explanation of its origin and evolution through the prism of these aspects is essential in this study, because it will facilitate the analysis and evaluation of the attitudes of the young high school and university students towards the priesthood and priests, forming the image of the religious awareness of all respondents.

a) The sociological dimension of institutional priesthood

The sociological dimension of the hierarchical priesthood is understood as an attitude and action formed and carried out under the influence of a confrontation between the personal needs and aspirations of appointed individuals with the needs and aspirations of their reference group. Under this assumption – as Piotr Taras notes – the priesthood can be defined as a predisposition of a man to: a) an appropriate way of life; b) acceptance and implementation of specific values and religious services, c) identify himself with a particular social group – with the state of priesthood.[4] Thus, the social dimension of the priesthood is closely related to a socio-religious group, so it has a community characteristic. The profession of a priest requires holding religious services for the faithful and a social mandate – authorization, approval and setting a goal. For this reason, the ministerial priesthood takes the form of a social contract or a contract as a social fact. This contract signifies a type of social commitment, which is governed by ecclesiastical law and religious and moral norms, directly designed by and exclusive to the clerical state. Practically, the

[2] Comp. E. Ciupak, *Kapłaństwo: powołanie i zawód* [Priesthood: Vocation and Profession], in idem, *Kult religijny i jego społeczne podłoże* [The Religious Cult and its Social Basis], Warsaw 1965, pp. 391–391.

[3] Ibidem, p. 393.

[4] Cf. P. Taras, *Społeczne uwarunkowania i motywy wstąpienia do zakonnego seminarium duchownego* [Social Conditions and Motivation for Entering a Religious Order Seminary], Poznan 1972, p. 14.

subjects of a priest's obligations, by the will of the Church, are ministries of the priesthood intended for the laity. A candidate for the priesthood, accepting the demands of the Church, undertakes to voluntarily and consciously respect and implement the laws relating to the priestly state – to adopt a proper lifestyle and fulfill the tasks belonging to the priest. As a result of accepting this, the bishop grants him priestly ordination, and allows him to enjoy the privileges of the clergy. Correct completion of these tasks requires the priest to possess relevant qualifications and abilities, time and strength, meaning analogous personal predispositions that are necessary for the effective performance of every profession. The priesthood in sociological terms is a profession of a religious nature, fulfilling all the parameters of the profession. This interpretation also includes the religious life of women and men in contemplative communities and active congregations, in which prayer as primary occupation is an ordinary effort, analogous to intellectual work, and by accomplishing it, priests and the religious are able to earn a living personally and in the religious community.[5]

Within the institutional priesthood can be identified all the basic features of a profession,[6] which, though very specific and exceptional, share the main objective of meeting the religious, moral, spiritual and other (even physical) needs of people gathering in a parish community or in other circumstances. Piotr Taras notes that these dimensions of the priesthood do not fail to work well even when performed in a religious community, because it helps the priest to work, protects him, provides for his existence, and gives him social prestige.[7] The parish priest has these conditions provided by the diocesan bishop and the residents of the parish, to whom he was sent by the power of ecclesiastical authority. It is impossible to ignore, in the analysis of the specificity of the hierarchical priesthood, its professional nature. Priesthood as a social fact and religious profession can be analyzed from a sociological point of view, namely in terms of contacts, relationships, activities and social institutions, which are secondary conditions and causes of its appearance and performance. Fulfilling these conditions, the gifted charismatic religious vocation can make a free decision to join the priestly state and remain in it for life. Sometimes these conditions make it difficult or impossible for an individual to become a priest or continue in the profession and vocation of the priesthood.

---

[5] Cf. J. Baniak, "Powołania zakonne w Polsce – analiza socjologiczna" [Religious Life Vocations in Poland – A Sociological Analysis], *Ruch Prawniczy, Ekonomiczny i Socjologiczny*, 1986, no. 1, pp. 279–300.

[6] Comp. O. Schreuder, "Le caractère Professionnel du sacerdoce," *Social Compass*, 1965, no. 1–2, pp. 5–15; R. P. Rankin, "Professionalization of the Calling: Functional Implication," *Social Compass*, 1963, no. 2, pp. 112–124; J. Baniak, "Aksjologiczny wymiar zawodu księdza" [The Axiological Dimension of the Priestly Profession], *Studia Socjologiczne*, 1989, no. 4, pp. 215–232.

[7] Comp. P. Taras, *Społeczne uwarunkowania...* [Social Conditions...], op. cit., p. 16.

Hierarchical priesthood is a specific historical and social reality, and therefore it is perceived as a peculiar "whole" made up of many different elements. The priesthood does not exist as a real or actual reality: only priests are real, those who play their professional role as priests, fulfilling their part in this framework as an intermediary between religious people and God, and yet forming a distinct social and professional group, which has features not found in other social groups and professions, distinguishing them from lay Catholics. The social dimension of the institutional priesthood is a particular value for those men who freely choose it as their own profession, their way of life and public career. Such men also take into account the social need for the profession of a priest and other tasks performed by him in the parish and in other circumstances for the operation of the Church, not forgetting that the religious ministry (work) of a priest follows directly from the nature and purpose of the priesthood.[8] A religious man chooses the priestly profession because he sees the ideals of goodness and beauty in working for other people, so he intends to make a career of this work and thus adheres to the expected values. He is interested in this profession because of the direct and extensive contacts with different people and the possibility of his influencing their attitudes and actions in different circumstances and situations. Through the prism of these opportunities, he sees value in the priesthood that does not exist in other professions that are within his capabilities. Thus, he makes the priesthood his own purpose and profession in life. In another situation, maybe due to coercion, pressure or developmental deficits, the choice of this specific profession would be impossible or illogical and senseless.[9]

The social status of the Catholic priesthood, meaning the occupied place in society, really depends on various factors, among which the following three are most important: a) the attitude of priests towards values accepted as essential in a given society, b) the ideas of the public about the role and functions of parish priests and in assessing the suitability of tasks for people's religion and morality, c) the degree of integration (unification) of priests into society and their participation in commonly accepted patterns of behavior. The social status of priests also significantly determines the type of group evaluating their social usefulness. Religious people and non-religious people, inhabitants of a rural or urban parish or industrial workers and intellectuals, the elderly

---

[8] Cf. J. Baniak, *Ksiądz w oczach młodzieży. Obraz kapłana w świadomości młodzieży licealnej i akademickiej na przykładzie Kalisza. Studium socjologiczne* [The Priest in the Eyes of the Youth. The Image of the Priest in the Awareness of High School and College Youth in the Example of Kalisz. A Sociological Study], Poznan 1993, p. 16.

[9] Comp. L. Dingemans, "Przyczynek do socjologii powołań," in F. Houtart (ed.), *Socjologia religii* [Sociology of Religion], transl. Z. Skórzyńska, Warsaw 1962, pp. 146–147.

and young people or children evaluate the priest differently. However, global society judges the social status of priests and monks, taking into account the nature of their religious life and their primary roles, the effectiveness of their impact on the religion and morals of people. The social status of a priest is also dictated by such factors as his relationship to cultural values as important in society, the type and level of humanistic education and vocational services, current civilization and economic changes, the appropriate attitude of people towards the institutional Church and the clergy, the political involvement of clergy in the country and their practical materialism and level of personal morality. These factors may reduce the authority of priests in a society and, consequently, cause loss of interest in the priestly profession in the religious environment of male youth.[10]

b) The psychological and religious dimensions of institutional priesthood

How do you determine the hierarchical nature of the priesthood from a psychological point of view? What is the priestly awareness of a priest in psychological terms? The answers to these questions is by no means simple and easy, but they can help us understand the essence of the priesthood in this very aspect, even as a specific way of life. The ministerial priesthood, seen from a psychological point of view, is a specific and unique way of life, and should have as its foundation a theological concept. The priesthood is not only the priest's personal way of life, but it will follow the path of the priesthood of Jesus, after whom the priest must follow if he wants to entrust his own priestly conduct to the priesthood of Jesus. The ministerial priesthood of a priest is psychologically understandable only through the prism of the priesthood of Jesus, which is for him the source and foundation of the priestly charisma. This interpretation of the priesthood and attitude of a priest towards his priesthood guarantees the priest acceptance and understanding in the community of the faithful laity. The priest therefore cannot understand and realize his priesthood differently than did Jesus himself – the Priest. Only then will he fulfill his tasks in accordance with the will of Jesus and the expectations of religious people. Consequently, a priest should be the servant of all people in need of help, give himself up for them, and serve them through his priesthood. In his priesthood, a priest fulfills the mission of Jesus, presently continuing it in the Church, among the faithful waiting for his religious ministry. In the name of Jesus, the priest must sacrifice for the people fully and undividedly in order to

---

[10] Cf. J. Baniak, *Ksiądz w oczach młodzieży...* [The Priest in the Eyes of the Youth...], op. cit., pp. 17–18.

exercise his priesthood. The priest therefore does not work alone, but through his priesthood Jesus works in him and Jesus Christ himself works with the priest, even when the life of a priest deviates from the Gospel message and Catholic moral principles.[11]

On the other hand, the priest must proceed so that his life will be in accord with the teachings of the Church and Catholic morality, which he officially proclaims to lay Catholics, and he must strive to ensure that his life be holy like the holiness of Jesus. The priest, theologians state, not only preaches the Gospel, but should show it through every aspect of his priestly life,[12] which distinguishes him from lay people. The priest ought to present a visible unity of vocation and existence, the connection of the sacramental and the objective holiness of his office and his personal holiness. This unity will allow him to influence the religiosity of the people effectively. Such holiness is demanded of priests by lay faithful, so that for them and through them he is different from them and encourages them to achieve it in everyday life. Hans Urs von Balthasar notes that the priest, by his holiness, is to be a sign of freedom, objective and disinterested activity for the good of other people, a sign of humility for properly understanding the meaning and purpose of this temporal life. Lay people want to see him as an authentic moral authority, a model of ethics as a reference for their own lives. He must convince others to accept the Gospel through his own consistency in matters of life and ethics, religiosity, and his commitment to the priesthood.[13] However, the priest is not obliged to be holy "differently" from other people, the lay faithful, to whom he explains the principles of holiness.[14]

The priesthood is a permanent way of life for a priest, it is an eternal "call" for a priest based on unity between his office and existence, between objective holiness and subjective holiness. For this reason priesthood involves a man called and unconditionally committed to exercise this ministry, meaning for his entire life, even when the priest leaves the priesthood and becomes a secular man again. G. Bachl believes that a man must give up all his time for the priest-

---

[11] Cf. G. Greshake, *Być kapłanem – teologia i duchowość urzędu kapłańskiego* [Being a Priest – the Theology and Spirituality of the Priestly Office], transl. K. Wójtowicz, Wroclaw 1983, pp. 131–132; J. Danielou, "Der priesterliche Dienst bei den griechischen Kirchenvätern," in *Das apostolische Amt*, Mainz 1961, pp. 114–115.

[12] Comp. H. U. von Balthasar, "Die Gegenwart des Jesus Christus in der Einheit der Kirche," in *In der Nachfolge Jesu Christi*, Mainz 1976, p. 41; idem, "Der Priester in der Kirche," *Lebendige Seelsorge*, 1972, no. 23, pp. 11–14.

[13] Cf. H. U. von Balthasar, "Das priesterliche Amt," *Civitas*, 1968, no. 23, p. 796.

[14] Cf. F. Haarsma, "Einige pastoraltheologische Thesen uber den Priester," in *Der Priester in einer sakularisierten Welt*, Maastricht 1968, p. 108; F. Klosterman, *Gemeinde ohne Priester?*, Mainz 1981, p. 46.

hood, meaning his whole lifetime, and constantly remain in this vocation, up to and including the last moments of his life, because as a priest he was called by Jesus to make a sacrifice of his life, and it is essentially a sacrifice of time.[15] God so "planned" the life of a priest that he cannot leave his vocation, even when he decides to depart from the clerical state. Lifelong perseverance in vocation to the priesthood sometimes becomes an unbearable burden for many priests, surpassing their personal capabilities, so they abandon it and return to the secular state. Their vocation is previously affected by a crisis caused by various factors, including mandatory celibacy and the loneliness which is part and parcel of it.[16] The priesthood, therefore, is a lifelong vocation in the priest's life, continuous through every stage of his priestly biography, and every priest must be aware of this fact and its consequences.

The unity of the vocation and existence of a priest, as the basis and criterion of his priestly spirituality, can be reduced to three components: a) the style of the priestly life, which is a form of imitation of the priesthood of Jesus throughout the entire life of a priest;[17] b) to accept the priesthood and its implementation in humility as special service to others and considering himself a representative of Jesus; c) the processes in the lifetime journey of a priest marking his identity and distinctness from people and the world. These elements of priestly identity help the priest to fulfill the mission of the Church among the Catholic laity.[18] Celibacy, modesty and poverty temper a model priest, readying him to follow Jesus in the service of others. Priestly service, in the psychological aspect, is always a dignity obtaining fullness only when the priest worships God through everything, acts in the name of Jesus and for Him alone.[19] The priest must be present among his parishioners, know their problems and needs, aware of the distinctiveness of his particular mission and role in the Church and the world. This distinctiveness is not a priest's escape from the laity, it is not scorn or disdain for their issues and problems, nor closing off or isolating a priest within the narrowly understood clerical state. The priest minister should also be social and politically active, but without entering into agreements with specific political

[15] Cf. G. Bachl, "Das Gottesbild und die Entschiedenheit christlicher Berufung," in *Priesterbild im Wandel*, Linz 1976, pp. 159–160.

[16] Cf. J. Baniak, *Wierność powołaniu a kryzys tożsamości kapłańskiej. Studium socjologiczne na przykładzie Kościoła w Polsce* [Faithfulness to Vocation and Priestly Identity Crisis. A Sociological Case Study of the Church in Poland], Poznan 2000; idem, *Rezygnacja z kapłaństwa i wybór życia małżeńsko-rodzinnego przez księży rzymskokatolickich w Polsce. Studium socjologiczne*, Cracow 2001.

[17] Cf. H. J. Venetz, *So fing es mit der Kirche an*, Zurich – Einsiedeln – Köln 1981, pp. 75–80.

[18] Cf. G. Lofhink, "Paulinische Theologie in der Rezeption der Pastoralbriefe," in *Paulus in des neutestamentlichen Spatschriften*, Freiburg – Basel – Wien 1981, pp. 80–81.

[19] Comp. H. U. von Balthasar, "Priesterliche Existenz," in *Sponsa Verb*, Einsiedeln 1961, pp. 399–403.

groups. Psychologists of religion add that the basic criterion of priestly self-understanding and self-determination, confirming the accuracy and authenticity of a particular priest's vocation to the priesthood, and his understanding the essence of his priestly ministry, is his personal prayer life, based on faith in God. Karl Rahner rightly stated that "[...] the faith of today's priest is the faith of the priest who prays, one could simply say – the priest of mystical contemplation, otherwise he does not have it at all."[20]

Edward Ciupak adds in this context that the psychological and sociological aspects indicate the subjective-objective placement of the charisma of priestly vocations in the personal and social life of a man "selected" for priestly ministry in the Church. In his view, the theological definition of the priesthood results in very important sociological consequences from which we learn the main characteristics of the priest. These features are as follows: "1) The priest comprises a cultural institution in the sense that the essence of his activity is communing with divinity [...], by which communing is conceived as something continuous and regular [...]; 2) the priest may be defined as a group of social roles, conditioned historically and by the current needs of the Church. The priest acts as a philosopher, because he deals with the interpretation of the world and man, explains the meaning of life and through his cultic activities gives this interpretation a symbolic meaning; in the role as guardian of 'God's Law' reflecting cosmic moral and ritual order; the technique of meditation, prayer and worship, able to 'effectively' use tools in contact with the deity; the organizer of public worship and individual religiousness; a teacher and educator; a judge, setting certain penalties for certain crimes to members of a group; the leaders of formal groups (parishes, dioceses, religious associations) and the leaders of informal groups in solidarity with religious ideology; and finally as a mediator and administrator in secular matters. This combination of roles is characterized by two extreme polar characteristics: contemplation and active work, the first of which characterizes a priest institutionally, the other functionally."[21] It seems that this can be considered a fully objective approach to the institutional priesthood, taking into account all the fundamental and inalienable characteristics – religious and secular – because it is embedded in these two spheres of human life.

---

[20] Comp. K. Rahner, *Knechte Christi*, Freiburg 1967, p. 42.

[21] E. Ciupak, *Kapłaństwo...* [Priesthood...], op. cit., pp. 397–398; comp. J.-P. Audet, "Priester in der christlichen Gemeinde," in *Der priestliche Dienst*, Freiburg – Basel – Wien 1970, pp. 116–175; O. Schreuder, "Le caractère professionel du sacerdoce," op. cit., pp. 5–10; W. Kasper, "Sein und Sendung des Priesters, Geist und Leben," *Zeitschrift für Askese und Mystik*, 1978, no. 51, pp. 206–208.

c) Institutional Priesthood in the Assumptions of Catholic Theology

In the opinion of theologians, the theological aspect is the foundation of the institutional priesthood and points to its sacramental character.[22] The theological definition assumes that "[...] In the Catholic Church, a priest is one who possesses the power of consecrating, absolving and administering the other sacraments, and priesthood is the authority and dignity of an intermediary between man and deity."[23] In terms of Catholic theology, the priesthood is a kind of office that an individual person established as priest fulfills among lay people in order to assist them in meeting their religious needs and ensures their religious and moral development. The priest's office, according to theologians, is a charismatic gift, or a unique talent, specific service and a special function, perceived among many other charisms in the Church community.[24] The main task of this office is to integrate, coordinate and stimulate a variety of charisms, talents, services, roles and functions among the members of the Church, in order to effectively lead them to unity, exchange and reciprocity.[25] The priest's office understood in this way does not spring from Christology and is not the vocation, mission and power granted to the priest by Jesus, but rather it is a form of representation of the institution of the Church, and only then represents Jesus, who is the source and foundation of the Church and her faith.[26]

Therefore, the priest holds an ecclesiastical office, and his priestly ministry is sacramental because the Church is by nature a sacrament, and Her sacramentality is made concrete by providing other people with sacraments, including the sacrament of holy orders. In this way, as Leo Boff teaches: "[...] priestly ordination in the person of the priest (the priestly material) is the focus of the entire Church and gives them the function to which they are called, a clear, public, organized and official character. This accompanies preaching and the celebration of the mysteries of Christ."[27] This concept prevents the excessive extension of the scope of the priestly office, placing it precisely in the community of the baptized and confirmed, and at the same time leading the priest beyond its structures. In this way, the reality of the

[22] Cf. G. Greshake, *Być kapłanem...* [Being a Priest...], op. cit., pp. 22–25; K. Rahner, "Theologische Reflexionen zum Priesterbild von heute und morgen," *Schriften zur Theologie*, 1970, no. 9, pp. 380–381; B.-D. Marliangeas, *Clés pour une théologie du ministère*, Paris 1978, pp. 46–52.

[23] Cf. M. Kowalewski, *Mały słownik teologiczny*, Poznan 1960, p. 184.

[24] Cf. G. Greshake, *Być kapłanem...* [Being a Priest...], op. cit., p. 22.

[25] Comp. H. Küng, *Wozu Priester?*, Zurich – Einsiedeln – Köln 1971, p. 69.

[26] Cf. E.J. Kilmartin, "Apostolic Office: Sacrament of Christ," *Theologie Studien*, 1975, no. 36, pp. 243–264.

[27] L. Boff, *Die Neuentdeckung der Kirche*, Mainz 1980, p. 106.

Church is greater than the office, because it includes this office and the laity. The office first of all serves the community of believers. Sacramental Holy Orders, as an introduction to the office, are an act of the Church. Hans Küng sees the act as "[...] a public calling of the believer to serve through directing, in which the Church recognizes and confirms God's call. This entails the establishment of the spiritual legitimacy of the religious community (parish) and of the priest himself."[28]

This concept of the office of priesthood is questioned by many theologians, who accuse it of ambiguity and lack of precision in terms of the central issue. In their opinion, they cannot agree with the proposition that the priest's office does not come directly from Jesus, but it is a function of the Church. These theologians maintain that the Church owes its existence solely to Jesus, who is the Head and the highest Authority. The Church is a community that is called, gathered and maintained by its very founder – Jesus Christ through his word and work. The Church has its reason for existing beyond itself, and not in itself.[29] Like the Church, the priest's office does not depend on the will of the community of believers, for Jesus calls and creates the Church, who is still living in the Church. Fulfilling this office requires being called and ordained. Validation of the office of priesthood is done by the will and grace of Jesus.[30]

In light of this concept, holy orders mean something more than public responsibility for carrying out the duties of the Church in performing the ritual prayer and imposition of hands by a bishop on the head of the ordained man. Rather, they represent a kind of "expropriation" of the person, taking him away from himself, so that in effect, he becomes a visible sign of Christ acting in His Church.[31] The priest's office, therefore, comes directly from Jesus and constitutes His representation in the structures of the Church. The priest represents Jesus, not by virtue of his personal abilities and characteristics, but by virtue of his office, which he received from Jesus through priestly ordination. For this reason, the priest does not work through his own power and abilities, but through the will and power of Jesus and in His name.[32] Hermann Josef Pottmeyer points out that the priest's office is not "[...] some ideology of rule, but an expression of the believing Church that Christ alone is Lord of the

---

[28] H. Küng, *Wozu Priester?*, op. cit., p. 77.

[29] Cf. G. Greshake, *Być kapłanem...* [Being a Priest...], op. cit., p. 28.

[30] Comp. H. Hoffman, *Repräsentation. Studium zur Wort Und Begriffsgeschichte von der Antike bis 19. Jahrhundert*, Berlin 1974, pp. 45–53.

[31] Cf. F. Hahn, "Neutestamentliche Grundlagen für eine Lehre vom kirchlichen Amt," in *Dienst und Amt*, Regenburg 1973, p. 35.

[32] Cf. J. Baniak, *Ksiądz w oczach młodzieży...* [The Priest in the Eyes of the Youth...], op. cit., pp. 33–34.

Church."[33] It seems that Max Weber also explained the essence of the priestly office erroneously, seeing in it the realization of authority with its source in charismatic qualifications,[34] because its realization has a rather theological character as a sign of Jesus beyond His physical body.

Other theologians believe that the Christological dimension of the priesthood simply and unilaterally explains the essence and meaning of that office. In their view, the priesthood is not only the authority of Jesus, but also the authority of the Church; therefore, a priest is a preacher of the Gospel with power on behalf of the Church. Hence, the priest cannot explain anything that is not rooted in the faith of the Church. Sacraments celebrated by a priest are both sacraments of Christ and the sacraments of the Church community. Thus, the priest must have the intention of doing what the Church Herself intends to do. This is the ecclesial aspect of the priestly office, which more accurately explains the essence of the hierarchical priesthood. Ecclesiology accepts the thesis that the entire religious community celebrates the Mass through the priest's hands, not just the priest himself at Jesus' command for the community.[35] According to this theory, the priest does not just act "in persona Christi," but also "in persona Ecclesiae." Thus, the priestly office is both the representation of Christ and also the representation of the sacramental Church.[36]

If the priest leaves being in unity with the Church or the Church withdraws his priestly *auctoritas*, he can no longer celebrate Mass and other sacraments, because he lacks the capacity to act in persona Ecclesiae.[37] However, irrespective of these two relationships (Christological and ecclesial), a priest is always a bearer of the office, and therefore his actions are primarily related to his ordination, and not with his person, with him alone. Theologians believe that the personal charism of the priest is of secondary importance, and plays a less significant role.[38] A full interpretation of the nature and purpose of the hierarchical priesthood was given by the Second Vatican Council, because it took into account all of its essential aspects and dimensions.

---

[33] H.J. Pottmeyer, "Der Papst, Zeuge Jesu Christ in der Nachfolge Petri," in *In der Nachfolge Jesu Christi*, Wurzburg 1976, p. 60.

[34] Cf. M. Weber, *Wirtschaft und Gesellschaft. Grundgriß der verstehenden Soziologie*, ed. J. Winckelmann, Köln – Berlin 1964, p. 184.

[35] Cf. Y. Congar, *Die Lehre von Kirche*, Freiburg – Basel – Wien 1971, pp. 30–40.

[36] Comp. F. Holbock, *Der eucharistlische und mystische Leib Christi*, Rom 1961, pp. 232–238.

[37] Comp. B.-D. Marliangeas, *Clés pour une théologie du ministère*, op. cit.; H. Legrande, "La presidence de l'eucharistie selon la tradition ancienne," *Spiritus*, 1977, no. 69, pp. 409–431.

[38] Cf. J.-P. Audet, *Priester in der christlichen Gemeinde*, op. cit., pp. 116–175; P.M. Gy, "La théologie des prières anciennes pour l'ordination des évêques et des prêtres," *Revue des Sciences Philosophiques et Theologiques*, 1974, no. 58, pp. 607–608.

Studying the cognisance of young Catholics in Poland concerning the priesthood and the image of the priest in the given time period, one should also take into account the views of this Council on this important issue.[39] In the conciliar concept of hierarchical priesthood, we see the following elements:

1) it takes into account the cultic function of the priesthood and the mission of forming the faith of the laity, and the central function of the priest is celebrating the Eucharist;

2) the priesthood in its essence is different from the monastic and religious life, because it is social, Apostolic and hierarchical, and on the other hand, priests can increase their own holiness based on the model of religious life. However, their sanctity should be closely associated with the specifics of the priesthood and functions of a priest, which are necessary in the community of believers. Obedience, poverty and celibacy are virtues obligatory for all priests, because they facilitate accomplishing pastoral tasks;

3) celibacy became a major part of the life of priests, although priesthood in itself does not require celibacy, therefore the priesthood of married priests in Eastern rite Catholic Churches is not of lower value than the celibate priesthood of the Roman Catholic Church;

4) unity in ministry and the priesthood life are important for every priest;

5) priesthood is closely recognized in union with the bishop, who has full authority in the local Church;

6) priestly ordination gives the possibility for direct participation in the priesthood of Jesus, regardless of union with the bishop, and he can perform his own mission in the world. His ordination as a priest, not a canonical mission, gives the priest the power to act in the person of Christ;

7) the hierarchical priesthood is a sharing in the apostolic and increasing ministry of the Church;

8) in the Catholic Church there is one priesthood, and not two different forms – diocesan and religious;

[39] Cf. P. Głowa, "Kapłaństwo według myśli Soboru" [The Priesthood according to Conciliar Thinking], in *Kościół w świetle Soboru* [The Church in the Light of the Council], Poznan 1968, pp. 194–200; B. Przybylski, "Wprowadzenie do dekretu »O posłudze i życiu kapłanów«" [Introduction to the Decree "Service in the Life of a Priest"], in *Sobór Watykański II: Konstytucje, dekrety, deklaracje* [The Second Vatican Council: Constitutions, Decrees, Declarations], Poznan 1969, pp. 474–486; J. Kurpas, "Charakterystyka dekretu [Characteristics of the Decree] »De presbyterorum ministerio et Vita«," *Ateneum Kapłańskie*, 1966, no. 69, pp. 193–203; J. Baniak, "Kapłani i kapłaństwo w świetle badań socjologicznych i postulatów Vaticanum II" [Priests and Priesthood in the Light of Sociological Research and Postulates of Vatican II], *Prace Naukowe Wyższej Szkoły Pedagogicznej w Częstochowie*, 1987, no. 1, pp. 81–102; M. Midali, "Crisi del sacerdozio e risporta dell Conzilio" [Christians on the Priesthood and the Voice of the Council], in *Il sacerdoti nelle spiriti del Vaticano II* [Priests in the Spirit of Vatican II], Torino 1968, pp. 307–345.

9) priests are not alone in fulfilling their duties and tasks as priests, but they are always supported by God, present in the Church, which they should always keep in mind. Without a doubt, the position of the Second Vatican Council on the priesthood and life of priests in the Church and society is evident in the model priest-minister, recommend by bishops to all priests working in various areas of ministry.

2. Research methodology in the youth environment

The theoretical concept of the institutional priesthood, based on current knowledge of the subject, is the basis of the methodological assumptions of sociological research, the results of which help elucidate the central issue. These principles establish the framework and goal of the empirical research, and are the guidelines for the development of this sociologial study. The theoretical assumptions, synthetically presented above, lead to the general question: how did the secondary school and university student youth test group in Poland during the study period of 25 years perceive and interpret the essence of the institutional priesthood and the parish priest? Are the concepts of the institutional priesthood and self-image of the priest consistent with the concepts of the priesthood and the priest present in the model based on Catholic theology and teachings of the Church? How do Catholic youth in Poland decide on a priestly vocation and do they remain in the priesthood given priests' living conditions?

Have cultural, social and economic changes in the country during the study period of 25 years influenced the attitudes and images of high school and university students towards the priesthood and priests? I will provide answers to these questions in the text based on this sociological study. The following issues shaped its methodology: the central issue and the issue of research, theoretical and empirical hypotheses, organization and implementation of environmental research and accepted test procedures, and the statistical description of the demographic and social characteristics of the young people. Methodological assumptions will facilitate a detailed analysis of the results of research on any matter within the central issue. The motivation for carrying out the empirical research presented here is purely scientific and cognitive in nature. However, these results also have practical, socio-religious and ecclesiastical-pastoral aspects, and as such they can be used for non-scientific purposes. These considerations, however, are beyond my justifications for choice of topic and research issues.[40]

[40] Cf. P. Nowak, *Metodologia badań społecznych* [Methodology of Social Research], Warsaw 1985, p. 26; J. Sztumski, *Wstęp do metod i technik badań społecznych* [Instroduction to Methods and Techniques of Social Research], Katowice 1999, p. 29.

Every scientific study, including sociological studies, has clearly marked primary and specific objectives.[41] The main objective of my research is the desire to broaden and deepen the current state of scientific knowledge on the attitude of high school and university students in Poland towards the priesthood and model parish priest, as an integral component of their awareness of religion, the Church and society, taking into account all three periods of research. The awareness of religion and the Catholic Church among the youth is a unique "whole," which occupies a significant place in their views and attitudes about the institution of the priesthood and a model priest. The priest – through his own priestly vocation, personal lifestyle in the parish, playing the role of a priest among the lay faithful in everyday observance of the principles of the Gospel, and in a sense representing the Church of Christ – defines the hierarchical priesthood he personally fulfills, aware of the assessments of attitudes and actions by parishioners, both adults and adolescents. I took these issues into account in my research, the results of which I present in this study. In relation to these assumptions, I again assume several hypotheses previously undertaken by other sociologists of religion, and also accept my own hypotheses, verifying all of these on the basis of the accepted independent variables and statistical indicators.

a) The central issue and the research problem

The research problem in science is variously defined by sociologists and humanists. Stefan Nowak writes that this problem is referred to as an issue that a research scientist has to solve with the help of appropriate field procedures and methods. This issue may take the form of a general question or a group of more specified questions, to which the researcher (sociologist) has to find an adequate answer, according to the subject of the academic discipline practiced.[42]

The central issue addressed in my research is the following question: in this period of 25 years, have the beliefs, attitudes and actions of the respondents in Polish high schools and university students concerning the institution of the priesthood and the model parish priest retained stability and unity, or have they undergone changes, and if so, what direction have these changes assumed?

From this general question a number of detailed questions arise, which together form the topic of my research.[43] These questions are as follows:

[41] Cf. W. Pytkowski, *Organizacja badań i ocena prac naukowych* [Organization of Research and the Evaluation of Academic Work], Warsaw 1985, p. 189; E. Babbie, *Badania społeczne w praktyce* [Social Research in Practice], transl. W. Betkiewicz and others, Warsaw 2007, pp. 110–113.

[42] Cf. P. Nowak, *Metodologia badań socjologicznych* [Methodology of Sociological Research], Warsaw 1970, p. 220.

[43] Cf. ibidem, p. 30.

1. What place does the institutional priesthood take in the religious awareness of the surveyed high school and university students?

2. How do the questioned secondary school and university students interpret the hierarchical nature of the priesthood?

3. What place does the priesthood take in the hierarchy of preferences of high school and university students?

4. What role does the priest play in the personal faith and religiousness of the studied high school and college students?

5. How do the surveyed high school and college students judge the authority of parish priests in Poland?

6. How do the surveyed high school and college students perceive and interpret the role of the parish priest in the secular community?

7. What is specifically characteristic of a model parish priest as proposed by the surveyed high school and college students, and is this consistent with the official model in the Church?

8. How are the studied high school and university students disposed to mandatory celibacy for parish priests?

9. How do the survetyed respondents understand the vocation to the priesthood and do they see in it the necessary conditions for selection of and persistence in the priesthood?

10. What required qualities and abilities should candidates for the priesthood show in the evaluation of the surveyed respondents?

11. How do the surveyed high school and university students define the institutional priesthood and explain its essence?

12. Do the young people evaluate the priesthood as a profession with sufficient existential value and life perspective for religious men to choose as their way of life?

13. Do the young people accept the mediation of the priest between God and man in religious matters?

14. Do the respondents display a desire to have a priest in their family, or were they against it?

15. Do the surveyed high school and college youth keep personal contacts and relationships with priests in parishes and academic pastoral ministry?

16. How do the respondents evaluate the professional advancement of priests in Poland over the period of 25 years in relation to other socially valued professions?

17. Do the respondents see priests as moral authorities possibly influencing the consciences of other people and their own consciences?

18. Do the respondents perceive Pope John Paul II as a personal model priest and pastor, worth following by other priests?

19. In the opinion of the surveyed respondents, should the Roman Catholic Church give up celibacy for its priests, in order to achieve religious ecumenism's assumptions?

20. Do the views and attitudes of respondents regarding the priesthood and priests depend on their demographic and social characteristics and on their religious beliefs and practices, and if yes, to what degree?

These questions have a diagnostic – descriptive aspect, but they are also supported and complemented by relevant empirical hypotheses, and thus are open to verification. These questions have a decisive character, and complement each other, involving different relationships and dependencies in the attitudes of the Polish youth towards the institutional priesthood and priests, with the accompanying internal and external circumstances.[44] These correlations will be tested in the statistical analyses in the final chapter of the book. It should be noted, however, that the selected problem does not explain all the issues falling within the scope of the main research problem. Rather, it points to an "epicenter" of interests of high school and university students in the institutional priesthood and its practice by priests in parishes and pastoral academic ministry based on an appropriate model of the priest proposed in the Catholic Church is identified.

b) Research hypotheses

The term "hypothesis" is defined in various ways by methodologists and researchers. Wiesław Pytkowski believes that the hypothesis is the "assignment" to accomplish, and is not the proof, but only the right to approximate the truth. A hypothesis is usually of a theoretical or empirical nature. A theoretical hypothesis is directly associated with the concept of the research, while a empirical hypothesis directs testing. The hypothesis is stated when we cannot explain certain facts by means of previously accepted statements accepted as true.[45] Methodological literature also presents other definitions of hypotheses, but there is no need to quote them here.

The hypotheses adopted in my research have both a theoretical and empirical character, and are closely related to the primary and special issues. However, in the meritorical dimension, they coincide with the general framework of this study.

The main hypothesis assumes that, based on the results of various studies, the beliefs, attitudes and actions of the Polish high school and academic

---

[44] Cf. J. Baniak, *Ksiądz w oczach młodzieży...* [The Priest in the Eyes of Youth...], op. cit., pp. 44–45.

[45] Cf. W. Pytkowski, *Organizacja badań...* [Research Organization...], op. cit., pp. 155–163.

students toward the institution of the priesthood and model parish priest were not stable in the accepted term, but changed, often negatively, and differed from assumptions and expectations of the Church regarding priesthood and priests.

The specific hypotheses are as follows:

1. I understand that during the research period, the ideas of the youth in Poland changed radically concerning the nature and structure of the institutional priesthood. The correctness of this interpretation is to some degree dependent on the level of education and religious commitment of respondents.

2. I assume that the high school and college students possessed the appropriate level of knowledge about the role of the priest in the parish and in the secular environment. This knowledge facilitated their acceptance of this role in both environments, and distinguished the relevant professional skills of parish priests. I also assume that the respondents accepted with limitations and objections the religious role of the priest in people's lives and in relation to their own religiousness.

3. I hypothetically assume that the majority of the surveyed high school and university students were sufficiently informed about the level of prestige and authority of the priesthood of priests in Poland in the given period. This knowledge also facilitated their own perceptions and personal assessment of the authority of priests, but their attitudes in this matter varied, depending on various factors, including their level of education, place of residence and level of religiosity.

4. I understand that the predominant majority of the surveyed high school and university students perceived the priesthood as a specific religious value with social significance. Such a positive approach to the priesthood made it easier, in their opinion, for religious men to choose the priesthood as their way of life and professional career.

5. I assume that their knowledge of the priesthood and the lives of priests made it possible for respondents to define and evaluate the model parish priest in their environment, with regards to personal virtues and vices. Vices were criticized by respondents and deemed inappropriate in a model priest. Virtues were considered necessary in the personal lives and work of priests. I also accept the fact that the respondents put forth recommendations for appropriate personal and social characteristics of candidates for the priesthood, taking into account the specificity of the profession of a priest and the eventual priestly identity crises of priests, showing loyalty to their own vocation.

6. I assume that the high school and college students were interested in the celibacy of priests, especially its universality and necessity, and its relationship to the essence of the priestly vocation. Respondents knew that this form of celibacy is present only in the Roman Catholic Church, and is not always

present in other Eastern Catholic rites or Christian churches. This difference was a concern for the respondents and led them to allow candidates for the priesthood a free choice between priestly life based on celibacy, or within the instituion of marriage and a family. Respondents attributed mandatory celibacy only to the people in religious orders of both sexes.

7. Only a small percentage of respondents showed a desire for personal contact and relationships with parish and academic ministry priests, while the remaining majority did not have such ties or did not foresee having such. Respondents avoiding relationships with priests most often did not trust them, for different reasons, including the scandalous conduct of some priests, clergy entering into the political affairs of the country or misunderstanding the problems of today's youth. These contacts were also generally difficult due to young people not understanding the language of the Church used by priests while preaching, in the liturgy and during religious education classes at school.

8. It can be assumed that during the decay of religious and moral authority, the respondents would observe a similar situation in the environment of the clergy, which lacked an appropriate model to follow. In the opinion of many respondents, the personal priest model worth following for today's priests, and the model for current and future priests, is Pope John Paul II. Many features of his personality, his love for truth and freedom, genuine faith and devotion and love for the Church and people, can attract a number of priests who are seeking proper reference for their own priesthood and place in the Church, wishing to see the benefits of their work in the parish and the local environment.

9. It seems that the dominant majority of respondents in both environmental groups consider God's call as a necessary prerequisite for a priest's choice of and endurance in the priesthood. The absence of such an appointment, in their opinion, should prevent a man from entering the seminary. Accepting Holy Orders without this calling seriously hampers the endurance of a priest in the priesthood, and in specific situations would make it easier for a clergyman to abandon the priestly state and return to the secular life.

10. Only a small percentage of high school and university students surveyed expressed a desire to have a priest in their family, but the remaining majority did not show such willingness in this regard. The respondents put forth various reasons for this reluctance, including reasons of a psychological, religious or social nature. In the opinion of many, "it is simply not worth becoming a priest" because it is a profession with a small-scale social need.

11. I assume that the dominant part of respondents in both environmental groups critically evaluated the political commitment of Polish bishops and priests during the study period, including their influence on the election awareness of lay Catholics, their taking sides with political parties, especially

those with a national and Catholic profile. Respondents believe that politics is not the responsibility of the clergy. Hence they were often offended by the clergy influencing the activities of politicians, parliamentarians and local council activists.

12. The attitude of respondents to the priesthood and priests significantly depended on their religious commitment and frequency of cultic and prayer practices. The higher the degree of faith and religion, the more positive was the attitude of respondents towards the priesthood and priests. Neglecting religious practices and the weakening of faith was associated directly with criticism of priests – their vices, procedures and activities, and lack of understanding of the institutional nature of the priesthood.

These hypotheses will be checked for accuracy and relevance of further parts of this study using statistical methods. They are based on the demographic and social characteristics of respondents as independent variables and explain only some of the issues related to the topic of research. Other hypotheses are "partial" and will be formulated and verified in subsequent chapters. Clarification of this issue will enhance the scientific knowledge in sociology of religion, sociology of religious vocations and the sociology of priesthood.

c) Organization and execution of research

The concepts presented here are based on many years of studies and empirical research on the subject, and were by no means simple or easy to implement. The real difficulty occured during testing in the two different youth environments. Explaining the problem and checking the validity of the main empirical hypotheses required consideration and application of many mutually complementing supplementary methods and techniques known in the social sciences, relevant also to sociology.[46] Gathering cognitively valuable source material that helped me to give answers to the research questions required the adoption of a complex procedure to remove a number of difficulties.

It was necessary to adopt and implement adequate methods, techniques and tools of research, both at the stage of conceptualization and implementation of studies, as well as during description and analysis of the results. Observation of objects used in the Church and worship proved to be necessary, as well as analysis of Church records and school topics related to the research, interviews with high school and academic youth and with Church and school

[46] Cf. J. C. McKinney, "Methodology, Procedures and Techniques in Sociology," in *Modern Sociological Theory in Continuity and Change*, New York 1975, p. 188; Ch. Frankfort-Nachmias, D. Nachmias, *Metody badawcze w naukach społecznych* [Research Methods in Social Teaching], transl. E. Hornowska, Poznan 2011, pp. 220–349.

staff, and long-term study of relevant literature. Research among young people is not an easy empirical initiative; if you want to win the trust and confidence necessary to obtain reliable answers to your questions and opinions on issues.

For this purpose, I applied research methods and techniques[47] that gave me insight into the true opinions and attitudes, beliefs and behaviors of young people as related to the institutional priesthood and parish priests, giving respondents full anonymity and freedom to express their own statements. All three studies used a so-called comprehensive method known in sociology, which includes the following specific methods: diagnostic survey, correlation, descriptive, historical-comparative, social engineering, and statistical-problematics tables.[48] Here I pay special attention to the method of correlation of variables,[49] since it allows for determining the existence and degree of statistically significant dependencies between the views, attitudes, beliefs and actions of high school and university students concerning the priesthood and priests, and their personal and social characteristics, such as the extent of their beliefs and religious practices.

In the analyses of correlations, I took into account associations between coefficients significantly exceeding the threshold for statistical significance.[50] At the same time, during the test, I used the following specific techniques: participant observation during simple, plain and in-depth interviews, analysis of documents, and statistical analysis,[51] because this combination would help me resolve the main problem of testing and verifying the validity of empirical hypotheses. The research tool was a questionnaire entitled "The Institution of the Priesthood and the Priest in the Awareness of High School and University Students," adapted essentially to the level of the personal and intellectual devel-

---

[47] Cf. P. Szulc, *Metody statystyczne* [Statistical Methods], Warsaw 1968, pp. 190–253; G. Lisowski, "Praktyczne problemy związane z doborem próby do badań" [Practical Problems Related with Selecting a Research Test Group], in *Metody statystyczne w socjologii* [Statistical Methods in Sociology], Warsaw 1986, pp. 58–70; H. M. Blalock, *Statystyka dla socjologów* [Statistics for Sociologists], transl. M. Tabin and others, Warsaw 1977.

[48] Cf. P. Szostkiewicz, *Procedury i techniki badań socjologicznych* [Procedures and Techniques in Sociological Research], Warsaw 1964, pp. 58–63; P. Nowak, *Metodologia badań socjologicznych* [Methodology of Sociological Research], op. cit., pp. 259–327.

[49] Cf. Z. Gostkowski, *Podstawowe metody statystyczne w psychologii i pedagogice* [Principle Statistical Methods in Psychology and Pedagogy], Warsaw 1964, pp. 146–163; T. Pacholski, *Statystyka. Wykład zagadnień podstawowych* [Statistics. Contribution of Basic Issues], Warsaw 1978, pp. 117–168; R. Mayntz, K. Holm, P. Hubner, *Wprowadzenie do metod socjologii empirycznej* [Introduction to Empirical Sociological Methods], transl. W. Lipnik, Warsaw 1985, pp. 240–265.

[50] Cf. G. Klaus, H. Ebner, *Podstawy statystyki dla psychologów, socjologów i pedagogów* [Basics of Statistics for Psychologists, Sociologists and Pedagogues], Warsaw 1972, pp. 107–108, 289–296.

[51] Cf. D. Katz, "Badania terenowe" [Field Studies], in *Metody badań socjologicznych* [Methods of Sociological Research], Warsaw 1968, pp. 348–349.

opment of both groups of respondents. In both environments the study was carried out in the auditorium during classes in my presence. Respondents were chosen using a random-intentional selection from a student registration list.

The research material presented in this study is of cognitive and academic value in the field of youth sociology and the sociology of religion. In addition, it presents objective information about their attitudes and actions with regard to priests, and documents changes in these attitudes that occurred during the study period. This material also allows you to present and evaluate the same phenomena on the basis of data from different sources, resulting in easy objective analysis and interpretation of indicators of relationships between variables and their external environment.

d) Statistical Description of the Respondents

This study was performed in Kalisz during three periods in the years 1983, 1998 and 2008, and included three separate groups of youth in high schools, the branch of Adam Mickiewicz University (UAM) in Poznan and the Higher Vocational State School (PWSZ). During this period, a total of 1390 respondents took part in the survey: 70.2% of this group were high school students and 29.8% college students in Kalisz. The proportion of respondents was different in later research: in 1983 they accounted for a percentage total of 38.6% (high school students 41.0% and college students 33.1%), in 1998, the percentage of the total was 32.6% (33.6% high school and 30.2% college) and in 2008, 22.8% (25.4% high school and 36.7% college). These tests included more high school students, hence their advantage over the total number of overall students.

In the group of 1390 respondents during the study period, women were in the majority – 948 (68.2%), including 656 high school girls (69.2%) and 292 female students (30.8%). The men numbered almost half this – a total of 442 (31.8%), including 320 high school students (72.4%) and 122 college students (27.6%). The numbers of men and women to high school students varied over the periods of research. Indicators of women were as follows: during the first studies, 40.5% women, in the second and third studies, 33.1% and 26.4% women, and there were always more high school students than woman college students. Male ratios were as follows: in the first period of study 34.6%, in the second and third 31.4% and 34.0% men. In every period more high school students were surveyed than college students.

Among all respondents, first-year students accounted for the majority – 870, or 62.6%, composed of 58.5% high school and 69.8% college students. Final-year students are in the minority – 520, composed of 37.4% of students about to graduate from high school, or 395 people (40.5%), and 125 final-year college students (30.2%). The quantitative distribution of the respondents in these groups of first-year and final-year students varied. In general, in 1983, first-year high school and college students constituted 38.8% of respondents; in 1998 they accounted for 32.6%, and in 2008 for 28.6%.

Indicators of high school and college students completing their education were as follows: 38.5% in the first period of research, 32.5% in the second, and 29.0% in the third. In the first and second periods, students from the Poznan branch of UAM were included and numbered 262, while in the third period the subjects were 152 students of the Higher Vocational State School (PWSZ). The university group consisted of 69 students studying elementary school pedagogy, 31 art students and 25 students of music. The group of students from PWSZ numbered 152 and included people who studied business management (42), local government management (50), nursing (36) and environmental protection (24).

Daughters and sons from families of intelligentsia (42.6%) clearly dominate quantitatively in the respondents, with a slightly larger proportion in university (45.2%) than high school students (41.8%). Every fifth respondent was from a working-class family, with 1.5% more high school than college students. Almost every fifth respondent was born and lived in the rural environment and came from a farming family, with 6.8% more in high school than among college students. Artisan families made up 11.2% of respondents, slightly more (1.7%) in high school than among the university students. A small percentage of respondents came from culturally and socially "mixed families," for example, families of peasant-workers or worker-intellectuals; in total, they comprised 6.0% of the total, 3.2% more among college students than in high school. The data indicate that children of parents with higher education, both in the city and the countryside, were more numerous in general education secondary schools and were more likely to enrol in higher education during this period.

The level of religious faith of the subjects was very diverse, with respect to both gender and academic level – meaning high school and university students. Persons who believe in God in the whole population amounted out to 59.6%. Among women, the percentage was 66.3% and among men 47.0%, a difference of 19.3%. Among the group of high school students believers accounted for 62.9%, and among college students 51.7%, a difference of 11.2%. Only one in six respondents declared to have a "deep faith," including marginally more women than men (3.0%), and this number was higher among high school than college students (1.9%). More than two-fifths of respondents said that their faith is "normal" or at a moderate level, meaning as required by the Church. A significant proportion of the study group can be categorized as religiously indifferent people – 24.9% are indifferent and doubt religious dogmas. This group is comprised of 24.2% high school and 26.6% university students, and 21.3% women and 32.4% men (11.1% more men).

Among all respondents were people stating they did not believe in God – a total of 11.2%, where men outnumber women (by 6.1%) and including 5.4% more high school than university students. The percentage of respondents declaring disbelief should be considered high, especially in the environment of high school student youth, since these students in general willingly attended or had to attend (parents' wish, peer pressure) Catholic religious catechesis classes in school.

It is easy to see that during the adopted period, there was a systematic decrease in proportions of respondents who believed, especially at the level of "deep" religious faith. Taking the year 1983 as the beginning of this period and 2008 as the end, we see that the percentage of believers decreased from 69.4% to 48.4%, or by 21.0%. The regression rate of "deep" faith is at a high of 14.3%. The percentage of people who believe decreased by 11.4% in the years 1983–1998, and deeply religious individuals by 11.2%.

At the same time, there was a regular increase in the percentage of people indifferent to religion and doubters of religious dogma: in 1983 the figure was 18.4%, then in 1998 it rose to 25.6% (or 7.2%). However, in 2008 they increased even more, to 32.5% (or by 14.1%). A particular concern was the dynamic growth of the proportion of non-believers – from 7.4% in 1983 to 12.0% in 1998 (a 4.6% increase), and in 2008 to 15.6% (an 8.2% increase). Throughout these 25 years, there have been important civilizational, cultural and social changes in Poland that have also affected the Catholic faith and religion, and the youth are no exception. This must be taken into account when analysing the decrease or loss of faith in a significant percentage of young people.

The participation of the youth in mandatory repeated religious practices was very diverse at that time, both among high school and college students, both women and men. Obligatory Sunday Mass was attended by 70.2% of respondents, including 74.5% of women, 61.1% of men, 73.9% of high school students and 61.7% of college students. Weekly Sunday Masses were regularly attended by less than one in five respondents, with more high school than college students (a difference of 3.9%) and more women than men (6.6%). Sunday mass was irregularly attended by every third respondent, while others participated in it occasionally. Most respondents took part in Sunday Mass irregularly – 50.5%, including 52.7% women, 45.9% men, 53.0% of high school students and 44.7% of college students. Moreover, among the respondents, 25.5% had not participated in the Mass in several years, including 21.6% of women and 33.7% of men (a difference of 12.1%) and 22.8% of high school students and 31.6% of university students (a difference of 8.8%).

Irregular participation rates and absenteeism rates in Sunday Mass begs the question whether the Polish youth see Sunday as a holy day, when participation in Holy Mass means giving glory to God and worshipping Him is obligatory for Catholics.[52] An average number of young people participate in the mandatory annual confession and communion at Easter. Total confessions for this occasion included 67.6% of respondents, 69.1% women, 64.4% men, 71.6% high school and 58.3% college students (13.3% less). By contrast, other respondents approached this religious practice with disrespect and followed it irregularly, perhaps every few years, particularly men and students. Among the respondents, 28.1% did not follow this practice at all, including 27.0% of women, 30.4% of men, 25.1% of high school students and 35.0% of college students. The indicated degree of this mandatory religious practice is evidence of the weak moral and religious condition of the youth in high school and college.[53]

In conclusion, it should be noted that the successive periods of research are essential in this analysis because they indicate the scale of changes in the views, attitudes and activities of the studied high school and university students towards the institutional priesthood and parish priests. There is no doubt that during this period of 25 years in Poland, important changes took place in the country and society. These changes also apply to Polish people's attitudes towards religion, the Church and the clergy – from positive to neutral and critical attitudes. This is especially true in the Polish youth, who are more radical than adults in responding to the negative aspects of life in the Church, including the attitudes and behavior of priests and lay Catholics. The answers of my respondents are evidence of these changes and the critical response of young Polish Catholics towards the Church and priests.

---

[52] Cf. J. Baniak, "Niedziela jako dzień święty w wyobrażeniach i ocenach katolików polskich" [Sunday as a Holy Day in the Ideas and Evaluations of Polish Catholics], *Teologia Praktyczna*, 2004, vol. 5, pp. 245–260.

[53] Cf. J. Baniak, *Między buntem a potrzebą akceptacji i zrozumienia. Świadomość religijna i moralna a kryzys tożsamości osobowej młodzieży gimnazjalnej. Studium socjologiczne* [Between Rebellion and the Need for Acceptance and Understanding. Religious and Moral Awareness and the Crisis of Personality Identity in Junior High School Youth. A Sociological Study], Cracow 2008, pp. 213 and 219. (These studies showed that 15.3% of boys, 9.1% of girls, 13.5% of city junior high school students and 7.6% of countryside junior high school students did not participate in the mandatory Sunday mass. The following percentage did not participate in Easter confession: 46.4% of boys, 39.8% of girls, 45.2% of city and 36.8% of country junior high school students, with a total lack of awareness of religious duty showed by a total of 39.8% of the participants, including 44.5% of boys, 37.4% of girls, 44.9% of city and 31.7% of countryside junior high schoolers).

Chapter II

Institutional priesthood in the perceptions and evaluations of the respondents

The theoretical analysis of institutional priesthood and the model of the parish priest in the first chapter provides a basis for the analysis and evaluation of the views, attitudes, and activities of the studied high school and college students concerning priesthood and priests. In this chapter, I will answer questions as to how the Polish youth perceived and interpreted the nature and structure of institutional priesthood during the study period, what determined their realization of the idea of priesthood, and whether this interpretation was always consistent with the theological concept of priesthood and the current model of the priest in the Roman Catholic Church.

1. The need for a religious vocation in choosing and staying in the priesthood

The Catholic Church, from its beginnings, has had a special religious mission to fulfill in the world among people of every time period, in different cultures and political circumstances. She teaches in her theological doctrine that Jesus Christ as the founder of the Church appointed her to do so. This mission of the Church consists of specific roles, functions, and tasks to be carried out systematically by its representatives – bishops, priests, and deacons. However, priests are mostly responsible for the success of this mission; without their personal commitment and professional work, the assignments of the Church would not be performed. Priests are essential in the structures of the institutional Church, and therefore Church authorities guard with great care over the professional and religious formation of the influx of new priests and religious personnel. The basic condition for the choice of priests is a specific "call from God," which a candidate for priesthood who intends to study theology in the seminary must possess.

The role of this vocation in choosing priesthood is aptly presented by Edward Ciupak when he indicates in his analysis that "[...] From a theological point of view, the most significant attribute of candidates is their vocation, and it is this that formally distinguishes the profession of priesthood from all others. Without going into a philosophical or dogmatic discussion, we can state that "vocation" is a term translatable into the language of sociology, since we explain it in the analysis of social conditions, gradually shaping an individual's decision. [...] Almost all of the factors which characterize the structure of dynamic processes in a given historical period, meaning the political situation, elitism or democratization of higher education, the economic situation, particularly the labor market, the style of general education, and the prevailing ideology have an influence on the selection of candidates for priesthood."[1] The priestly vocation is therefore a fundamental condition for a candidate's choice of priesthood, and for the priest remaining a clergyman.

In the light of these assumptions, it is worth assessing whether the surveyed high school and college students, as young Catholics, accept the necessary condition of vocation for institutional priesthood, and how do they themselves understand the nature of this vocation?

Studies have shown that the greater percentage of high school students (63.8%) and college students (47.0%) acknowledged the calling of God as a necessary condition for the choice of priesthood. Half the percentages of respondents (21.3% and 26.9%) held a different opinion. The remaining respondents did not take a position on this matter (14.9% and 26.1%). However, the percentages of high school students (32.6%) and college students (23.0%) who accepted the need for a vocation in the choice of priesthood during the period of testing systematically decreased, while at the same time, the percentage

---

[1] E. Ciupak, *Kapłaństwo: powołanie i zawód* [Priesthood: Vocation and Profession], in idem, *Kult religijny i jego społeczne podłoże* [The Religious Cult and its Social Basis], Warsaw 1965, pp. 400–402. The author explains that the term "vocation" comes from a "charisma," which in theology is a supernatural "call of God" directed to a specific person. Externally it is expressed in a candidate's decision to voluntarily report to the seminary. Then the author recalls that "in the literature on the subject, there are two basic types of charisms: the personal charisma based on personal skills, and the charisma of office, which is attributed institutionally by higher ecclesiastical authorities. From the Catholic point of view, the charisma of the priest has several meanings: it includes lasting and indestructible abilities for performing cultic prayer activities, it is an extraordinary supernatural gift (a gift given to the priest temporarily), the ability of extraordinary mental ecstasy." Ibidem, p. 425, footnote 13.

of those who rejected this necessity increased – by 24.0% and 14.5% – and those who did not take a position on this matter by 8.6% and 8.5%. These indicators also confirm the accuracy of the empirical hypothesis, which assumed such a situation with regards to the attitudes of respondents in both groups towards the condition of necessity of a religious vocation when choosing priesthood.

2. The structure of institutional priesthood as understood by the respondents

An unequivocal explanation of the structure of institutional priesthood is a difficult problem for theologians and sociologists of religion. Both see priesthood from their own point of view, and often do not appreciate a different perspective. Theologians prefer the distinctly religious dimension of priesthood (as a "divine call" and as "the authority of Holy Orders"), while sociologists of religion view the office of priesthood as an "ordinary occupation" of a religious nature for which at a given time there is public demand, especially in an environment of people who are religious and connected to the Church. Among researchers on the priesthood are those who incorporate both of these qualities into its structures – religious and secular – presenting them as a kind of cultural "whole." How do the surveyed high school and college students perceive the institutional structure of priesthood?

Research shows that a dominant proportion of high school students (63.1%) and college students (57.3%) see both the religious aspect (vocation) and the professional aspect in priesthood. On the other hand, the percentages of those who view priesthood as only a religious vocation (10.7% and 10.3%) or only an ordinary occupation (22.3% and 27.1%) is several times lower in the entire study group. Other respondents – 3.9% and 5.3% – did not take a position on this matter. Studies have also shown that within the adopted period of 25 years, attitudes towards the individual constituents of the structure of priesthood changed: first, the percentage of high school students (15.8%) and college students (19.2%) who perceive both of these aspects in priesthood decreased. The percentages of those high school students (3.0%) and college students (3.1%) who view priesthood only as a religious vocation also decreased. On the other hand, in both groups the percentages of respondents who viewed priesthood only as an ordinary occupation, necessary in the Church and religious communities, increased – by 20.7% and 19.8%. The results confirm the validity of the hypothesis on the perception in the majority of respondents in both groups of priesthood as a whole consisting of these two aspects, and also record a change in attitude to the structure of priesthood within the adopted time for a significant percentage of them.

3. The constant presence of the charisma of the priesthood in the daily life of a priest

A relevant matter in this analysis is also the constant presence of the charisma of priesthood in the life of a priest in various circumstances and situations – religious and secular. It is therefore necessary to question whether the priest is a priest always and everywhere, as the Church states in its doctrine on priesthood, or whether he is a priest only in circumstances strictly connected with religion and the Church, excluding typically secular situations?

Adult Catholics in Poland researched in the late 1980s identified the following circumstances conditioning the religious dimension of priesthood as exercised by the priest: a) he is a priest in the parish church – 42.2%, b) he is a priest in the parish office – 6.0%, c) he is a priest in the catechetics classroom – 17.4%, d) he is a priest during the New Year's and Christmas Carol visits to parishioners – 8.0%, e) he is a priest in his private life every day – 14.5%, f) he is a priest in public life – 10.4%, g) he remains a priest always and everywhere – 0.5%.[2]

Under which circumstances and situations is the charisma of priesthood present according to the surveyed high school and college students? Have their attitudes towards this issue changed over the period of 25 years?

The respondents saw the charisma of the priesthood in the life of a priest through various functions which a priest fulfills in the Church and secular society. The greatest percentage of high school (44.2%) and college students (43.6%) indicated religious functions that make evident the priestly charisma. In the second place a large percentage (26.7% and 30.7%) pointed to these Church functions as a "deposit" of this charisma. So a total of up to 70.9% of high school and 74.3% of college students stated that the priesthood of the priest expresses itself in particular in the religious and Church functions, and it is through these functions, fulfilled according to the conditions of the Church, that the priest is fully a priest. In these circumstances the faithful see him as a priest, playing his major role in the parish community. In other circumstances, the priesthood of priests was perceived in smaller proportions of respondents in both groups – in situations outside of Church activities (9.0% and 8.0%), in his personal life (9.4% and 7.1%), always and everywhere (7.0% and 6.5%).

The remaining respondents (3.7% and 4.1%) did not take up a position on this issue. On the other hand, studies have shown a change in the attitudes of respondents to the circumstances conditioning the charismatic priest. During

[2] See J. Baniak, *Obraz kapłana w świadomości katolików świeckich – na przykładzie Kalisza, Kotłowa i Przedborowa. Studium socjologiczne* [The Image of the Priest in the Awareness of Lay Catholics based on Kalisz, Kotłów and Przedborów. A Sociological Studies], Poznan 1994, p. 93, table 12.

the research period of 25 years, the perception that the priesthood is expressed in the Church functions of the priest dropped among students in high school (by 9.5%) and college (by 11%). At the same time there was an increase (of 13.4% and 8.2%) in those who believe that priesthood is expressed through religious and cultic functions, celebrated by a priest in the parish church. Other features played a minor role, as seen in the declining percentage of respondents who saw in priests the charisma of priesthood.

From a theological point of view, the priesthood is "a permanent process," that is, the priest satisfies his own priesthood constantly and consistently, both in his personal life and in the exercise of the priestly role, not only during religious and church functions, although these are the most important features of the role. However, the vast majority of the college and high school students reject the concept of the priesthood "beyond all boundaries," limiting priesthood to clearly religious and Church boundaries. The priestly charisma of a priest, according to most of these students, does not stretch beyond these limits. These young Polish Catholics interpret the essence of the priestly role and nature of the institution of the priesthood wrongly, and contrary to Church teaching on this subject. Fr. Władysław Piwowarski's observed 40 years ago in reference to this idea that "[...] in urban and industrial environments, the view continues to spread that the priesthood is a profession, but peculiarly understood. In such a context, there is change in the traditional way of looking at a priest. The priest is treated as a priest when he plays a strictly religious role, and apart from this, he seems to be a common man. This evolution can be regarded as a kind of desacralization of priesthood."[3]

An important question is whether this process of desacralization of the ministerial priesthood in Poland, especially among young people, is stable or developing. Which percentage of Polish Catholics, including the youth, will notice in the priest a "common man" who, while engaging in religious matters, also forgets about his priestly charisma, without which he would simply be a "professional" executing a religious profession? This question will likely be answered reliably by other researchers of the Church and parish clergy.

4. Institutional priesthood in the context of social meanings

Institutional priesthood, in axiological terms, has a certain social prestige in a religious community, the parish and in global society. The prestige of the priest is

[3] W. Piwowarski, "Religijność miejska w warunkach uprzemysłowienia (na przykładzie Puław)" [Urban Spirituality with Instustrialization Conditions (the Situation in Pulawy)], *Studia Warmińskie*, 1973, vol. 10, pp. 438–439.

a reflection of the values and religious needs of the community of believers. Leo Dingemans says that the prestige of the priest is expressed in the positive attitude of people towards him, in giving him honor and respect, or wide recognition.[4] A further analysis of the phenomenon of institutional priesthood is necessary to take into account its importance in the context of social and economic conditions. This would include the parish priest's prestige in society, career advancement in the priesthood in Poland over the 25-year period, the current status of the profession as seen through the eyes of young Polish people, and statements by the respondents who want to have a priest in their family regardless of constantly changing living conditions. I will present these issues in the next section.

a) The prestige of parish priests in the society during the research period

Candidates for the priesthood are constantly looking for reasons for their vocation and their choice for it as their personal way of life. The prestige of the priesthood in society and in the parish community, and people's trust in priests, often serves as such "strong" justification and support for their own career decisions. The prestige of priests in society is the basis on which priestly vocation is born and matures in an aspirant priest. His ideas concerning the true choice of the priesthood as his personal path in life and career crystallize and mature. On such a foundation of religious prestige, usually centered on a particular priest role-model. Sociological studies confirm this relationship and indicate that the priestly vocation is closely related to the social prestige of the priesthood and priests, due to the respect conferred on them by the parish and the local community. This relationship was confirmed 40 years earlier by the sociological studies of Fr. Peter Taras among the alumni of religious order seminarians. According to his results, as many as 91.8% of priestly vocations came from families that accord priests high prestige[5], and this was confirmed by the research carried out at the time in many dioceses of the Catholic Church in Poland,[6] and by Fr. Andrzej Postawa's 2004 study on alumni of the Salesian Society in Poland.[7]

[4] See L. Dingemans, "Przyczynek do socjologii powołań" [Contribution to the Sociology of Vocations], in F. Houtart (ed.), *Socjologia religii* [Sociology of Religion], transl. Z. Skórzyńska, Warsaw 1962, p. 154.

[5] See P. Taras, *Społeczne uwarunkowania i motywy wstąpienia do zakonnego seminarium duchownego* [Social Conditions and Motivation for Entering into the Religious Life Seminary], Poznan 1972, pp. 86–88.

[6] See J. Baniak, *Dynamika powołań kapłańskich i zakonnych w Kościele rzymskokatolickim w Polsce w latach 1900–1994. Studium socjograficzne* [The Dynamics of Priestly and Religious Vocations in the Roman Catholic Church in Poland in the Years 1900–1994], Cracow 1997, pp. 168–176.

[7] See A. Postawa, *Powołania kapłańskie w Towarzystwie Salezjańskim w Polsce. Studium socjologiczno -pastoralne* [The Priestly Vocation in Salesian Society in Poland. A Sociological-Pastoral Study], Cracow 2005, pp. 259–265.

A. Postawa writes in this respect that "[...] The perception of the priesthood requires conforming to a specific, attractive model for life, which encourages others to follow. We are concerned not only with the external perception of the priesthood, but also the priest's friendliness and ability to approach young people. In this respect, giving shape to the vocation is treated as a function of pastoral care and the high authority of a priest. [...] Nearly 84% of the alumni of the Salesian Society, before entering the novitiate, maintained a close relationship with a religious person, usually a priest."[8] Wojciech Świątkiewicz notes that Catholic clergy is a social group that for a young man, especially from the lower social strata, means social advancement and gaining respect in society and the home parish[9]. In this context one would be curious as to how the high school and college respondents evaluated the prestige of Catholic priests in Poland during this period.

The prestige of priests in Poland over the 25-year study period can be characterised as "high" to "very high," the so-called optimal level. This level was designated by a total of 59.8% of high school and 50.4% of college students. In subsequent periods of research, the percentages decreased and were as follows: among high school students, 73.5%, 60.3% and 40.6%, meaning that during the entire period, the proportion of respondents declined by 32.9%; among college students, 61.5%, 48.6% and 41.2%, thus a decline of 20.3%. Therefore, 58.1% of high school and 50.4% of college students surveyed said that Catholic priests in Poland at that time were respected, accepted and valued in society and in the parish. The remaining respondents in both groups judged the prestige of priests to be lower: as average prestige (9.6% and 9.2%), as low prestige (9.5% and 12.0%) and very low prestige (9.1% and 10.8%). In total, low prestige was designated by 28.2% of high school and 32.0% of college students. In addition, 10.8% of high school and 15.0% of college students said that during the study period, Catholic priests were assessed negatively in society, and that ultimately people refused them prestige and recognition. Criticism of the priests and their authority clearly intensified in the late eighties and early nineties of the twentieth century and remains so up to the present. College students and men were more critical towards the prestige of priests than high school students and women.

As with other socially recognized professions, the social prestige of the priesthood and priests depends on many different factors. My respondents

8 Ibidem, pp. 259–260.

9 See W. Świątkiewicz, "Portret księdza" [Portrait of the Priest], in W. Zdaniewicz, S.H. Zaręba (ed.), *Kościół katolicki na początku trzeciego tysiąclecia w opinii Polaków* [The Catholic Church at the Beginning of the Third Millenium in the Opinion of Polish People], Warsaw 2004, pp. 107–120.

depicted the prestige of the priesthood as based on four factors: the amount of income, the difficulty in earning it, work stability, and its demand among youth and family. Studies have shown that, taking into account these four criteria, in the 10 most popular professions in Poland at that time, respondents located the profession of the Catholic priest in the following positions: a) by amount of revenue: high school students in eighth place (66.7%) and college students in 6th place (72.5%). However, during the entire period this criterion declined by 9.2% and 14.7%; b) according to the difficulty in earning revenue: high school students in sixth place (71.4%) and college students in eighth place (63.2%), but over the whole period considered, the percentages decreased by 13.1% and 10.8%; c) according to stability of employment: high school students in third place (67.6%) and college students in second place (74.3%), although the percentages also declined throughout the period, by 16.6% and 11.8%; d) according to the needs of youth in their environment: high school students in eighth place (63.0%) and college students in ninth place (61.5%). During the research period, there were no significant changes in the assessment of this last criterion.

Interest in the priestly profession among the youth has decreased steadily over the given period, but it decreased the most during the late nineties of the twentieth century and remains at a low level. The measurable effect of this decrease is also a quantitative decline in priestly vocations in Poland during this period.[10]

b) Professional advancement of the institutional priesthood in Poland during the study period

I also asked respondents in each study period how they evaluate the professional advancement of the institutional priesthood with regards to other secular professions socially valued at that time. This advancement was evaluated by respondents using the Likert scale with its five degrees: very high, high, average, low, very low.

Research shows that over half of high school students (50.5%) and less than half of college students (47.5%) evaluated promotion in the priesthood at very high and high levels. 29.0% and 33.9% of both groups rated it at a low level, meaning average or very low. If we add up all these factors, it appears

[10] See J. Mariański, *Emigracja z Kościoła. Religijność młodzieży polskiej w warunkach zmian społecznych* [Emigration form the Church. The Religiousness of Poland's Youth in Conditions of Social Change], Lublin 2008, p. 432, table 50; J. Baniak, "Vocation for the ministry in Poland during the pontyficate of John Paul II (1978–1987)," *Christian Life in Poland*, 1989, no. 264, pp. 16–24; idem, "Determinants of Social Origin and Evolution of Sacerdotal Vocations in Poland," in W. Cross (ed.), *Perceived Influences on the Career Choice of Polish Priests*, Illinois 1990, pp. 12–47.

that the institutional priesthood advanced on the scale of promotion during this period in the assessment of 79.5% of high school and 81.4% of college students, compared to other professions respected at that time in Poland. At the same time, 14.6% of high school students and 13.2% of college students said that the Catholic priesthood declined during this period, based on the level of attractiveness compared to other professions, and this would discourage religious men from opting for the priesthood. Other studies have also shown that the interest of respondents in professional advancement in the priesthood declined steadily in subsequent periods, while increased interest among high school and college students showed a diminishing of prestige of the profession in society and a decline in its attractiveness in the youth environment.[11]

c) The current need for the priesthood and the importance of the work of priests in the assessments of respondents

Janusz Mariański argues correctly that "[...] From the sociological point of view, it is interesting to comment on the issue of young Poles' position towards the institution of the priesthood. Is the priesthood considered an essential and necessary institution, or rather as something unnecessary and even harmful in society? Here we are concerned with the issue of having a priest in the family, as seen through the prism of one's own family. Do young people fully approve of such a possibility, do they reject it, or regard it as emotionally neutral? It can be assumed that with a higher degree of modernization in society, Catholics will have a tendency to consider the priest more and more marginalized with regards to the values considered important in society. People will increasingly show a tendency to isolate themselves from priests, and desire to maintain distance from a priest in family circles."[12]

It should also be noted that recent sociological studies show progressive desacralization in the daily and festive life of Polish Catholics, including

---

[11] See A. Sarapata, "Zawód jako wyznacznik miejsca w społeczeństwie" [Profession as a Place Indicator in Society], in A. Sarapata, *Socjologia zawodów* [Sociology of Professions], Warsaw 1972, pp. 149–151. (The author notes that in the 1960s, there was a decrease in the prestige of being a priest, which was brought about, among others, by state policy, the development of rational thought, science and knowledge and other facts which give rise to confusion and caused breeches in spiritual needs and comforts). Cf. J. Baniak, *Obraz kapłana w świadomości katolików świeckich...* [The Image of the Priest in the Awareness of Lay Catholics], op. cit., pp. 101–102. (Catholic adults in Kalisz evaluated the professional advancement of the priesthood in 1994, according to the following scale: very high – 53.7%, high – 25.7%, average – 9.1%, while a decline was designated by 5.1% of respondents).

[12] J. Mariański, "Postawy młodzieży wobec duchowieństwa parafialnego" [The Attitudes of Youth Towards Parish Clergy], in idem, *Emigracja z Kościoła...* [Emigration from the Church...], Lublin 2008, pp. 431–432.

schoolchildren and university youth. Desacralization also includes the institutional priesthood and priests (in their personal lives), resulting in increasing numbers of Polish Catholics who see the priesthood from the secular point of view, that is, as a "normal" profession, which is now substantially less in demand than in the first half of the twentieth century.[13] Do high school and college youth respondents see the need for institutional priesthood at the present time, or not?

The attitudes of respondents to this question differ. Only 34.8% of college students and 42.0% of high school students expressed strong approval of the priesthood in today's highly secularized times, while 13.8% and 14.2% saw the need for a large reduction in priests. In total, 56.2% of high school and 48.6% of college students identified a need for priests. A different opinion was expressed by 26.6% of high school students and 33.4% of college students, who made it clear that they do not see the need for the institutional priesthood today, because the work of priests does not give much to religious people. The remaining respondents (17.2% and 18.0%) did not take a position on this issue.

The demand for the priesthood has fallen steadily in the subsequent periods of research. The number of respondents definitely seeing the need for priests decreased in both groups: among high school students by 21.9% and among college students by 13.6%. At the same time there was an increase in both groups, by 20.2% and 11.2%, of respondents who did not see such a need and define the priesthood as basically useless or socially unsuitable today. There was also slight increase in those who had difficulty in stating their position on this matter: by 6.0% and 0.3%. These data also confirm the relevance of the empirical hypothesis, which assumed loss of interest in the priesthood in a society under the influence of state and social changes during this period.[14]

---

[13] See J. Baniak, *Desakralizacja kultu religijnego i świąt religijnych w Polsce. Studium socjologiczne* [Desacralization of Religious Cult and Holy Days in Poland. A Sociological Study], Cracow 2007, pp. 13–36.

[14] Cf. J. Baniak, *Między buntem a potrzebą akceptacji i zrozumienia. Świadomość religijna i moralna a kryzys tożsamości osobowej młodzieży gimnazjalnej. Studium socjologiczne* [Between Rebellion and the Need for Acceptance and Understanding. Religious and Moral Awareness and the Crisis of Personality Identity in Junior High School Youth. A Sociological Study], Cracow 2008, p. 130, table 125. (The research shows that demand for the profession and work of the priest is accepted by 62.1% of junior high schoolers, including 63.2% of girls and 59.8% of boys, and a surplus of priests and their work was identified by a total of 21.6% of respondents, including 21.9% of girls and 21.0% of boys, 20.6% of rural and 22.2% of urban college students. Only one in five respondents in these times considered priests expendable, and their work in the parish no longer an absolute necessity).

What place does the professional priesthood take among the 15 most popular professions in the period examined, according to high school and college students?

Respondents, assessing the social usefulness of 15 different professions, placed the priesthood in seventh place (54.8%), while high school students placed the priesthood in sixth place (58.3%) and college students in eighth place (51.3%). However, in subsequent testing the percentages of respondents in both groups decreased: among high schoolers 12.2%, and 18.0% among college students. Above the priesthood, the respondents ranked as more important and more useful seven lay professions in the following areas: university professor – 86.2% of high school students and 85.6% of college students, medical doctor – 75.0% and 83.2%, lawyer – 71.6 % and 75.7%, businessman – 70.9% and 70.6%, pharmacist – 41.7% and 64.2%, teacher – 64.3% and 63.7%, nurse – 57.7% and 55.8%. The following professions were ranked lower than the priest: film director – 45.2% and 50.0%, plumber – 51.5%% and 47.6%, construction worker – 50.5% and 53.5%, farmer – 43.2% and 38.2%, trader – 38.7% and 33.9%. The respondents judged that the priesthood is a profession more necessary and socially valued than these secular professions.

I also asked respondents whether it is presently worth becoming a parish priest or a priest in a religious order. The youth participate in school catechesis, during which they receive information about these two possibilities of service in the priestly office, and about priestly studies undertaken by alumni in diocesan and religious seminaries. Therefore I was also able to ask this question.

Studies have shown differences in the respondents' evaluations of the greater "benefits" of becoming a priest in the diocese versus in a religious community, considering the financial criterion of the clergy in these two Church structures. 53.6% of high school and 43.9% of college students felt that it is currently better to be a parish priest than a priest in a religious order, which was given lower approval by both groups: 35.0% and 27.4%. However, there is an inverse proportion between the percentage of the respondents who said that at present it is not worth choosing the profession of parish priest – 31.6% and 38.8% – or the religious order priesthood – 52.2% and 59.6%. The decisions of the respondents on this issue changed during the study period of 25 years, showing decreased interest (of 13.7% in high school students and 21.5% in college students) in the choice for the diocese, and also for religious orders (of 11.2% and 10.5%).

At the same time the percentage of respondents who feel that it is currently not worth becoming either a diocesan priest increased (by 20.1% and 15.1%), and the same holds for becoming a priest in a religious order (by 12.4% and 8.5%). Life in religious communities, the greater restriction of personal freedom of religious priests, and above all full vows of poverty are the principle factors that discouraged such large percentages of respondents from the priesthood.[15]

5. Approval and disapproval of a priest in the family

Janusz Marian argues convincingly that "[...] An important indicator of the positive or negative attitude of young people towards the clergy is the approval or disapproval of having a priest in their family. This specifies the question of whether priests are needed at all. Approval of a priest in the community does not necessarily mean approval of a priest in his own family."[16] As Władysław Piwowarski reasoned "[...] the more common the desire to have a priest in the family and the more this desire is religiously motivated, the stronger is the acceptance of the ordained ministry and the higher the degree of identification with the clergy."[17] Therefore, if the institutional priesthood enjoyed such high prestige, comprising a significant proportion of respondents' central existential value, constituting a sought-after way of life for almost a third of them, we should ask which percentage would wish to have a priest in their immediate family.[18] Would the respondents like to have a priest among the members of their immediate family – their brother, cousin, uncle, etc.?

The position of respondents in both groups on this issue differs markedly. Only 44.9% of high school students and 41.0% of college students desired to have a priest in their family. Furthermore, the percentage expressing this desire decreased over the period in both groups: among high school students it was less by 11.0%, among college students by 6.2%. The absence of such a desire is evident in 31.0% of high school and in 36.2% of university students, increasing by 14.4% and 6.1% over the study period. Less than 10% of respondents were indifferent to this matter, consisting of 10.8% of high

[15] Cf. J. Baniak, "Powołania zakonne w Polsce – analiza socjologiczna" [Religious Life Vocations in Poland – A Sociological Analysis], *Ruch Prawniczy, Ekonomiczny i Socjologiczny*, 1986, no. 1, pp. 280–285.

[16] J. Mariański, *Emigracja z Kościoła...* [Emigration from the Church...], op. cit., p. 435.

[17] W. Piwowarski, *Religijność miejska w rejonie uprzemysłowionym. Studium socjologiczne* [Urban Spirituality in an Industrialized Region. A Sociological Study], Warsaw 1977, p. 320.

[18] See W. Piwowarski, "Księża w opinii parafian wiejskich" [Priests in the Opinions of Countryside Parishoners], *Homo Dei*, 1963, no. 2, p. 112 (The author informs that 93.7% of people countrywide wished at that time to have a priest in their family, including 43.9% for non-religious motivations, and only 34.5% with typically religious motivations); idem, *Religijność ludowa – ciągłość i zmiana* [Folk Religiousness – Continuity and Changes], Wroclaw 1983, pp. 134–135. (According to the author's research, it turns out that in 1977 in Pulawy, 66.3% of Catholics in the city expressed a desire to have a priest in their family).

school students and 8.5% of college students. Other respondents did not take up a position on this issue – 13.3% and 14.3%, respectively. Respondents justified their reluctance to have a priest in the family in various ways, most often it was due to the alleged decline in the prestige of priests in Poland, as well as the immoral conduct of some priests and religious persons.[19]

6. Factors causing changes in the attitudes of respondents to the priesthood and priests

The attitudes and beliefs of the surveyed high school and college students concerning the institutional priesthood and priests have changed over 25 years. Another important cognitive question is which factors caused these changes in the religious and social awareness of the respondents? In the second and third survey period, I asked respondents to identify the main causes and reasons that brought about the changes in their attitude toward the priesthood and priests. The reasons and causes indicated by them can be categorized in two broad groups – religious and secular – within which there are several specific factors. The percentages of respondents indicating specific reasons and causes allow for ranking them in order of importance, both for high school and college students. The same reason sometimes has a different meaning in different groups, and only some are identically rated.

Concerning religious reasons and causes, respondents identified eight factors, assigning them various meanings, namely: the lack of a religious vocation – high school students 59.5% (1st place) and college students 66.0% (2nd place); inauthentic, faked piety – 52.7% (4) and 56.2% (4), weak religious faith – 36.5% (7) and 52.0% (5), immoral behavior – 57.0% (2) and 70.0% (1), neglect of worship – 39.5% (6) and 46.8% (6), neglecting catechesis in school – 44.4% (5) and 42.8% (7), conflicts and discord in the rectory – 52.8% (3) and 58.6% (3), other reasons – 23.4% (8) and 26.4% (8), no indication – 13.7% and 12.5%. These reasons were indicated by a total of 45.7% high school and 52.4% of university students, but there was an increase (of 16.7% and 23.4%) in the number of respondents who indicated the reasons for this in 2008.

The reasons and causes of the secular respondents included several factors, among which eight were indicated most frequently in both groups. These

[19] See J. Baniak, *Między buntem a potrzebą akceptacji i zrozumienia...* [Between Rebellion and the Need for Acceptance and Understanding...], op. cit., p. 304, table 127. (Rural and urban junior high schoolers, when asked whether they wished to have a priest in their family, replied as follows: I want to – 40.2%, I do not want to – 34.1%, I am indifferent – 10.7%, It is difficult to say – 10.7%, Lack of data – 4.3%).

reasons were also rated differently by respondents. They are: pride and conceit – 70.5% of high school (4th place) and 72.1% of college students (6th place), secular way of life – 62.0% (7) and 73.7% (4), too much political involvement – 72.6% (2) and 78.6% (1), intolerance for those who think differently – 63.1% (6) and 65.1% (7), practical materialism – 72.0% (3) and 75.4% (3), intimate relationships with women – 66.6% (5) and 78.0% (2), alcoholism and drug addiction – 74.4% (1) and 72.4% (5), poor professional and humanities education – 39.6% (8) and 45.5% (8), other reasons – 20.0% (9) and 14.3% (9), no display – 11.5% and 12.1%. The percentage total of secular reasons indicated by high school students was 61.0% and by college students 63.9%. During the study period, there was an increase in the percentage of respondents who were aversely inclined towards the priesthood and priests for these reasons – 25.7% among high school students and 32.4% among college students. It is precisely these reasons and causes that often provoked a crisis in the priestly identity of priests and pressured them to abandon the priesthood for the life of marriage and family.[20]

In conclusion, from the analysis in this chapter, it can be noted that the institutional priesthood is both a religious vocation and necessary profession in the religious community. Theologians attempt to explain the essence of the priesthood as a "gift" from God to a man, or by referring to the visible charisma as the set of features allowing him to carry out religious functions for the worship of God and service to the Church. Psychologists see the priesthood as a specific way of life, based on religious and spiritual ideals, through which the priest himself must pass, since he freely and consciously chose it. Sociologists, on the other hand, perceive the priesthood through the prism of social significance, contact and relationships, professional roles and functions, which the priest fulfills every day for the good of other people.

Catholic adults and youth perceived and evaluated the recognized institutional priesthood differently, sometimes contrary to the teachings of the Church on the priesthood. In this chapter, research presented the views, attitudes and actions of high school and academic students towards the priesthood and priests over the study period of 25 years. During this time, the living

[20] See J. Baniak, "Źródła i przyczyny kryzysu tożsamości kapłańskiej księży rzymskokatolickich w Polsce. Studium socjologiczne" [Sources and Reasons for the Roman Catholic Priestly Identity Crisis in Poland. A Sociological Study], in M. Libiszowska-Żółtkowska (ed.), *Tożsamości religijne w społeczeństwie polskim. Socjologiczne studium przypadków* [Religious Identity in Polish Society. A Sociological Case Study], Warsaw 2009, pp. 67–107. (Economically active priests in the Church and priests who left the priesthood and returned to secular life identified a number of reasons for their identity crisis and crisis of priestly vocations, which had a religious, Church and typically secular profile. Among these, they also pointed to alcoholism – 58.6 %, consisting of priests currently working in the Church – 62.2%, and "former" priests – 55.3%).

conditions of Poles changed under the influence of systemic transformation in the country. These changes played a role in Poles' religious life and attitudes towards the institutional Church, including the clergy. This was also shown to be the case for the Polish youth. In a large percentage of the surveyed high school and college students, these changes are negative and critical towards the priesthood and ptriests. The majority in both groups understand the priesthood and the role of the priest according to the teachings of the Church.

Chapter III

The priest as a social role type in the perception of the respondents

The role of a priest has many definitions and depends on the field of knowledge that deals with the problem of defining this role – theologians, sociologists of religion, and canon lawyers all define its nature and range of possibilities differently. Leo von Deschwanden describes the priestly role rather broadly and distinguishes two types: specific and diffusive. The specific role is associated with institutional religiosity and is characterized by a totality – it includes many role segments that the priest fulfills in religious and local groups. This role of the priest consists of the following functions: teacher of faith, celebrant of sacraments, head of the parish community, superior of a religious congregation, director of penitents' consciences, and counselor in temporal matters. On the other hand, the diffusive role is associated with individual religiosity, often selective and subjective,[1] and as a result it is innovative in nature. This role includes various pastoral initiatives of the priest and contributes to the modernization of the methods and tools of his parochial activity, as well as the shaping of new forms of this activity. Emphasis is placed on the personal and individual pastoral care of the faithful. In this role, the priest has a chance to reach out with religious service to various individuals making up the parish community, to help them solve difficult religious and moral dilemmas.[2]

---

[1] CF. S. Grotowska, *Religijność subiektywna. Studium socjologiczne na podstawie wywiadów narracyjnych* [Subjective Religiousness. A Sociological Study Based on Narrative Interviews], Cracow 1999, pp. 56–68.

[2] See L. von Deschwanden, "Die Rolle des Gemeindepriesters zwischen Kirche und Gesellschaft," in J. Wossner (ed.), *Religion in Umbruch*, Stuttgart 1972, pp. 395–409; idem, "Eine

1. Institutional priesthood as the basis for the role of a priest in a religious group

The basis for the social role of a priest in a religious group is institutional priesthood as a specific ecclesiastical office. Institutional priesthood is interpreted from many perspectives. In this analysis, its sociological understanding is important. Henri Spencer derives vocational priesthood from original polytheistic religion, and points out that it originated as a result of the social division of activities within a wider social group with a religious character. In his view, the functions of the priest were originally associated with the functions of the sorcerer, exorcist, prophet, physician, magician, tribal leader, teacher, philosopher, etc. The coming into existence of a social hierarchy and the emergence of religious and magical activities in the cyclical process of specialization became a basis for the formation of a special and exclusive group of people who occupied themselves exclusively or almost exclusively with cultic activities, the aim of which were to multiply the glory of God (or a deity[3]). Edward Ciupak adds that "[...] in the social division of labor, activities beyond productive labor fell to the priests, with the result that they became actively involved in the development of culture, science, and education. In Catholicism, priesthood is a professional institution satisfying two basic criteria: activity intended for others and activity based on prior preparation in the form of professional education and religious, spiritual, and moral formation."[4]

From a theological viewpoint, a priest is "[...] a man called by the Church to actively mediate between people and God through the sacrifice of the Holy Mass and through his existential relationship with Christ, the only Mediator living in the Church."[5] In this context, M. Kowalewski adds that "[...] in the universal Church, a priest is one who by virtue of ordination has the authority to consecrate and absolve, as well as to provide other sacraments, while priesthood is the office and dignity of mediator between divinity and man."[6]

Practically speaking, the cult over which the priest presides is institutionally defined and distinguished from other products of culture. This fact requires of

Rollenanalyse des katholischen Pfarreipriester," *Internationales Jahrbuch fur Religionssoziologie*, t. IV: Beitrage zur religionssoziologischen Forschung, Köln – Opladen 1968, pp. 125–135.

[3] See H. Spencer, *Instytucje religijne* [Religious Institutions], Warsaw 1981, pp. 34–35.

[4] E. Ciupak, *Kapłaństwo – powołanie i zawód* [Priesthood – A Vocation and Profession], in idem, *Kult religijny i jego społeczne podłoże* [Religious Worship and Its Social Basis], Warsaw 1965, p. 393.

[5] See W. Granat, *Sakramenty święte. Cz. 1* [The Holy Sacraments. Part 1], Lublin 1961, p. 343.

[6] M. Kowalewski, *Mały słownik teologiczny* [A Small Dictionary of Theology], Poznan 1960, p. 184.

the priest theological knowledge and practical skills. He is therefore described as a set of social roles, historically conditioned and dependent on the current needs of the Church. The implementation of these roles is essential for the Church and its various structures, and at the same time it is not indifferent to the priest himself nor to the religious people living in a particular parish community.

a) The nature, components and process of implementing the role of the parish priest

The social role of the priest is dependent on various factors, and above all, it is institutionalized and takes the form of specific patterns of action established in religious communities. The basis of its institutional nature in the past was both the requirements of theology and ecclesiastical norms, as well as the requirements of local traditions and customs. The priest's role was in fact much more extensive than defined by the regulations of the Church. Over time, it underwent many changes and has evolved to such a degree and extent that the primary and secondary tasks which the priest performed in the religious group have merged. Descriptions of this evolution of the priest's role can be found in what are now classic works of sociology,[7] which call attention to the essential scale and importance of this process to the role of the priest.[8]

Therefore, it is the social and religious dimension of priesthood that is the source of the priest's social role, since it is this dimension that contains the priest's fundamental purpose, the religious position and extent of his hierarchically assigned competences, and the extent of his priestly authority in a parish as granted by the diocesan bishop. On this basis, the priest acts formally ("officially") in a religious group, performs his own professional duties and the religious and secular functions which make up his social role. These functions also determine the integrity of his role as a coherent whole. The variety of functions indicates the complexity and significance of the priest's social role and the parish as a basic structure of the institutional Church.[9]

In sociological terms, the functions of the parish priest forming his primary role can be described in three general categories: 1) basic functions: liturgical and ritual, parish administration, charismatic, charitable, management

[7] See F. Znaniecki, *Chłop polski w Europie i Ameryce* [The Polish Peasant in Europe and America], vol. 1, Warsaw 1985, pp. 14–21; J. Chałasiński, *Młode pokolenie chłopów* [The Young Generation of Peasants], vol. 4, Warsaw 1958, pp. 24–29.

[8] See J. Baniak, "Problem roli społecznej kapłana" [The Problem of the Priest's Social Role], *Teologia Praktyczna*, 2002, vol. 3, pp. 257–258.

[9] See W. Goddijn, "Rola kapłana w Kościele i w społeczeństwie" [The Role of the Priest in the Church and Society], *Znak*, 1966, no. 139–140, p. 207.

of material goods and economic resources of the parish; 2) complementary functions: paraliturgical, social and economic, educational, cultural, recreation and leisure, parish management; 3) private functions: they vary and depend on the self-awareness and spiritual identity of the priest, on his attitude towards the tasks of priesthood and the priestly ethos. Furthermore, these functions are also dependent on the attitude of lay Catholics to the Church and the clergy, on the social status and living standards of the lay, their religious involvement, and the level of religious and secular morality.[10]

In practice, the social role of the priest and its daily realization depends on a combination of situations in a given country, the living conditions of the people and their attitude towards Church institutions and parish priests. Acceptance of priests and their practices differs widely in different environments; all the more so given the variety of social roles of the priest. Not all people accept priests, and some acknowledge their social role and the tasks directly related to it in different ways. Such attitudes of the lay affect the status of the institutional priesthood and the social self-esteem of priests in a global society and in the parish community.

b) The internal and external conflict in the social role of the priest

The priest is vulnerable to a double conflict – internal and external – in his social role in the Church. The internal conflict of the priest's role includes the following problems: 1) Assuming the position of a "link" connecting the bishop to the faithful sometimes minimizes or reduces the value and importance of the priest's role, while overestimating the importance of superior authority or the role of the laity in the Church. An intermediary status creates a certain ambiguity of this role of the priest; 2) The institutional priesthood has certain characteristics similar to so-called liberal professions, as well as bureaucratic work. This similarity significantly affects the process of realizing the role of the priest in a religious group and in the local community. The realization of the priest's social role in the church and secular environment also encounters an external conflict when the priest performs everyday professional duties, as then he finds himself between two systems of norms and expectations that are mutually exclusive, or contradictory. The priest must resolve this

[10] See E. Pin, *La Paroisse catholique. Le formes variables d'un système social*, Rome 1965, pp. 81–83; W. Piwowarski, "Więź z przywódcami religijnymi" [The Bond with Religious Leaders], in idem, *Religijność wiejska w warunkach urbanizacji* [Rural Religiosity in the Conditions of Urbanization], Warsaw 1971, pp. 273–276; J. Majka, "Socjologiczna analiza duszpasterskiej roli proboszcza" [A Sociological Analysis of the Pastoral Role of the Parish Priest], in idem, *Socjologia parafii. Zarys zagadnienia* [Parish Sociology. An Outline of the Topic], Lublin 1971, pp. 176–183; J. Mariański, *Żyć parafią* [Living with the Parish], Wroclaw 1984, pp. 134–146.

contradiction to his own advantage, although he knows that this task is very difficult. This conflict is caused by the necessity of combining the secular role with the religious role, which results from the different positions of the priest in the parish and secular group. In Poland, priests often take the secular role too far and are excessively involved in political activities, leading to criticism from lay Catholics for neglecting their religious role, which is considered the fundamental role in their Church activity.[11]

Sociologists of religion and pastoral theologians point to the many sources of both conflicts in the priest's social role. The main source of these conflicts, in their view, is the current priestly formation of students in seminaries, where they are systematically trained for pastoral work in parishes.[12] In the seminary, students familiarize themselves with the nature of the priestly role, the methods of performing the role in the parish, the professional competences that will be entitled to them as parish priests, and also learn the specificity of the priestly life in stages – its pros and cons, bright and dark sides, conveniences and difficulties, and above all, the original attributes of the parish priest's profession, which are not present in typically secular occupations and groups in society, such as celibacy, solitude, strict obedience to the authority of the bishop, or poverty. In the seminaries, superiors and lecturers consciously and purposefully shape the personality of the priest in seminarians according to the current model of the parish priest in the Church, in which there is a clearly presented religious and social role for priests.[13]

The problem is that there is a great difference between the objectives of priestly formation of the students in the seminary and the practice of priestly life in the parish, one that young priests soon see and experience themselves. This discrepancy results in conflicts in performing their own roles in the parish and the local community, which they sometimes are unable to resolve to the benefit of themselves and the faithful, without neglecting the interests of ecclesiastical authority. Seminary formation of students in Poland is very unilateral and emphasizes poorly, or sometimes completely ignores, the prospect of

---

[11] See J. Baniak, "Problem z politycznym zaangażowaniem Kościoła instytucjonalnego w Polsce" [The Problem with Political Involvement of the Institutional Church in Poland], *Społeczeństwo i Kościół*, 2007, vol. 7, pp. 7–13; idem, "Zaangażowanie społeczne i polityczne Kościoła i księży w Polsce w wyobrażeniach katolików" [Social and Political Involvement of the Church and Priests in Poland in the Perception of Catholics], *Społeczeństwo i Kościół*, 2005, vol. 2, pp. 107–154.

[12] See G. Słowiński, "Ksiądz wczoraj i dziś. Społeczne konstruowanie powołania do kapłaństwa" [The Priest Yesterday and Today. Social Construction of the Vocation to Priesthood], in M. Libiszowska-Żółtkowska, S. Grotowska (ed.), *Religijność i duchowość – dawne i obecne formy* [Religiosity and Spirituality – Past and Present Forms], Cracow 2010, pp. 408–424.

[13] See J. Majka (ed.), *Osobowość kapłańska* [The Priestly Personality], Wroclaw 1976.

priestly life and work in the sociocultural conditions of the parish and secular group, the living conditions of lay Catholics and other residents of the parish. Little or no attention is paid to a life completely different from the life of the clergy within a kind of enclave, the life to which the seminarians are accustomed according to Church methods of seminary education and socialization.[14] Parish life quickly falsifies this idea of priestly formation, exposing them to various conflicts, including the sharp conflict of their own conscience, or a conflict with the demands of ecclesiastical authority.

The image of the social role of the priest is a model image. This image results from an analysis of the normative system of the Catholic faith and the parish community system. When confronted with the life of the parish, this model contributes to a double conflict in the priest's roles. Consequently, only some parish priests fulfill these roles properly, while in other cases, their realization encounters the resistance of both Church regulations and the expectations of the lay faithful. Most likely, only a percentage of parish priests fulfill their spiritual and professional duties according to the model of the priestly role which is currently binding in the Roman Catholic Church. As current sociological research indicates, this situation also occurs in Poland.

2. The scope of the role of the priest according to the youth

What do high school and college students imagine the role of a parish priest to be? What ingredients do they include in the structure of a priest's role? Do their perceptions of the role of the priest correspond to the official description in the teachings of the Catholic Church? These questions produce a theoretical analysis of the religious and social role of the priest. I asked my respondents these questions during all my research studies, and will present their replies in the further analysis of the results.

a) Religious mediation of the priest between God and Man in the assessment of the respondents

The theological concept of the institutional priesthood assumes that the authority of the priest's office is based on objective premises and comes from religious functions that he fulfills in the Church. By virtue of the priesthood, a priest is a "mediator" or "intercessor" between religious people and God; he

[14] See A. Królikowska, "Współczesna katolickość – w kierunku enklawy. Przypadek Polski" [Contemporary Catholicism – Towards an Enclave. The Polish Example], in L. Gołdyka, I. Machaj (ed.), *Enklawy życia społecznego. Kontynuacje* [Enclaves of Social Life. A Follow-up], Szczecin 2009, pp. 323–342.

is a kind of "helper" who facilitates people along the way that leads them to eternal salvation. The Church reminds the faithful that the mediating role of the priest is required, so they ought to take advantage of it in their religious life. In the light of these assumptions, the question is whether Catholic Polish youth accept the necessity of the role of the priest in their personal religiosity, or do they regard it as useless on their quest for salvation?

he study revealed that the surveyed high school and college students' attitudes towards this issue are very differentiated, and thus clearly differ from the Church's doctrinal assumptions. The need for the mediating role of the priest in their religiousness and the pursuit of salvation was claimed as necessary or required by only 52.0% of all respondents, including 58.9% of high school and 45.1% of college students, a percentage that decreased over the assumed period of 25 years by 13.8% and 4.8%. At the same time, 32.9% of respondents, including 28.2% of high school and 37.7% of college students, stated clearly that the role of priestly mediation is clearly superfluous in their religion and their quest for eternal salvation, because they can establish a relationship with God themselves and care for their own salvation. The percentage of respondents manifesting this attitude towards this role of the priest increased throughout the period in both groups – among high school students by 7.0% and among college students by 5.2%. The remaining respondents did not address this issue – 12.1% and 17.2% of all respondents.[15]

Surveyed high school and college students look at the mediating role of the priest through the prism of the different functions that he fulfils in the parish community and people's secular lives. These functions form the scope of the role of a priest, or decide on the scale of its competence in the parish. Which issues and problems do respondents include in the scope of the mediating role of the priest?

---

[15] See. S. Dobrzanowski, "Młodzież o kapłaństwie i kapłanach" [The Youth on Priests and Priesthood], *Chrześcijanin w Świecie*, 1977, no. 2 (50), p. 97. (This author states that in 1973, among 300 of his young respondents, 72.3% accepted the mediating role of priests, and 21.7% rejected this role, so the remaining did not take a stance on this point); J. Baniak, *Między buntem a potrzebą akceptacji i zrozumienia. Świadomość religijna i moralna a kryzys tożsamości osobowej młodzieży gimnazjalnej. Studium socjologiczne* [Between Rebelion and the Need for Acceptance and Understanding. The Awareness of Religious and Moral a Crisis of Personal Indentity in Junior High School Youth. A Sociological Study], Cracow 2008, pp. 311–312, table 130. (Priestly mediation in people's salvation was claimed to be absolutely necessary by 38.6% and necessary by 18.6% of the studied junior high schoolers in Kalisz, including 42.0% and 16.8% of girls and 32.0% and 22.3% of boys. However, it was deemed superfluous by a total of 31.5% of the respondents, including 30.8% of girls and 32.9% of boys and 27.8% of country students and 33.8% of city students. The remaining did not get involved with this issue).

Matters that respondents included in the scope of the mediating role of a priest can be summarized into three general groups: religious and church, religious and moral, and typically secular. The largest percentage of respondents were in favor of the first group of cases – in total they were appreciated by 55.0% of respondents, including 53.4% of high school and 56.6% of college students; during the study period, these percentages by 19.9% and 20.9%. Respondents placed religious and moral matters in second place: these aspects met with the approval of 15.9% of the total respondents, including 18.8% of high school and 13.0% of college students, but interest in them declined during the study period in both groups, by 20.0% and 11.2% respectively. Typically secular issues were included in the role of the priest by only a small percentage of respondents – averaging 8.0%, including 7.4% of high school and 8.7% of college students, and their percentage declined during the study period by 4.2% and 2.8%. The remaining high school (17.4%) and college students (18.7%) did not indicate any matter that might be part of the mediation role of the priest.[16]

b) The mutual contact of the respondents with priests in varying circumstances

In sociological terms, it can be assumed that the mutual attitudes of young people and priests manifest into complex relationships and social contacts, which have the effect of creating closer bonds and ties between the two parties. These contacts in the case of the young people I studied are made possible in different circumstances and situations: in the parish of origin, during school catechesis and in formal or informal religious groups of which the priest takes care or control. This occurs in the priest's parish of residence during the youth's instruction in school, during the activities of university ministry, etc. Under these circumstances, there are real opportunities for youth to interact with priests, while at the same time creating an opportunity for priests to influence the religious, moral and secular attitudes and actions of youth. Which types of mutual contact with priests did the respondents indicate?

Respondents indicated, depending on group membership, the various circumstances that facilitate their contact and affiliation with priests in the parish or at centers of student pastoral care ministries during this period. Among the many circumstances, eight things were indicated by both groups as most popular, although with different emphasis as to their importance. Catechesis classes in school as the occasions for meeting priests were most frequently

[16] Cf. J. Baniak, *Ksiądz w oczach młodzieży. Obraz kapłana w świadomości młodzieży licealnej i akademickiej na przykładzie Kalisza. Studium socjologiczne* [The Priest in the Eyes of the Youth. The Image of the Priest in the Awareness of High School and College Youth in the Example of Kalisz. A Sociological Study], Poznan 1993, pp. 108–113.

indicated by high school students (65.9%) and pastoral ministries centers by college students (43.5%), and these circumstances were indicated by a total of 49.0%, respectively. Respondents placed the church building in second place, where they met with priests during the Holy Mass and when receiving the sacraments, which included 47.6% of respondents, meaning 59.1% of high school and 36.1% of college students. Third place went to the priest's annual Christmas carol visits to the family home, indicated by a total of 41.4% of respondents, including 55.1% of high school and 27.7% of college students. Pre-marriage courses were a good opportunity to test young people's frequent contact with priests, indicated by a total of 33.7% of respondents, including 24.7% of high school and 42.6% of college students. Youth retreats were placed fifth, indicated by a total 32.4% of respondents, including 39.4% of high school and 25.3% of college students.

Religious activities and church youth organizations were convenient circumstances for contact with priests for 31.0% of respondents, including 36.8% of high school students and 25.1% of college students. More than one in four respondents (25.2%) had the possibility to contact the priest during the walking pilgrimage to Jasna Góra in Częstochowa, as indicated by 21.3% of high school and 29.1% of college students. Some respondents (24.5%) met the priest in the parish office to arrange various matters related to their own religious or family problems, and this circumstance was indicated by 19.6% of high school and 29.5% of college students. In addition, 25.2% of respondents, including 24.3% of high school students and 26.1% of college students mentioned other circumstances that facilitated their contact with priests. During the whole study period, some circumstances were less favorable for contact between respondents and priests, and others contributed to reinforcing existing mutual bonds between the parties. High school students were more interested in contact with priests than college students, thus pointing to these different circumstances which make contacts possible.[17]

c) The need for a personal relationships between the respondents and parish priests

During each period of study, I also asked respondents whether they felt the need to establish and keep a personal relationship with parish priests as their ministers, teachers and religious educators or caregivers in youth groups in par-

[17] See A. Przybecki, *Urzeczywistnianie się Kościoła w środowisku akademickim* [The Church Coming to Life in Academic Student Centers], Poznan 1986, pp. 42–50; A. Grzesik, *Między kryzysem a odrodzeniem moralności. Wartości moralne w świadomości studentów* [Between a Crisis and the Re-birth of Morality. Moral Values in the Awareness of Students], Rzeszów 2002, pp. 271–312.

ishes and other circumstances. Did informal and occasional contacts develop into lasting relationships between respondents and their priests?

The study found that 46.8% of respondents, including 50.0% of high school students and 43.1% of college students had felt the need for establishing or maintaining a personal relationship with priests in different circumstances, although the frequency of this desire varies significantly. This need appeared frequently in 12.4% of respondents, including 13.5% of high school and 11.0% of college students; irregularly among 19.0% (18.2% and 19.8%), and occasionally among 15.4% (18.3% and 12.3%). The dominant response indicates irregular and occasionally maintained personal relationships with priests, comprising a total of 34.4%, including 36.5% of high school students and 32.1% of college students. Percentages of respondents in favour of these close ties decreased throughout the period in both groups among high school (by 15.7%) and college students (by 23.4%). At the same time, up to 42.6% of respondents, including 41.1% of high school and 43.6% of college students said they had never made, or did not seek to establish, direct ties with priests, since they did not feel such a need, or did not trust priests for a variety of reasons, including moral reasons. This percentage increased in both groups during the study period, by 9.8% and 12.6% respectively.[18]

3. Political involvement of priests in Poland in the assessments of the respondents

The attitude of Poles towards the political involvement of bishops and priests, and more generally towards the entire institutional Church, has always been critical, especially concerning Church influence on the voting preferences of citizens. The radicality of this criticism has intensified significantly since 1989 and continues presently. In the 1980s, the Roman Catholic Church in Poland was a strong political and moral opposition to the socialist state with its central

---

[18] See J. Przybyłowski, *Znaczenie nowej ewangelizacji dla duszpasterstwa młodzieży. Studium pastoralne* [The Meaning of New Evangelization for Student Youth Ministry. A Pastoral Study], Lublin 2001, pp. 278–290; F. Bednarski, *Wychowanie młodzieży dorastającej* [Educating Adolescent Youth], Warsaw 2000, pp. 36–43; J. Baniak, *Między buntem a potrzebą akceptacji i zrozumienia...* [Between Rebelion and the Need for Acceptance and Understanding...], op. cit., pp. 371–401, table 13. [The research shows that 47.6% of all junior high school students, including 49.9% of girls and 43.3% of boys and 56.6% of students from rural areas and 42.0% of students from cities reported the need to establish and reinforce personal relationships with priests. But 43.5% (42.1%, 46.1%, 37.1%, 47.4%) stated that they still had such a need. People declaring this need justified it for religious reasons (49.0%), moral reasons (12.1%) and typically secular reasons (30.3%). The remaining 8.6% did not take a position on this issue].

and local government. Due to this, the Church retains Her own autonomy and independence when assessing political events that took place in the country. The moral evaluations of these events often turn into severe critique of state power activity and the political system.

The political situation of the Church and the clergy changed significantly in the 1990s under the influence of political transformations in the country. At that time, the Church's protective barriers in society disappeared almost completely, but authorities could not agree to these changes. Such a "protective request" attitude towards the state is the current situation, demanding separate privileges for the Catholic Church, the largest religious community in the country. Researchers indicate that only since November 1995 could a stabilization in social ratings of involvement of priests and the Church be observed, when the percentage of Catholics evaluating them critically decreased.[19] We see a similar situation in the early years of the first decade of the twenty-first century, even though the "front" of criticism towards the Church and clergy is gaining strength and increasing in scale in the state umder the new political and economic system.[20]

The political commitment of bishops and parish priests intensified considerably in the second half of the twentieth century, when the hierarchy clearly interfered with the legislative activity of Poland's lower Parliament house and the Senate, and influenced important government decisions. Parish priests also instructed the faithful as to whom they should vote for in presidential and parliamentary elections as well as for local councils. Consequently, Poles today protect the Church less often, and increasingly criticize its excessive political involvement and interference in state affairs without shame. Today, the position of the Church and clergy in Poland is morally overburdened, due to the blurring of clear boundaries between the two institutions, and the trespassing of mutual competencies. Researchers are constantly informing us that Poles are concerned with this situation and perceive the Church's "entering into" state

---

[19] See B. Wciórka, *Kościół w III Rzeczypospolitej. Komunikat z badań Centrum Badania Opinii Społecznej* [The Church in the III Republic od Poland. Communique from Studies of the Center of Social Opinion (CBOS)], BS/78/1999, Warsaw 1999; also idem, "Opinie o roli Kościoła w Polskiej Rzeczypospolitej Ludowej (PRL)" [Opinions about the Role of the Church in the People's Republic of Poland], *Zestaw Materiałów CBOS* [Set of CBOS Materials], Warsaw 1998, no. 3, p. 7. (The study reported that 56.3% of adult Poles were against this and 20.6% agreed that the Church should state Her opinions in political matters).

[20] See B. Roguska, *Stabilizacja opinii o wpływie Kościoła na życie kraju. Komunikat z badań CBOS* [Stabilization of Opinions about the Church's Influence on the Life in the Country. Communique from CBOS Research], BS/79/2004, Warsaw 2004; Cf. J. Baniak, "Zaangażowanie społeczne i polityczne Kościoła i księży w Polsce..." [Social and Political Involvement of the Church and Priests in Poland...], op. cit., pp. 108–154.

matters incorrectly. At the same time, they also ask if they are now "living in a church-state," or a "state-church"? Objectively speaking, Poles' fears seem justified, since the blurring of the boundaries between the Church and the democratic Polish state is becoming more evident, an unacceptable situation according to public opinion.[21]

What is the attitude of my respondents towards the political commitment of the Church and priests in Poland? Are the assessments of the high school and college students surveyed during this period concerning this issue identical to the assessments of adult Poles, established in a number of sociological studies?

The study found that 63.9% of respondents, including 61.3% of high school students and 66.6% of college students, are convinced of the excessive politicization of the Church and priests in Poland. This percentage steadily grew in both groups during this period, by 10.9% and 9.5%. It is worth noting that as manyas 36.5% of high school and 41.2% of college students spoke of the excessive politicization of Polish bishops and priests, and their percentage increased during the test period of 25 by 23.8%, and 19.1%. In contrast, limited politicization practice was noted by only 10.8% of respondents, including 10.1% of high school and 11.4% of college students, and this percentage declined during the study period by 2.2% and 2.6%. At the same time, 28.0% of respondents, including 30.6% of high school and 25.4% of college students openly claimed that they do not see any politicization in the Church – neither among bishops nor among parish priests, and expressed surprise that the "enemies" of the Church in Poland are "accusing" her of political engagement, which they consider a lie.

The percentage of people not perceiving political commitment among Polish bishops and priests declined between 1983 and 2008 in both groups: among high school students by 12.2% and among college students by 10.0%. Most likely, these numbers joined those who were convinced of the involvement of Polish clergy in political issues and of their influence on the political preferences of lay Catholics in various environments, mostly parishes. The remaining respondents (8.1% and 8.0%) did not take a position on this issue.[22]

---

[21] See S. Kwiatkowski, "Stosunek do religii a orientacje polityczne Polaków" [The Attitude of Religion and the Political Orientation of Poles], *Edukacja Polityczna*, 1989, no. 10, p. 314–326; S. Kwiatkowski, E. Kościerza-Jaworska, "Polacy o religii i miejscu Kościoła w życiu kraju," [Poles in Religion and the Place of the Church in the Life of the Country], *Nowe Drogi*, 1989, no. 2, pp. 96–117; J. Mariański, "Patologia kierownictwa parafialnego" [Pathologies in Directing a Parish], in idem, *Żyć parafią* [Living with a Parish], op. cit., pp. 185–223.

[22] See B. Badora, "Młodzież o polityce i demokracji" [The Youth on Politics and Democracy], in *Młodzież 2003. Opinie i diagnozy nr 2. CBOS* [The Youth 2003. Opinions and Diagnostics no. 2. CBOS], Warsaw 2004, pp. 49–60. (Youth in middle and secondary schools survey by CBOS in 2003, expressed by 72.0% of its population, the idea that the Church should

Respondents also answered the question of whether priests influenced the electoral preference of parishioners by indicating the person they should vote for in presidential, parliamentary and local government elections.

The dominant percentage of respondents in both groups stated that many parish priests and many bishops gave specific "instructions" to the faithful during the election campaign on election day, telling Catholics for whom they should cast their electoral votes.

75.0% of respondents are convinced that the Polish clergy intervene in elections, including 71.9% of high school and 77.0% of college students, and this percentage has increased during the study period in both groups: 10.1% and 9.1%. However, priests usually instruct the faithful in the following circumstances: Sunday sermons – 34.8% (including 31.8% of high school students and 37.8% of college students), special interventions – 13.9% (14.5% and 13.3%), letters from bishops read in Church – 12.6% (11.2% and 14.0%), religious education – 6.0% (6.9% and 5.1%), and at the parish office – 7.2% (7.5% and 6.8%). The opposite view on this issue was demonstrated by only 21.7% of respondents, including 24.1% of high school and 19.3% of college students, stating that priests in their parishes were quite apolitical and encouraged faithful people to vote for the Church, or for members of the party "friendly" to the Church or priests . The percentage of these respondents decreased during the study period in both groups by 11.0% among high school students and 9.6% among college students – most of these numbers probably joined the ranks of people confirming the impact of clergy on the voting preferences of the faithful.

The same applies to priests influencing the faithful during local elections. Up to 71.8% of respondents spoke of such "pressures," including 70.1% of high school and 73.7% of college students, and this percentage grew during the study period in both groups – by 12.5% and 5.7%. According to respondents, this impact is most strongly exerted during Sunday sermons and homilies at mass (33.9%, including 30.9% of high school students and 36.8% of college students), with special agitation propaganda in the local community (22.8%, including 24.3% and 21.3%). Meanwhile, 24.3% of respondents, including 25.9% of high school students and 22.6% of college students, did not notice the influence of priests on the faithful during local elections, a number which declined during the study period in both groups, by 13.4% and 6.2%.[23]

---

be separated entirely from the state, and 15.0% stated that the Church should influence state policy, while 12.0% was not able to take a position on this issue).

[23] See J. Baniak, *Między buntem a potrzebą akceptacji i zrozumienia...* [Between Rebelion and the Need for Acceptance and Understanding...], op. cit., pp. 317–319, table 132. [Junior high respondents said that priests influence voters in parliamentary and presidential elections in such

From an objective point of view, the scale of this phenomenon in Poland is considered highly alarming, which consequently raises questions in society, including among Catholics, about the true role of the Church in a democratic state and civil society. Other researchers also write about the current level of politicization of the Church and clergy in Poland, including those professionally connected with its structures,[24] pointing out that we should again normalize relations between Church and State, making them autonomous in all respects.

To sum up this analysis, it should be stated that the investigated Polish secondary school, high school and college students generally accept the religious and social roles of the priest in the parish and the local community, but judge it not to be in accord with the doctrinal guidelines of the Catholic Church. The dominant percentage of the respondents reduce a priest to his religious and ecclesiastical matters, and exemplifies him from civil and moral matters and problems. Many respondents believe that the Church should not expand the role of priests to include political affairs or enter into the areas of state competence. Also, a significant proportion of respondents do not accept the mediation of priests on their personal way to salvation, or, generally speaking, in their religious life. People accepting the mediating role of priests in matters of salvation often justify their choice according to religious motives and the legitimacy of Church teachings.

---

circumstances: sermons (26.2%), agitations (20.3%), letters from bishops (11.2%), religious education classes (7.8%). In turn, 29.7% said that priests did not affect the voting preferences of the faithful, including 32.4% of girls and 24.4% of boys, 37.1% of students from rural areas and 25.1% of students from the city].

[24] See J. Mariański, *Kościół katolicki w Polsce a życie społeczne. Studium socjologiczno-pastoralne* [The Catholic Church in Poland and the Social Life. A Sociological and Pastoral Study], Lublin 2005, pp. 181–182; *Religion. Polish Survey. Codebook*, Warsaw 1992, pp. 20–21. (Poles asked in 1992 whether priests should not try to influence how people vote in elections, gave the following replies: strongly agree – 36.9% agree – 34.8%; I neither agree nor disagree – 5.6%; I disagree – 8.7%, strongly disagree – 8.5%; hard to assess – 4.4%, no response – 1.4%); P. Stachowski, "Dylematy zaangażowania. Kościół katolicki wobec wyborów parlamentarnych i prezydenckich w Polsce: 1989–2001" [The Dilemma of Getting Involved. The Catholic Church towards Parlamentary and Presidential Elections in Poland: 1989–2001], *Przegląd Polityczny*, 2003, no. 1, pp. 73–88.

Chapter IV

The authority of the priest in the perceptions and evaluations of the respondents

1. Authority as a multidimensional phenomenon and subject of sociological research

What is authority in its essence and purpose? What does it mean to "gain" and "exercise" authority, or to "delegate" it to a person? What is the "intervention" of an authority and what are its basic types? What is the source of the authority of an individual? Such questions precede the establishment of the nature and extent of a priest's authority in a religious group and local community, as well as the discussion of ideas and opinions of the Polish youth surveyed on the authority of Catholic priests in Poland. In a general sense, as Janusz Mariański states, "[...] authority means someone's (a given individual's or institution's) advantage over other individuals or social groups. This advantage warrants their right to issue decisions, to control and enforce their execution (the right to give orders) and is expressed in the ability to influence, gain the recognition and obedience of subordinates, and to control others' conduct."[1] In sociological terms, the source of a person's authority is found in social experience, in the structure of a social group in which certain individuals demonstrate an advantage over other individuals. Consequently, these individuals assume a specific position in the structure of a social group, playing important social roles consisting of various functions or sets of functions, and specific competences and tasks.[2]

---

[1] J. Mariański, "Koncepcja autorytetu księdza" [The Concept of a Priest's Authority], in idem, *Żyć parafią* [Living with the Parish], Wroclaw 1984, pp. 108–109.

[2] See K. Z. Sowa, *Wstęp do socjologicznej teorii zrzeszeń* [Introduction to the Sociological Theory of Associations], Warsaw 1988, p. 123.

Authority as a subject of sociological research is a multidimensional phenomenon. From the time of Max Weber, researchers have indicated three groups of authority: traditional, legal, and charismatic. Traditional authority is based on people's belief that an individual or group of persons inherits or for a long time has had authority over other people or social communities. Legal authority is based on official documents legitimizing a particular kind of power. Charismatic authority is based on the acceptance of extraordinary or supernatural qualities of persons who have specific power over other people. Over time, researchers have pointed to other, contrasting categorisations of leadership and authority such as static and dynamic, general and specialized, continuous and periodic, conscious and unconscious, professional and amateur, personal and impersonal, formal and informal, religious and secular, traditional and modern, directive and non-directive, natural and institutional, instrumental and expressive.[3]

The authority of an official position is directly and strictly connected to a social role, institutionalized and performed in a group. It is "assigned" an office by the act of introduction and functions to a certain extent regardless of whether the entity with authority enjoys personal authority or has no such recognition.[4] According to Władysław Piwowarski, "[...] Authority can be viewed from two sides: the persons who exercise authority and the functions that these persons fulfill in a social group and in society."[5]

Some researchers point to a crisis of authority in the modern world, with the result that it is questioned, and even in extreme cases absolutely rejected. J. Mariański argues that deepening individualism and withdrawal into the realm of privacy affects the attitude of people towards contemporary institutions, their structures and authorities; they are recognized not in themselves, but only to the extent that they provide reliable and vital answers to problems important to the individual.[6]

Peter Berger maintains that young people emphasize their own individual needs particularly strongly and value autonomy of their actions without the support of various external authorities – secular and religious. The author em-

---

[3] See R. Holly, "Badania nad przywództwem nieformalnym w małych grupach" [Studies on Non-Formal Leadership in Small Groups], *Przegląd Psychologiczny*, 1979, no. 3, pp. 457–478; idem, "Funkcjonalne teorie przywództwa. Typologia przywództwa" [Functioning Theories of Leadership], *Studia Socjologiczne*, 1981, no. 2, pp. 43–61.

[4] See J. Mariański, *Żyć parafią* [Living with the Parish], op. cit., p. 109.

[5] W. Piwowarski, "Tradycyjny autorytet księdza w procesie przemian" [The Traditional Authority of a Priest in the Process of Changes], in idem (ed.), *Religijność ludowa – ciągłość i zmiana* [Folk Religiousness – Continuity and Change], Wroclaw 1983, p. 129.

[6] See J. Mariański, *Religijność społeczeństwa polskiego w perspektywie europejskiej. Próba syntezy socjologicznej* [Religiousness of Polish Society in the European Perspective. An Attempt at Sociological Synthesis], Cracow 2004, p. 362.

phasizes that "[...] the young individual can and certainly should decide about how to live, what to believe, and ultimately who to be. This is the most radical, truly Promethean stage of the development of Western individualism."[7] In another of his works, Berger adds in this context that Western societies not so much cultivate the spirit of self-denial, "[...] but rather are characterized by a pursuit of self-gratification and unhindered individual freedom."[8]

In light of these theoretical assumptions, it is necessary to inquire as to the authority of the priest: what is it in essence, and what are its sources and the extent of its powers or competences in a religious and local group?

2. The nature and source of authority of the priest in a religious group

The types of authority mentioned above are applicable to the concept of a priest's authority in a religious group and at the community level. In the first dimension, authority includes two components: charisma of office (authority), associated with the position officially held by the priest in the Church, and his personal charisma (his own authority), associated with his representing religious groups on the outside. In practice, the priest fulfills his own functions based on these two types of authority simultaneously, in accordance with the desires and expectations of the parish. Walter Goddijn points out that, in the needs of the faithful, a kind of "communis opinion"[9] is expressed, which directly concerns the authority of the priest. Lay Catholics are particularly interested in the scope of the authority of the priest and ask if it includes only religious matters, or also secular matters. They do not forget the personality traits of the priest directly connected with his priestly profession,[10] thus also taking into account the personal authority of the priest, his own charisma. The second dimension of authority indicates the religious and social roles of the priest in the Church and secular environments. These roles of the priest comprise specific functions that he fulfills in a parish and secular community.[11]

[7] P. Berger, "Człowiek Zachodu: wyzwolenie i samotność" [Western Man: Liberation and Loneliness], *Aneks. Kwartalnik Polityczny*, 1986, no. 43, p. 8.

[8] P. Berger, "Etyka społeczna w postsocjalistycznym świecie" [Social Ethics in the Post-Socialist World], *Teraźniejszość. Człowiek. Twórczość. Kwartalnik Myśli Społeczno-Pedagogicznej*, 2000, no. 3, p. 16.

[9] W. Goddijn, "Rola kapłana w Kościele i w społeczeństwie" [The Role of the Priest in the Church and in Society], *Znak*, 1965, no. 18, pp. 2–4.

[10] See J. Baniak, "Aksjologiczny wymiar zawodu księdza" [The Axiological Dimension of the Priestly Profession], *Studia Socjologiczne*, 1989, no. 4, pp. 215–222.

[11] See J. Mariański, "Autorytet księdza – aspekty socjologiczne" [The Priest's Authority – Sociological Aspect], *Chrześcijanin w Świecie*, 1977, no. 50, pp. 75–94; W. Piwowarski, "Tradycyjny

Sources of a priest's authority have a religious, Church and secular character. The priest is not simply an ordinary leader of a religious group. In theological terms, a priest represents the leading authority by power granted him to fulfill a special mission, which he received from the Church, with which he identifies, accepting these objectives and implementing them. Ultimately, the authority of the priest comes from Jesus Christ, so the priest shares in Christ's priestly authority (under the power of Holy Orders and with authority to govern). The scope of the authority of the priest comes from his position in the overall hierarchy of positions in the Church, to some extent regardless of his personal values and personality traits. The priest, guiding a certain religious community, not only executes the commands given to him by a bishop's authority, but also leads his community and gains people's recognition and respect on the basis of his qualifications, abilities, skills, personal characteristics, and in this way acquires personal authority in the parish.[12]

In certain circumstances and situations, the real authority of a priest goes beyond religious matters, and includes typically secular affairs, on which his opinions, views and decisions are accepted. A priest is granted respect and his judgment concerning their life problems is considered binding by parishioners. His decisions are not questioned or rejected as conflicting with the expectations and wishes of lay Catholics. This approach to the authority of the priest is called "irradiation of authority" by Józef Majka.[13]

In the first half of the twentieth century, priests in Poland possessed considerable, almost "spontaneous" authority, especially in traditional rural communities. This was granted simply by "being" a priest, due to the "delegated" authority of the bishop, and particularly because priests "represent" Jesus on Earth. At the time, Catholics believed in such authority and did not question it even if knowing about bad moral conduct of a priest in the parish and beyond the rectory, for example, that he lived in the rectory with a woman, or had his own children. The priest was possessed a unique "holiness" which they respected and valued as a model of holiness and religion. Holiness understood in this way guaranteed the priest invulnerability, power and authority in the parish and the village.

autorytet księdza w procesie przemian" [The Traditional Authority of a Priest in the Process of Changes], op. cit., pp. 129–131; J. Baniak, "Autorytet i rola kapłana w społeczności religijnej" [The Authority and Role of a Priest in the Religious Community], in idem, *Religijność miejska w warunkach uprzemysłowienia i ruralizacji na przykładzie Kalisza* [Urban Religiousness in Industrialized and Rural Conditions based on the Example of Kalisz], Cracow 1990, pp. 199–203.

[12] See J. Mariański, *Żyć parafią* [Living with the Parish], op. cit., p. 110.

[13] J. Majka, *Socjologia parafii. Zarys zagadnienia* [Parish Sociology. A Scope of the Issue], Lublin 1971, p. 185.

The parish was an institution strongly associated with the organization and collective life of the countryside, thanks to the authority of the priest as its pastor. The authority of the pastor gave him almost unlimited powers to interfere in the lives of parishioners as individuals and the whole parish community, or even in the family community. His influence involved religious, moral and typically secular matters. Jan Krucina wrote in the seventies of the twentieth century: "In the so-called homogeneous society, closed, existing prior to processes of technicalization and urbanization, social control played a big role. The ostensibly natural surveillance of a group made it easier for its members to restrain ideals, which motivated conduct. The authority of the Church and the prestige of its official representatives were considered nearly indisputable."[14]

In these environments, the official authority of the pastor was complete, and so he was perceived by the faithful to be their personal authority. Obedience to the pastor's authority and discipline in complying to his orders favored the formation of authoritarian structures in rural parishes. Kazimierz Dobrowolski wrote in the sixties of the twentieth century that in the traditional rural culture of clergy, authority flowed not only from the function of mediation between the parish community and God, but had its roots in tradition and social and economic status.[15]

A similar interpretation of the authority of the priest in rural communities appeared in the seventies of the twentieth century. William I. Thomas and Florian Znaniecki wrote that "[...] since the priest represents Jesus, he possesses moral superiority, implicitly accepted when he appears not only as a private individual, but in a religious and official capacity. Therefore, his teachings, advice, praise and blame, imparted in the Church, from the pulpit or in the confessional, are understood by the people as the words of Jesus himself: they rarely or never question their validity, and do not challenge the orders – in fact, theyare fulfilled more willingly than the orders of secular authorities. Such influence extends beyond the Church and manifests itself in all the social activities of a priest, although here it loses some of its power,

---

[14] J. Krucina, "Przenikanie się powszechnego i lokalnego wymiaru Kościoła według społecznej zasady pomocniczości" [Penetration of the Universal and Local Church According to the Social Dimension of the Subsidiarity Principle], *Colloquium Salutis. Wrocławskie Studia Teologiczne*, 1972, vol. 4, pp. 47–48.

[15] K. Dobrowolski, "Przeobrażenia świadomości społecznej ludności chłopskiej w południowej Małopolsce po drugiej wojnie światowej" [The Transformation of Social Consciousness in the Peasant Population in Southern Lesser Poland after World War II], in A. Sarapata (ed.), *Przemiany społeczne w Polsce Ludowej* [Social Transformations in the People's Republic], Warsaw 1965, p. 432.

because peasants are not certain whether the priest is still a representative of Jesus beyond Church matters."[16]

The priest as the representative of Jesus possessed the charisma of his office, from which stemmed his sacramental and liturgical assignments and the function of proclaiming the system of religious ideas and moral norms. In turn, as a representative of the community, he was also distinguished by a personal charisma. These two types of authority made up his entire role as a priest. Janusz Mariański adds that "The respect of the rural population towards the pastor resulted from his belonging to the upper class and the intelligentsia. The Church in the minds of the faithful was reduced to the clergy, so the Church and the pastor were seen as one and the same thing. The position of the pastor in the parish was predominant. The global community of the Church presented itself as a somewhat abstract organization. The role of the priest displayed a diffusive and non-specialized characteristic, usually confined to strictly religious and Church assignments."[17]

The authority of the priest differs in urban and industrialized environments, especially in the big cities. The city priest is no longer the "expert" on everything, but is perceived as a "specialist" on religious issues and problems of a moral nature. Secular matters are not included in the scope of his priestly authority and power. A priest entering into secular affairs, especially of a political and legislative nature, is perceived negatively and seen to bestraying from his professional duties and responsibilities. In an urban environment, criticism of a priest and his authority is direct and comes from many sides. His authority is often questioned, even in religious matters. Researchers speak of a strong desacralization of the priesthood and the religious authority of the priest.[18]

According to Janusz Mariański, in recent decades in Poland "[...] the authority of a priest has lost its intra-Church and religious label function, and is now measured according to specific functions. From the institutional point of view, the authority of the Church is sometimes recognized as a depersonalized and bureaucratic management apparatus. From the individual point of view the authority of the priest is seen not as a consequence of the fact of priestly consecration, but in terms of exercising the functions of leadership."[19] Under

---

[16] W. I. Thomas, F. Znaniecki, *Chłop polski w Europie i Ameryce* [The Polish Peasant in Europe and America], vol. 1: *Organizacja grupy pierwotnej* [Organization of the Original Group], Warsaw 1976, pp. 226–227.

[17] J. Mariański, *Żyć parafią* [Living with the Parish], op. cit., p. 111.

[18] See J. Baniak, "Prestiż Kościoła instytucjonalnego i księży w Polsce a zmiana społeczna. Studium socjologiczne" [The Prestige of the Institutional Church and Priests in Poland and Social Change. A Sociological Study], *Poznańskie Studia Teologiczne*, 2002, vol. 13, pp. 153–195.

[19] J. Mariański, *Żyć parafią* [Living with the Parish], op. cit., pp. 112–113.

the influence of civil, political, cultural and economic changes in Poland over the past 76 years, especially at the turn of the century, the traditional authority and social position of priests in the parish and in the local community have been subject to progressive collapse, resulting in a clear crisis in the urban environment.

Against the backdrop of these theoretical analyses, we ought to ask: how do respondents, the high school and college students from Kalisz, perceive and evaluate the authority of a priest in Poland in the last 25 years?

3. The authority of parish priests in the awareness of the respondents

The theoretical concept of the authority of the parish priest raises two important questions: a) how did the young people perceive and evaluate the authority accorded to priests by Polish Catholics during this time? b) what kind of authority did the respondents grant parish priests? Respondents therefore judged the opinions and evaluations of contemporary Poles concerning the authority of parish priests, relying on their own observations and knowledge on the subject. At the same time, they revealed their personal attitudes towards the authority of priests. In this way, one could see if these assessments were similar, or showed some contradiction.

a) The authority of priests in the years 1983–2008 in the light of the assessments of the youth

Sociological studies have shown that Polish Catholics in this time displayeddifferent and changing attitudes towards priests and their authority in the parish and the local community. High school and college students responded to the survey by taking up a position and giving their own assessments. Further analysis will show how the young people exhibited the ideas and the evaluations of Polish society concerning the authority of parish priests in these years.

According to the respondents, during this period Polish society valued the authority of parish priests on the following scale: very high – 38.3%, high – 12.6%, average – 12.0%; low – 13.6%, very low – 10.2%, while 11.0% refused to grant priests authority (none). If we combine the assessment levels "very high" and "high," we get a so-called average optimal social assessment of 40.9%. This level was more commonly given by high school (57.8%) than college students (44.1%). The difference (13.7%) indicates that college students, as exponents of public opinion, more cautiously and critically assessed the authority of priests than the Catholic community in the majority of municipal and rural Churches.

The accuracy of this conclusion is confirmed by the percentage of college students who, in greater numbers than high school students, claimed that Poles assessed the authority of priests as average (0.7% higher), as low (1.4% higher) and as very low (1.1% higher). College students are also more numerous (by 3.0%) than high school students, and we found that a percentage of Poles completely refused to acknowledge the authority of parish and religious priests during this period. In addition, respondents in both groups reported that the percentage of Polish Catholics who judged priestly authority as very high or high decreased significantly: among high school students, 25.4% registered a change, and 29.2% among college students. At the same time, they pointed out that there was an increase in the percentage of Catholics who denied the authority of priests: 9.2% of high school students and 11.6% of college students.[20]

The results of the study allow us to identify two facts mentioned by my respondents connected with the social assessment of the authority of parish priests in Poland at that time. Firstly, in the 1980s, Poles granted priests relatively high authority, regardless of the perceived personal, moral or professional shortcomings of many priests. In the 1990s, criticism of the Catholic clergy in Poland has intensified under the influence of various external factors, and also due to the faults of priests themselves. Such faults include over-engaging in the new political arena, i.e. the political, legislative and economic spheres of society, which is "not their business," and the ever-increasing numbers who ignored the ethical principles of the clerical state.

The criticism of the clergy dramatically intensified in the first decade of this century, when we noticed a decrease in the levels of tolerance and indifference of Poles towards the political excesses of a number of bishops and parish priests expressing the material and property expectations of the Church, the daily secular lifestyle of many priests, and the undercutting of the role of lay Catholics in parish structures. All these circumstances contributed significantly to the rapid decline in the authority of priests, to reducing their respectability and importance in some groupings and social environments of Polish society. This criticism continues, edging Catholics away from priests and the Church, and even away from religion. Secondly, college students reported the decline in

---

[20] See J. Baniak, *Obraz kapłana w świadomości katolików świeckich – na przykładzie Kalisza, Kotłowa i Przedborowa. Studium socjologiczne* [The Image of the Priest in the Awareness of Lay Catholics based on Kalisz, Kotłów and Przedborów. A Sociological Studies], Poznan 1994, p. 237. (Catholics in the city of Kalisz, respondents in the 1980s, judged the authority of priests as follows: very high – 55.4%, high – 13.4%, average – 9.8%, low – 7.4%, very low – 6.4%, and total lack of authority was indicated by 5.4%. Meanwhile, "high" authority is indicated by 80.5% of rural Catholics and 64.4% of urban Catholics, hence the difference between these percentages is high, in fact it amounted to 16.1% higher amongst rural Catholics).

the authority of priests in Polish society during this period in greater numbers than high school students, probably more comprehensively taking into account the political mood and other conditions of life in the country and the attitude of Poles towards the clergy, which displayed systematic negative trends. These changes will probably be evident for a long time in the relationship between the clergy and lay Catholics.[21]

In addition, studies have not confirmed the accuracy of the empirical hypothesis which accepted the authority of priests and the positive attitude of Catholics towards them during this period. Studies inform us of the reverse situation, i.e. a slow but systematic regression of the authority of Catholic priests in Poland, especially in urban environments. This crisis is based on many causes, but to a large extent it was brought about by priests themselves, by their attitudes towards the laity and their lifestyles which were incompatible with the principles of the Gospel they were persuading lay people to accept.

b) The authority granted to priests by respondents

During the research, I asked respondents in both groups if they were able to show what kind of authority they themselves granted priests who are their teachers, religious educators, academic center ministers and parish pastors, using the same evaluation scale according to which they designated the level of priestly authority in Polish society.

Studies showed that young respondents and Catholics hold priests in higher esteem than the majority of the public in Poland. In general, respondents assessed the authority of priests according to the accepted scale in the following way: as very high, 42.2% (3.9% morethan the indicated public opinion); as high, 12.7% (0.6% higher); as average, 11.6% (0.4% lower); as low, 12.1% (1.5% lower); as very low, 8.4% (1.8% lower); no opinion, 9.2% (1.8% lower). The level of education of respondents in this case also differentiates their evaluation concerning priestly authority.

---

[21] See J. Baniak, *Między buntem a potrzebą akceptacji i zrozumienia. Świadomość religijna i moralna a kryzys tożsamości osobowej młodzieży gimnazjalnej. Studium socjologiczne* [Between Rebelion and the Need for Acceptance and Understanding. The Awareness of Religious and Moral a Crisis of personal Indentity in Junior High School Youth. A Sociological Study], Cracow 2008, p. 306, table 128. [In the opinion of the junior high school participants, Poles in the late twentieth century granted priests authority according to the following assessment scale: very high – 32.9%; high – 12.9%, average – 11.0%; little – 11.2%, very little – 9.7%, none – 15.2%, lack of evaluation – 4.5%, no data – 2.6%. However, "optimum" authority was granted priests by: 50.8% of girls and 35.8% of boys, 49.4% of students from rural areas and 43.5% of students from the city, and total lack of authority indicated, respectively, by 14.3%, 16.9%, 13.8% and 16.0%].

This granted authority is higher in high school youth environments than among college students. These differences are documented by the percentage of high school students granting priests authority during this period at a very high level (49.4%) and high (12.6%) compared to the percentages of college students at 39.5% and 13.1%. In addition, a higher percentage of high school (62.0%) than college students (52.6%) evaluated the authority of priests at the optimal level. College students were more likely (10.6%) than high school students (7.5%) to deny priests authority in religious and secular matters completely.

Over the given time period, the attitude of respondents towards the Church and priests changed. This change is manifested in the authority granted to priests. If we compare indicators of such authority in the years 1983 and 2008 (border dates), it is easy to see that both high school and college students gave higher evaluations to priests during the first period of research. This conclusion is justified by various percentages of respondents in both groups granting priests authority according to the applied scale of evaluation, meaning: very high – high school students 59.9% and 38.7% (regression of 21.3%) and students – 51.2% and 21.6% (regression of 29.6%); high – 13.0% and 10.0% (regression of 3.0%) and 14.6% and 10.4% (regression of 4.2%); average – 10.2% and 9.2% (regression of 1.0%) and 12.4% and 13.0% (increase of 0.6%); low – 9.2% and 15.2% (increase of 6.0%) and 7.3% and 18.6% (increase of 11.3%); very low – 4.2% and 10.4% (increase of 6.2%) and 7.3% and 13.8% (increase of 11.0%); none – 3.5% and 15% and 14.0% (increase of 10.5%) and 5.8% and 19.4% (increase of 13.6%). The more critical attitude of students towards priests influenced students to grant priests very high and high authority less often, and in many cases this led to denying priests authority.[22]

c) The scope of professional competence of priests identified by respondents

The authority of the office of priesthood has a specific range competence, which the laity can use when dealing with their religious needs and moral dilemmas or spiritual matters, and to some extent with some of their secular problems. Catholic laity, even those who are deeply religious and regularly attend religious worship, consider the priest an "expert" only in matters of

[22] See J. Baniak, *Między buntem a potrzebą akceptacji i zrozumienia...* [Between Rebelion and the Need for Acceptance and Understanding...], op. cit., p. 306, table 128. [Researched junior high schoolers granted authority to priests in the following way: very high – 29.0%; high – 10.8% (optimal – 39.8%), average – 12.0%; low – 12.3%; very low – 10.8%, none – 17.5%, no evaluation – 5.0%, no data – 2.6%, very high: girls – 34.1% – and boys 18.8%, students from rural areas – 31.2% and from the city – 16.0%, none – 16.0%, 20.6%, 16.0% and 18.4%].

religion and the Church, and they often benefit from his help in their private religious lives. In matters of moral authority, people consulted priests significantly less. Furthermore, he is becoming almost completely irrelevant in typically secular matters, and the great majority of Catholics do not recognize priests as "experts" in these areas. We should ask, therefore, how broad is the range of powers assigned to priests according to the high school and college students surveyed during this period?

Studies show that the dominant percentage of respondents in both groups reduced the competency of priests to issues and problems directly related to religious faith, worship, the Church, religious education in schools and the Catholic upbringing of children and adolescents. Priests' competence in these matters was accepted by 81.1% of the respondents, including 84.9% of high school and 77.4% of college students.

In the opinion of 70.0% of the respondents, including 73.4% of high school and 66.6% of college students, priests ought to help the poor and socially excluded in solving difficult problems with living situations and promote the common good in parishes and local communities, especially among wealthy individuals and groups, who have a surplus of economic resources and material goods. This is in accord with the principle of mercy in the Church. In these aspects, according to the dominant percentage of respondents, priests in Poland are still generally recognized and valued authority figures. They are seen as "influential" experts, to whom people in need of support and assistance will always turn with confidence and hope, without fear of being ignored or disregarded.

The powers and competences of priests shrink significantly in typically secular matters, and therefore, there is a lower percentage of high school (42.3%) and college students (34.5%) surveyed who would ask the priests for support and assistance in these matters or with personal problems. Over half of the survey respondents (50.4%), including more high school (58.0%) than college students (42.9%) felt that priests could also through their counsel and different point of view help secular authorities in solving problems related to social pathology. These problems have affected different social environments in the country, including youth environments. Respondents in both groups are aware of the danger in the escalation of these social evils, related to the conditions of democratization of public life, and the broadening of the horizons of personal liberty of citizens, which took place around the turn of the 20th and 21st centuries.

This issue relates primarily, in their opinion, to drug addiction, addiction to medication, alcoholism and drunkenness, smoking, and a general casualness in the areas of eroticism and sexuality, resulting in ethical liberty and permissiveness or a hedonistic approach, especially among young people, towards life. These plagues have affected all categories and groups of Polish youth,[23] including students of primary and junior high schools. Priests may, in the opinion of the respondents, help children and young people in solving moral and existential dilemmas directly related to these pathologies.

The competence of priests dealing with issues and problems related to marriage and family life are shrinking significantly. Competence in this sphere was granted to priests by 47.7% of respondents, including more high school (50.0%) than college students (45.4%). With regards to morality, they exclude eroticism and sexuality, leaving decisions related to this to their spouses and other people, exercising their personal freedom. Competence in this sphere of morality is attributed to priests by only 24.7% of high school (a 70.2% decline) and 13.4% of college students (an 84.5% decline).

This issue also relates to the priest's influence on people's consciences, at least during regular periodic confessions,[24] through properly shaping a person's conscience and raising the awareness of the need to apply ethical principles in everyday life, opting for good rather than evil. Unfortunately, competence in this area was granted to priests by only 52.7% of respondents, and 46.7% of them refused them authority, arguing that people are free and should be responsible for the moral state of their conscience. In difficult and ambiguous cases, they may ask for help from psychologists in explaining certain ethical dilemmas, but not a priest, because in these matters he is not an expert.

An even lower percentage of respondents recognize the competence of priests in moral aspects concerning employment and unemployment. Only 40.5% turned to priests for advice about these issues, including more high school students than college students. Issues of work and unemployment are assessed by 58.6% and 64.4% of high school students as pertaining to secular authorities, and not to religious ministers. If these issues are dealt with by priests, then it concerns confession of sins, when priests can give their penitents absolution for work poorly performed or for financial fraud and other moral problems related to work.[25] This view was shared by 54.4% of high school and

---

[23] See J. Kurzępa, *Zagrożona niewinność. Zakłócenia rozwoju seksualności współczesnej młodzieży* [Threatened Innocence. Disruption of the Development of Contemporary Youth Sexuality], Cracow 2007; T. Szlendak, *Supermarketyzacja. Religia i obyczaje seksualne młodzieży w kulturze konsumpcyjnej* [Supermarketization. Religion and Sexual Mores of Young People in Consumer Culture, Wroclaw 2008, pp. 135–170.

[24] See W. Pawlik, *Grzech. Studium z socjologii moralności* [Sin. A Moral Sociology Study], Cracow 2007, pp. 97–150; J. Mariański, *"Struktury grzechu" w ocenie społecznego nauczania Kościoła* [The "Stucture of Sin" in the Evaluation of the Church's Social Teaching], Plock 1998.

[25] See J. Mariański, *Etos pracy bezrobotnych. Raport z badań empirycznych* [The Ethos of Work by the Unemployed. Empirical Research Studies Report], Lublin 1994, pp. 209–257; J. Sieg,

61.3% of college students, while other respondents did not perceive priestly competence in these cases.

Only a few high school and college students granted priests competence in such matters as people's personal lives (35.8% and 26.7%), people's mental health (25.0% and 21.2%), economics and the market economy (16.8% and 9.6%), politics (17.3% and 10.3%), and other secular matters (24.9% and 23.5%). Only those respondents who could not find other authorities on the matter benefited from the advice of priests in these secular matters and problems.

Studies also showed that 36.5% of respondents, including 34.6% of high school and 38.5% of college students did not consider clergy to be competent on every matter, and hence these people do not benefit from the clergy's advice or any other form of assistance.

The attitude of respondents towards the authority of the priestly office has changed during the study period, which is shown by the percentage of those who approve of or reject the competence of priests between the first year (1983) and the third year (2008) of the study. The sharp increase in the percentages of people who in the final period of the study would benefit from the advice and assistance of priests as competent professionals is in the following areas: faith and religion – high school students increased by 3.9% and college students by 8.8%, during school catechesis – an increase of 1.8% and 1.2%; parish affairs – an increase of 12.4% and 5.7%, the ethos of work and unemployment – an increase of 1.9% and 3.0%, works of charity – an increase of 12.9% and 8.2%.

Meanwhile, there was a decrease in the percentages of respondents who would turn to a priest for advice, and this concerns the following issues: morality – high school students declined by 0.5% and college students by 15.8%, matters of conscience – by 1.4% and 6.6%, marriage and family – by 10.3% and 4.5%, school and education – 8.7% and 10.5%, personal life – 10.0% and 10.8%, mental health – 10.8% and 4.2%; politics – 14.6% and 5.9%, social pathologies – 18.5% and 11.8%, other problems – 14.6% and 10.6%. Priests are not competent in these secular issues, hence these respondents did not benefit from their advice and assistance in such matters. During this period, the percentage of high school and college students who openly refused priests any type of competence, including in religious matters grew steadily.[26]

"Praca zawodowa jako wyraz wiary chrześcijanina obecnego w świecie" [Work Experience as an Expression of Christian Faith Present in the World], *Śląskie Studia Historyczno-Teologiczne*, 1973, vol. 6, pp. 33–41.

[26] Cf. J. Baniak, "Zaangażowanie społeczne i polityczne Kościoła i księży w Polsce w wyobrażeniach katolików" [Social and Political Involvement of the Church and Priests in Poland in the Ideas of Catholics], *Społeczeństwo i Kościół*, 2005, vol. 2, p. 136, table 6.

d) The impact of the moral authority of a priest on people's consciences in the assessments of the respondents

The impact of priests on the consciences of people, including during personal confession of sins, is real and far-reaching, as results of sociological research show.[27] Stanisław Witek notes that in matters of conscience, priests exercise special authority over people – as confessors or as their religious and spiritual leaders, although this authority does not have a formal dimension.[28] Catholics are, however, obliged to go to a priest for personal confession of their sins at least once a year, although the Church recommends confession more frequently for the "good of their souls" and for the proper care of their conscience. Moral sociologists point out that, through the influence of a priest, a Catholic conscience receives the opportunity to be properly trained, to properly respond to all forms of good and evil, to check them in relevant moral activities according to proper ethical qualifications.[29] The power of religious leaders is reflected in their being approved of by the Catholic laity as members of a religious group. When Church authorities present their top-down decisions, the faithful are consciously obliged to follow them.

Moral sociologists point out that acceptance of the influence of religious authorities on people's consciences and their personal morality is significantly dependent on many factors, including, to a great extent, the religious level of believers. The scope of this acceptance is greatest among the deeply religious, who systematically perform religious practices and receive the sacraments, and it gradually decreases in other categories of religious involvement, or even completely disappears among people who are apparently quite religious or even non-believers who live in conflict with Catholic moral principles. These people deny and reject religious authorities, undermine Catholic moral authority and do not want to be concerned with their consciences. They do not want religion to have an impact on their ethical attitudes and moral behavior. Their attitude is a result of different motives and reasons, including the desire to

[27] See J. Mariański, "Zakres władzy przyznawanej osobom duchownym" [The Scope of Authority Granted to Religious], in idem, *Żyć parafią* [Living with the Parish], op. cit., p. 121; W. Szewczuk, *Sumienie. Studium psychologiczne* [The Conscience. A Psychological Study], Warsaw 1988, pp. 24–36; G. Lubowicka, *Sumienie jako poświadczenie. Idea podmiotowości w filozofii Paula Ricoeura* [Conscience as a Credential. The Idea of Subjectivity in the Philosophy of Paul Ricoeur], Wroclaw 2000, pp. 79–99.

[28] See S. Witek, *Duszpasterstwo w konfesjonale* [Pastoral Ministry in the Confessional], Poznan 1988, pp. 24–26.

[29] See M. Ossowska, *Social Determinants of Moral Ideals*, London 1970, É. Durkheim, *L'education morale*, Paris 1922; T. Kotarbiński, *Sprawy sumienia* [Matters of Conscience], Warsaw 1956.

solve the problems in their personal consciences independently. They have the desire for full autonomy and privacy in moral matters, and the will to become independent from religious and ecclesiastical factors in this sphere of life, which is essentially represented by priests, especially confessors. We can also not exclude the influence of the process of secularization, including the desacralization of daily life and neglect of festive Catholic holy days. These people themselves contributed to the rejection of many previously approved moral and religious authorities.[30] Unfortunately, some deeply religious people, who fulfill religious practices, are also under the influence of these processes, including young people who are involved in religion.

In the light of these assumptions, we may ask whether and to what extent the high school and college student respondents during the period of 25 years accepted a priest as a moral authority in matters concerning their personal consciences. Did they perceive the impact of parish priests and priest confessors on their ethical attitudes and moral behavior that affects their personal ethos and the ethos of marriage with family?

The study found that respondents in both groups and in subsequent time periods adopted a critical attitude towards the intervention of priests as religious and moral authorities in matters of people's conscience and morality. As a result of this attitude, only 48.2% recognized the moral authority of the priest in the parish, including more high school students (53.0%) than college students (43.4%). At the same time, 40.0% of respondents, including 35.8% of high school students and 44.3% of college students, decidedly rejected this authority, claiming at the same time that priests "in the past assigned themselves such moral rights which allowed them to influence people's consciences." Meanwhile "priests themselves often cannot be moral models for the laity in the parish due to their bad example and unethical and immoral behavior." This assessment was made by 67.3% of high school and 74.7% of college students.

---

[30] See W. Piwowarski, "Moralność jako sprawdzian żywotności religijnej katolików Południowej Warmii" [Morality as a Test of the Religious Life of Catholics, Southern Warmia], *Studia Warmińskie*, 1966, vol. 3, pp. 95–183; H. Smarzyński, "Problem zagrożenia moralnego współczesnej młodzieży" [The Problem of the Moral Hazard of Modern Youth], *Ruch Pedagogiczny*, 1974, no. 1, pp. 33–50; J. Mariański, *Moralność w procesie przemian. Szkice socjologiczne* [Morality in the Process of Change. Sociological Sketches], Warsaw 1990, pp. 406–433; J. Baniak, "Katolicy niewierzący i praktykujący? Między wiarą i ateizmem" [Practicing Catholics and Non-Believers? Between Faith and Atheism], *Homo Dei*, 2007, no. 1 (282), pp. 23–42; idem, *Desakralizacja kultu religijnego i świąt religijnych w Polsce. Studium socjologiczne* [Desacralization of Religious Worship and Religious Festivals in Poland. A Sociological Study], Cracow 2007, pp. 42–46.

The remaining respondents did not take a position on this issue – 11.2% and 12.3%. Acceptance of the moral authority of the priest decreased in both groups of respondents in subsequent periods of research. Among high school students in 1983, Church authority was accepted by a total of 58.4% of respondents, and in 2008 this percentage decreased to 47.5%, a decrease of 10.9%. At the same time, there was an increase in the percentage of high school students who did not accept the moral authority of the priests from 27.0% to 44.1% (a 17.1% difference) and a percentage decrease of 6.2% of people who did not take a position on this issue. In the student group, the acceptance and rejection rates of priestly authority are slightly different. If in 1983, priestly authority was accepted by a total of 52.4% of the students, in 2008, the percentage declined to 36.6% (or a 15.8% difference), while there was an increase from 36.4% to 52.8% of those involved who strongly questioned the authority of priests (16.4%).

Respondents also pointed to the influence of priests on their own consciences and personal morality, accepting them as religious and moral authorities. Overall, this impact was perceived by 51.5% of respondents (a total of 32.5%), including 54.3% of high school students (a total of 35.0%) and 48.6% of college students (a total of 29.7%). At the same time, 48.6% stated that priests did not affect their consciences and personal moral behavior at all, and this group included 45.7% of high school students and 51.4% of college students. This statement was expressed in the group in 1983 by 40.8% of high school students – in 2008 by 50.6% (an increase of 9.8%), and in the group of college students – 46.7% and 57.2% (an increase of 10.5%). At the same time, there was a decrease in both groups of the percentage confirming the influence of priests on their consciences and personal morality: among high school students from 59.2% to 45.4% (a decrease of 13.8%) and among college students from 53.3% to 42.8% (a decrease of 10.5%).

Respondents also indicated that the priest (confessor, pastor, vicar, catechist teacher) has the greatest and most frequent influence on their conscience and morality. Their statements show that confessors most often influenced the conscience of 63.4% of respondents, including 70.5% of high school and 56.3% of college students. In second place, the respondents pointed to their parish priest as the person who was able to influence their conscience and morality, including 44.0% of respondents, meaning 47.7% of high school and 40.4% of college students. Over 1/3 of respondents (37.9%) pointed to the importance of the parish vicar, including 41.5% of high school and 34.2% of college students. The least influence was attributed to the priest catechist, as indicated by 32.7% of respondents, including 35.3% of high school and 30.0% of college students.

Unfortunately, during the study period, the impact of these religious and moral authorities on the consciences and morality of the respondents steadily declined in both groups. The percentage of high school students indicating the influence of individual priests decreasing in the first and third study periods is as follows: the confessor from 78.6% to 62.4% (16.2% less), the pastor from 53.7% to 41.7% (12.0% less), the parish vicar from 47.6% to 36.6% (11.0% less), the catechist from 38.8% to 32.4% (6.4% less). The percentages of students who also pointed to the impact of these priests decreased respectively: the confessor – from 67.4% to 48.8% (18.6% less), the pastor of the parish – from 43.6% to 36.8% (6.8% less), the vicar – from 38.7% to 29.4% (9.3% less), the catechist – from 32.3% to 27.2% (5.1% less). Perhaps the respondents indicating no effect of the priests on their conscience and morality neglect to go to periodic confession, or even completely ignore this mandatory religious practice, which can be brought about by many different factors, including their personal decision.

e) Trust and distrust of the respondents towards the Church and parish priests

Acceptance and rejection of the authority of the institutional Church and Her priests as representatives of the parish is directly in line with lay Catholics' trust and distrust. We can accept the hypothesis that the weaker the authority of institutions and officials representing the Church on the outside, the greater the increase in the degree of distrust, while at the same time there will be a decrease in the level of trust of people related to the Church in various ways – formally and informally.

What is trust and how do people express it in practice? In sociology, there are two known meanings of "trust." In the theory of social bonds, trust is ascribed to attitudes, which sometimes involve entrusting partners with such deep interaction that they do not betray the recognized values and principles of behavior in emergency situations, which relate to the good of the wider community. This type of trust relates to the virtues of the individual. The second type of trust indicates the component of "social capital," meaning the specific features characterizing a given human population, group, local community, and civic or religious community.[31] Robert D. Putnam adds in this context that in groups where members trust each other mutually, they achieve higher values than in groups where trust is lacking or limited. Trust, in his opinion, is an

[31] See J. Baniak, "Zaufanie młodzieży gimnazjalnej w Polsce do Kościoła instytucjonalnego" [Confidence in the Institutional Church among School Children in Poland], *Społeczeństwo i Kościół*, 2009, vol. 6, pp. 98–99.

essential component of social capital. In small, integrated communities, trust stems from personal acquaintances. However, in larger communities and more diverse systems, it is necessary to have more impersonal or indirect forms of trust. This author believes that trust fosters cooperation – the greater the level of trust in a community, the greater the likelihood of cooperation.

However, common activity increases the level of trust between people.[32] According to Adam Bartoszek, trust as a collective virtue increases the ability to cooperate and provides the opportunity for the community to obtain benefits, and achievement of these benefits without trust would be virtually impossible.[33] Piotr Sztompka "argues that trust plays an important role in interpersonal and intergroup interactions. Entering into relationships with other people, we must constantly play a unique kind of game, make bets, and count on their honesty, give partners we meet our confidence, or deny it. This author believes that confidence, on the one hand, and trust on the other, perform very important functions in an individual person's life: these allow a person to reduce uncertainty, to hope that others will work for their benefit, or at least be indifferent. Under such circumstances, a person works peacefully and freely, with optimism and hope of success.

On the other hand, distrust generates a sense of danger in people and at the same time activates the will for self-defense against it. Distrust helps reduce the degree of danger, but at the same time causes the individual to withdraw from interaction with other people. Confidence can improve communication between people, bring them together, facilitate spontaneous interaction between people, give them more security and confidence, a chance to participate in the life of various organizations and groups, promotes tolerance and mutual acceptance, generates solidarity, and in effect supports democracy. [...] Trust and distrust play an important role in the social lives of people with different levels of dependency and social influence."[34]

---

[32] See R. D. Putnam, *Demokracja w działaniu. Tradycje obywatelskie we współczesnych Włoszech* [Democracy in Action. Civic Traditions in Modern Italy], transl. J. Szacki, Warsaw 1995, pp. 258–259.

[33] See A. Bartoszek, "Zaufanie jako czynnik aktywności obywatelskiej na lokalnej scenie politycznej" [Trust as a Factor in Civic Activity on the Local Political Scene], in E. Nycz (ed.), *Budowa lokalnego społeczeństwa obywatelskiego w perspektywie integracji europejskiej* [Construction of the Local Civil Society in the Perspective of European Integration], Opole 2003, p. 139.

[34] See P. Sztompka, "Kulturowe imponderabilia szybkich zmian społecznych: zaufanie, lojalność, solidarność" [Cultural Imponderables of Rapid Social Change: Trust, Loyalty, Solidarity], in P. Sztompka (ed.), *Imponderabilia wielkiej zmiany: mentalność, wartości i więzi społeczne czasów transformacji* [Imponderables of a Great Change: Attitudes, Values and Social Bonds of Transition Times], Warsaw 1999, pp. 95–109.

The issue of trust and confidence also applies to various religious and church institutions. Mariusz Kwiatkowski states that "[...] the category of social trust seems to be particularly useful in describing the Church, which seeks its place in the new social and cultural reality. [...] In light of the ongoing discussion about the Catholic Church in recent years in Poland and Her place in the emerging civil society, first and foremost is the need to verify the present thesis of an increasing 'trust deficit' in the Church. Equally important and interesting seems to be isolating specific factors of trust and distrust in the Church in Poland, and also an attempt to determine whether and to what extent the Church is an institution which contributes to building a culture of trust."[35]

Janusz Mariański, writing 15 years ago about trust and distrust in the Church, claimed that survival and development in a post-modern, culturally and socially diverse, radically pluralistic society can only happen in an open and multi-centered Church that accepts inner-Church pluralism and the autonomy of various trends, not in a lost Church. In the hospitable Church, the author suggests, it seems necessary to change the attitude of many priests towards the laity – from the paternalistic and prescriptive style to a style of dialogue and partnership, and to replace the passivity of the laity in the Church with their active participation in Her various structures.[36] In another of his academic research papers, J. Mariański aptly writes that in sociological terms, trust towards the Church and priests can be studied on different levels: trust between people who identify with the Church and clergy (trust in the Church), trust in Church institutions and the Church as a whole (trust towards the Church). This trust may have a personal, positional, institutional and systemic character. The author argues that the Church is a social and religious institution, and therefore trust in the Church should be studied on religious and social levels.[37]

Confidence in the Church as a whole is reflected in the confidence of the faithful towards Her structural institutions. This includes the clergy participating in the authority of the Church at various degrees and levels of leadership and management: the pope, the primate of the national Church, the diocesan bishop, the head of the conference of Catholic bishops or the parish pastor

[35] M. Kwiatkowski, "Zaufanie i nieufność w Kościele. Perspektywa socjologiczna" [Trust and Distrust in the Church. A Sociological Perspective], in J. Baniak (ed.), *Katolicyzm polski na przełomie wieków. Teologiczny, instytucjonalny i wspólnotowy wymiar Kościoła* [Polish Catholicism at the Turn of the Century. Theology, Institutional and Community Aspects of the Church], Poznan 2002, pp. 103–104.

[36] J. Mariański, "Kościół ludowy w poszukiwaniu nowej tożsamości społecznej" [The Folk Church in Search of a New Social Identity], *Znak*, 1997, no. 1, pp. 45–48.

[37] See J. Mariański, *Kościół katolicki w Polsce a życie społeczne. Studium socjologiczno-pastoralne* [The Catholic Church in Poland and Social Life. A Sociological and Pastoral Study], Lublin 2005, pp. 110–111.

and his associates – vicars and including teachers of religion. The confidence expressed by Catholics towards these representatives of the ecclesiastical authority can bear witness to the extent of this conviction towards the whole Church. However, distrust may indicate a weakening or a loss of confidence in the Church or the loss of ties with the Church as an institution.

In light of these theoretical findings, it is important to ask whether the surveyed high school and college students trusted the Church and priests, or not.

The attitudes of the surveyed high school and college students towards the institutional Church vary highly, which affects their level of confidence in the Church. Only 54.6% of respondents, including 59.3% of high school and 49.9% of college students, always trusted the Church, while 35.0%, including 31.1% and 38.8% in both groups, showed a total distrust of the institutional form of the Church, Her religious and moral doctrines and methods of administering authority by priests in parishes. The remaining respondents (9.6% and 11.3%) did not take a position on this issue. Taking into account the boundary dates of research, we see that in both groups the increase in percentage of respondents showing distrust in the Church was as follows: among high school students, they came to 17.4%, and 19.5% among college students; throughout this period, mistrust was manifested by 31.1% of high school students and 39.8% of college students (greater by 7.7%). At the same time, at every period of the study, we could see a decrease in the percentage of people who trusted in the Church. Taking into account the boundary dates of research (1983 and 2008), this decrease is significant, and in both groups of subjects it was different: 18.6% among high school and 19.7% among college students, hence in general, 59.3% and 49.9% of youth in both groups seemed to trust the Church during this period. Other respondents – 9.6% and 11.3% – refused to comment on this issue.[38]

[38] Cf. D. Pollack, "Religios–kirchlicher Wandel im Mittel- und Osteuropa – ein Uberblick" [Religious-Church Changes in Central-Eastern Europe – an Overview], *Ost–West. Europäische Perspektiven*, 2000, no. 2, pp. 88–90. Detlef Pollack emphasizes what he calls the sinister decline of trust in the Church in Poland, saying that in the years 1989–1994 the percentage of Catholics who declared their confidence in the Church decreased from 87.8% to 40.5% (a drop of 47.3%). In 1991, only 10.4% of Poles granted the Catholic Church confidence, 22.2% – high, 40.7% – low, 15.1% – very low, 11.5% – none. The author argues that the trust declared before 1989 rarely associated individual religiosity or a personal relationship with the Church, which means "impersonal" and "un-individualized" Church-going. Even the genuinely religious person does not always associate personal religiousness with the institutional Church. According to a survey of the Public Opinion Research Centre (OBOP) in June 2004, the majority of Poles trusted the Church – 39.0% definitely yes, 39.0% – rather yes, and 1/5 did not confide in the Church; 12.0% – rather distrusted the Church, 7.0% – definitely did not seem to trust Her. See *Opinie Polaków o Kościele. Komunikat z badań OBOP* [Poles' Opinions about the Church. OBOP Research Communique], July 2004, Warsaw, pp. 2–3.

The differentiation of trust of towards the institutional Church becomes important with regards to trust in the representative of ecclesiastical authority, the parish pastor. Studies showed that such confidence was much weaker than towards the Church understood globally. During this period, confidence, broadly understood, was granted the pastor by a total of 59.0% of respondents, including 63.6% of high school and 54.3% college students (less by 9.3%). In this group, 46.5% of respondents granted pastors full confidence and 12.5% granted pastors limited trust. The granting of full confidence was more common among high school students (53.4%) than college students (39.5%). The confidence of both groups of respondents declined steadily in subsequent periods of research, which can best be observed when taking into account the first and third terms of studies. While in 1983 trust was granted to pastors by 71.2% of high school students (including 60.5% full confidence), in 2008 this percentage decreased to 55.7%, meaning a drop of 15.5% (including 44.7% full confidence). In the first study period, 63.0% granted pastors personal trust (50.8% full confidence), while in the third period they numbered only 48.2%, less by 14.8% (including full confidence at 31.6%). At the same time, studies showed that less than 1/3 of respondents at that time did not trust their parish pastor, including a higher percentage of college students (35.9%) than the percentage of high school students (26.8%).

The percentage of the respondents who felt distrust towards their pastors increased in both groups in subsequent periods of research: among high school students from 20.3% in 1983 to 34.6% in 2008 (an increase of 14.3%) and among college students from 26.4% to 43.4% (an increase of 17.0%). The remaining respondents (9.8% and 9.6%) did not respond to this question. The drop in trust towards the pastor was justified by respondents with different reasons, although four reasons were indicated most often by the two groups: excessively "practicing" secular politics (54.6% of high school and 72.4% of college students), a curt and arrogant approach towards parishioners (44.8% and 63.2%), excessively high fees for religious and sacramental services (40.5% and 58.8%), frequent "problems" with maintaining fidelity to celibacy (39.7% and 52.4%). These and other reasons contributed to the distrust of this percentage of surveyed high school and college students towards parish pastors.[39]

[39] Cf. W. Świątkiewicz, "Portret księdza" [Portrait of a Priest], in W. Zdaniewicz, S.H. Zaręba (ed.), *Kościół katolicki na początku trzeciego tysiąclecia w opinii Polaków* [The Catholic Church at the Beginning of the Third Millennium in the Opinion of Poles], Warsaw 2004, pp. 107–120. The author informs us that in the light of the results of the Centre for Social Studies, in the 2004 survey, we learn that the trust of Poles towards the parish priest was manifested by: 55.8% completely and 29.2% in a limited way, 8.2% manifested distrust, others did not take a clear position (6.1%) or did not answer the question (0.7%).

In conclusion, based on the analyses in this chapter, it should be stated that the authority of parish priests and the confidence granted them by these Polish youth were not stable or permanent over the assumed period of 25 years. On the contrary, they were characterized by the peculiar dynamics of changeability, in the direction of limitation with sharp criticism, especially due to the excesses of priests in using their exercising their competence and in breaking partnerships with Catholic laity. In assessing the replies of high school and college students, including junior high school students, the authority of parish priests in Poland during this period can be described by the following sociological probability: non-religious issues and problems were the first degree (according to the concept of the "indifference zone") and involved commands that were most difficult for young people to obey (which also holds for elderly people). These commands often proved impossible to achieve. Issues concerning marriage and family, parenting, eroticism and sexuality, and the ethos of work and unemployment are on the neutral plane – priests should not excessively interfere or intervene in these areas.

Yet there are issues and problems directly related to religious belief and religious worship in which authority is still accepted. The statements of the surveyed youth show that the advice of priests has lost its former social significance and values, that there has been a steady decline in the percentage of high school students and college students who want to listen to the indications of priests concerning their religious needs whole-heartedly, and they often located their religious beliefs beyond the official framework of priests' work, not wanting to be in lasting personal relationships with them. The authority of priests in the Polish academic environment of high school and university students has sharply declined during this period, and confidence in them has definitely diminished or even disappeared, while at the same time there is an increase in the percentage of those who no longer want to trust priests, or do not expect help from them in solving their personal problems in life or in explaining moral and axiological dilemmas. Most of these young Polish Catholics treated their own consciences as the last instance for solving existential and ethical issues. On the other hand, we cannot exclude the conclusion – Janusz Mariański rightly points out – that the attitude of Polish youth towards the authority of priests might be "[...] an expression of distrust towards the official representatives of their religion, and also includes the risk of decreasing their actual authority. Managers of parish communities are presented matters in such a way, that they cannot count on the obedience and submission of subordinates."[40]

[40] J. Mariański, *Żyć parafią* [Living with the Parish], op. cit., p. 121.

The approach of Polish Catholics towards the parish clergy has changed over the study period, resulting in an increased percentage of people dissatisfied with the clergy's professional ministries, and critical evaluation of the personal morality of priests who violate the rules of celibacy and disregard the entity of lay Catholics in the parish and the Church. In these matters, secondary school and university students responded to the Polish clergy in a similar way. Their critical attitude towards priests who disregard their professional obligations and the rules of the priestly ethos, as well as important problems of the youth, has been presented and discussed in detail in this chapter, which was devoted to the authority of priests and the trust these young Catholics grant them. In Poland today, a priest no longer impresses the youth as a professional competent on various issues of life and moral values, as was evident during the youth of their parents or grandparents. On the contrary, the formal authority of the priest is perceived by contemporary youth to be very limited. Young people today consider a priest only to be a specialist on issues and problems concerned with religion and the Church, and at the same time want priests to be marked by a genuine religious vocation, with many necessary personal qualities and talents in the priesthood, as a result of which he will deserve their full confidence.

A priest marked with a vocation, in the judgment of the respondents, should be well versed in the methodology of his priestly profession and personal role in the parish, yet cannot eliminate lay people from active parish life or show them contempt through his own pride and arrogance. The priest, as a member of the clergy, cannot show the laity his "superiority" or ill-conceived "power," but should be fair, obliging, ready to help and serve, because these qualities and actions result from the nature of his mission in the Church. The surveyed youth question and reject the extensive authority of priests over the laity and at the same time emphasize the importance of their personal charisma, which contributes significantly to their bestowing of trust in life. These people do not want priests to cross the limit of their professional competence and scope of their official authority consciously, but want priests to be concerned with the religious life of the faithful. Priests should not, therefore, in assessing these young people, embody typically secular and moralizing roles, especially in the political and economic spheres, because these do not belong to the scope of their professional competence and to the essence of the priesthood. Many respondents said that authentic priests will always be needed by religious people who will rely on their religious and ethical authority, trusting them fully, especially in difficult matters and issues that require a thorough theological and religious analysis.[41]

[41] See J. Baniak, *Obraz kapłana w świadomości katolików świeckich...* [The Image of the Priest in the Awareness of the Lay Faithful...], op. cit., pp. 187–212.

Chapter V

The model of the parish priest according to the respondents

Authority and the role of a priest are directly connected with the official and environmental model of the parish priest. In principle, it is authority that lies at the basis of the model priest functioning in the religious and social awareness of lay Catholics. The official model of a priest is, in this analysis, an ideal reference point for parishioners to identify with their ministers. The environmental model of a priest has at its basis the theological and canonical status of the hierarchical priesthood along with local customs and traditions that express the faithful's desires to relate to the personal role-model and social role of a priest.[1]

In light of these assumptions, the question arises whether and to which extent this model of a priest was accepted by the interviewed high school and college students during the study period?

1. The concept of the "model" and the "personal role-model" in sociological studies

There is no doubt that every age creates more or less widely accepted personal role-models and models, some of which are hardly propagated, and others which are in fact accomplished. These two concepts and conditions of real-

---

[1] See P. Taras, "Problem modelu kapłana w Kościele katolickim [The Issue of the Priest Model in the Catholic Chruch], *Znak*, 1968, no. 20 (171), pp. 1116–1132; B. Tomczyk, "Model kapłana w świetle dokumentów Soboru Watykańskiego II" [The Priest Model in the Light of the Documents of the Second Vatican Council], *Studia Warmińskie*, 1975, vol. 12, pp. 304–324.

ity are differently defined by researchers of people's social lives, including sociologists.

Antonina Kłoskowska writes that the "personal role-model" is "[...] a certain regularity, meaning a relatively lasting structure of human behavior which is conditioned by social and cultural factors. [...] Models of human behavior expand, they propagate. This means that they have a dynamic characteristic; they are not only expressions, but also a factor shaping uniformity in human behavior. [...] They are a widespread pattern in a certain social circle of typical ways of actually behaving."[2] Referring to Thomas Merton, the author indicates two types of cultural personality patterns: models of open behavior, which are made conscious, and models of hidden behavior, which are unconscious.

In the understanding of Alicja Kuczyńska: "A life model is a picture of the way of being or acting in the world, it is an image that tends to be socially treated as a value or group of values worthy of imitation."[3] The author further mentions two types of imitating: "[...] passive, blind, mechanical, unconsciously duplicated pictures, repeating observed activities or imitation resulting from a conscious acceptance of a certain scale of values."[4] According to her, "Behavioral patterns are universalized in various ways. Imitation and empathy play their role without reflection. In the majority of cases, however, activists are aware of the existing behavior pattern that they achieve. Even people who are not quite able to reflect on their own actions are able to state how they most often behave in their society in a given situation, how one ought to behave."[5] Therefore, the personal role-model is realistic behavior, a set of concrete traits which can be present in a person, and it is indicated by a set of norms and ideas related to fulfilling specific social roles and functions. The personal role-model for an individual or group is usually an individual person, who embodies their ambitions.

Antonina Kłoskowska points out that "at the moment when we go from the sphere of direct activity to reflection and the impression of regularly performed behavior in a symbolic grasp of whatever kind, the concept of the role-model is replaced by the concept of the type or model."[6] As the author indicates, the model refers to the imaginings of behaviour. Therefore, unlike the

---

[2] A. Kłoskowska, "Wzory i modele w socjologicznych badaniach rodziny" [Patterns and Models in Sociological Family Studies], *Studia Socjologiczne*, 1962, no. 2, p. 37.

[3] A. Kuczyńska, *Wzory modne w życiu codziennym* [Popular Patterns in Daily Life], Warsaw 1983, p. 34.

[4] Ibidem, p. 38.

[5] Ibidem, p. 39.

[6] A. Kłoskowska, "Wzory i modele..." [Patterns and Models...], op. cit., p. 44; see eadem, "Modele społeczne i kultura masowa" [Social Models and Mass Culture], *Przegląd Socjologiczny*, 1959, no. 2, pp. 49–56.

personal role-model, it does not reflect reality, but propagates certain ways of behaviour in this reality. A. Kłoskowska defines a model as "always being a conscious model, which comprises a set of norms or ideas referring to a specific social sphere of activity, formulated in a verbal way or expressed as an image, for extra-cognitive goals [...]."[7] A model, therefore, is only an outline for behavior, a set of traits and attitudes, which are conceptualized, and next created by a concrete person. The author indicates two types of models: propagated and environmental. Propagated models are created for use by strangers and popularized in the press and by other means of mass social communication. On the other hand, environmental models are the unique creations of groups and environments to which this activity is directed. The author further clarifies that there also exist other so-called "clean" models, meaning models that are devoid of counterparts in the sphere of social role-models. These models are propagated, but at the same time rejected by society.[8]

Claude Levi-Strauss distinguished two types of models, dependent on the relationship of the individual to the researched phenomena. The first types are mechanical models, which "[...] lie on the plain of researched phenomena, meaning that they comprise the expression of regularity perceived by members of collective studies, in which they took on the role of normative systems. An example of this model is the set of rules for entering into marriage in primeval families, referring to individuals whose place in the family structure is strictly defined. The second types are static models situated beyond the sphere of consciously realized actions which do not have a counterpart in rules and norms. An example of this is the family life of primeval people. In addition, the author also points out that there are conscious and unconscious models. Conscious models, also known as 'homemade productions,' can represent the adequate understanding of social relationships, and express the evaluations and norms that preserve and universalize the beliefs and customs, but do not explain the phenomena. Unconscious models do not have a counterpart in norms."[9] Józef Majka accepts that a model is an image of some phenomenon, thing or group of activities which comprises a certain whole.[10]

In the contemporary world, personal role-models and models play an important role in the life of every person; they are a certain type of original style.

[7] A. Kłoskowska, "Wzory i modele..." [Patterns and Models...], op. cit., p. 45.

[8] Ibidem.

[9] Cited from ibidem, p. 40.

[10] J. Majka, "Wpływ środowiska i przemian społecznych na kształtowanie się modelu kapłana – duszpasterza" [Environmental Influence and Social Changes on the Formation of the Model Priest – Minister], in J. Majka (ed.), *Osobowość kapłańska* [The Priestly Personality], Wroclaw 1983, p. 106.

We can ask why this happens. A person consciously or unconsciously imitates other people. Do people want to model their personal behavior and actions based on others? Do we want to be equal to them or "chase after" them in striving for specific goals? Alicja Kuczyńska writes that "[...] the model of a more intense and unceasing imitation of others is the result of the disappearance of traditional authorities, which ensure people safety, but others appear in their place, who no longer guarantee such safety, and in addition weaken the feeling of the autonomous personal 'self,' and this deepens the need for imitating existing role-models. Consequently, a person adjusts to existing role-models, therefore they can be certain of themselves only when they live as others expect them to. If we would not live according to this image, not only would we be exposed to the danger of criticism and even greater isolation, but risk the loss of identity, which is synonymous with the threat of losing our sound reasoning. Striving to be the same as others, assumes, due to various reasons, the rank of the basic principles of life."[11] This is a common phenomenon, which appears in every social group; hence these also apply to people in spiritual ministry.

2. The model and the personal model of the priest – its essence, structure and applicability

The formal definition of the personal model and the model synthetically described above must now be adapted to the personal pattern and model of the priest, incorporating theological and social content. Wladysław Piwowarski states that the term "model priest" may be used in a threefold sense: a) as an official model, expressed in Catholic social doctrine, b) as a promotional model, expressed in various forms of ecclesial significance, c) as an environmental model, spontaneously formed by the specific environment of the Church.[12] Piotr Taras notes that "[...] the model of the priest is set up institutionally or required (or in some sense approved of) by social types and modes of action, the behavior and attributes of a clergyman, serving the social role of a priest. This model may have a simple structure, fulfilling only one function, or complex, fulfilling several functions. It can be established in a formal, institutional or informal way. It can have a static or dynamic, ideal or existential character. [...] Lack of significant difference or discrepancy between the ideal, institutional and existential models is evidence of the proper functioning of the system."[13]

[11] A. Kuczyńska, *Wzory modne w życiu codziennym* [Popular Patterns in Daily Life], op. cit., p. 23.

[12] W. Piwowarski, "Moralność jako sprawdzian żywotności religijnej" [Morality as a Test for Religious Longevity], *Studia Warmińskie*, 1966, vol. 3, pp. 97–98.

[13] P. Taras, "Problem modelu kapłana..." [The Issue of the Priest Model...], op. cit., p. 1117.

Józef Majka, analyzing the essence of the model parish priest, asks: which elements comprise his role? Which are essential and immutable, and which are variable and secondary? Under the influence of which factors do changes occur in the model pastor? Who controls these changes and who can approve or reject them? Which models of priests exist in our Polish reality today, and what has shaped them? What can we say about the model priest – the pastor needed in our present times, and which model suits the needs of the future? What is characteristic of the model priest of Catholic youth in Poland, and to what extent is it consistent with the official features of the priest model in the Catholic Church?

In response to these questions, Józef Majka proposes a precise and exhaustive typology of the elements constituting a model parish priest, first dividing them into three general categories, and identifying various specific elements within these. The general categories of these elements are as follows: 1) absolutely invariant elements, meaning the theological components of the model priest and pastor, 2) actual invariant elements, that is, resulting directly from the theological elements, implemented in ways defined by the Church, with regards to specific actual circumstances, but not changing the standards that determine how a priest acts and behaves, 3) variable elements of the model priest, resulting from the "signs of the times" with multiple environmental differences under which the priest proclaims the Gospel and carries out parish ministry.[14]

In conclusion, the author points out that "[...] the number of environmental factors that shape models of priests is very high, so it would be difficult to enumerate them exhaustively: some function more directly and others indirectly, but together they are invariable elements. They all constitute the practical model of the priest, combined into one functional whole, giving a certain product, which is the particular personal pattern of a priest, functioning in a given period and in a given community."[15]

The author further identifies five key factors that significantly influence the development of the model of a parish priest. These factors essentially result from the functions he fulfills in the parish community: 1) the participation of the priest in the Church's salvific mission, from which stems his principal functions and tasks, 2) the concept of the Church and Her image functioning in the minds of priests, 3) social needs and expectations of the lay faithful directly addressed to the priest, which may be many and varied, yet changing over time, 4) the possibilities and means of action at the disposal of the priest in the parish, influencing its pastoral and social activity – which tends to be

[14] See J. Majka, "Wpływ środowiska i przemian społecznych..." [Environmental Influence and Social Changes...], op. cit., pp. 108–116.

[15] Ibidem, p. 116.

different in rural parishes than in a city, 5) the process of cultural urbanization, evoking among others mental changes in the faithful concerning faith, religion, morality, and people's attitudes towards the Church and the clergy, ranging from positive to neutral to critical or negative. These factors converge and cause a rapid process of transformation of the "old" model of the priest into the model that is suited to the living conditions of people in a particular time.[16]

The model of the parish priest is complex in nature, because it takes into account various aspects of the institution of the priesthood, but does so in a greatly simplified way. These arguments can be explained with the help of W. Sadowski's thesis, which states that "[...] the model reflects a fragment of reality that we are interested in, but avoids the less essential elements of this reality."[17] This model for the priesthood applies to standards and images concerning the behavior of a priest desired by the faithful. Practically speaking, we are dealing with an empirical "picture" of the priest, not the theological meaning of the priesthood, with an attempt to determine the stereotypical image of a priest, which is, as pointed out by J. Mariański, "[...] the presentation of objective reality from the subjective perspective of those who judge."[18]

What is the typical environmental model of the parish priest in the mentality of Polish high school and college students, or junior high school students? Is this model consistent with the official model of the priest, currently held in the Catholic Church? Is the model of a priest functioning in the young generation of Polish Catholics significantly different from the model created and disseminated in the generation of adult Catholics? I will answer these questions in my further analysis of the phenomenon.

3. The psychosocial image of the person of the priest in the perceptions and evaluations of the respondents

During my sociological research, I asked high school, college and junior high students to identify the positive characteristics (virtues) that a parish priest should be "equipped" with and the activities that he should perform in the parish and the secular community. The second question concerned the personal vices of parish priests and negative behavior that should not occur at all. Respondents had complete freedom in choosing both types of features and activities in priests, so the total number of these indications is greater than the general number of respondents in both groups.

---

[16] Ibidem, pp. 117–120.

[17] W. Sadowski, *Teoria podejmowania decyzji. Wstęp do badań operacyjnych* [The Theory of Decision-making. Introduction to Operational Research Studies], Warsaw 1964, p. 11.

[18] J. Mariański, *Żyć parafią* [Living with the Parish], Wroclaw 1984, p. 147.

a) Personal and professional virtues of parish priests identified by the respondents

In the 1970s, Stefan Dobrzanowski carried out sociological research on the perceptions and evaluations of high school students concerning the personal and professional characteristics of parish priests. The research shows that the young respondents clearly preferred the secular personal characteristics and professional activities of parish priest. His religious traits and activities were placed second in their classification.[19] Young Catholics, preferring the secular traits and actions of priests, want to see him as a good man first, with a high level of personal morality and sense of self-dignity, but at the same time respecting the dignity and freedom of other people, and only then do they see a priest as a professional performing his priestly task, caring for the faith, religion and spirituality of the faithful laity. In the seventies of the last century, the youth's assessment of priests was largely dependent on his individual characteristics and his official authority based on his personal charism. In light of the results of these studies, it makes sense to ask the Polish youth I surveyed, the representative average group from secondary schools and universities, if they looked for this same model of the parish priest in the periods of 1983–1998–2008.

Based on these studies, we found that, during the study period, respondents in both groups valued the religious qualities and activities of parish priests more highly than their secular characteristics and natural or secular activities. The characteristics and activities of priests in their religious model were generally preferred by 69.4% of respondents, including 71.4% of high school and 67.4% of college students. By contrast, the secular features and activities were appreciated by a total of 64.0% of respondents, including more college students (64.8%) than high school students (63.2%). The personal model of a priest, made up of these two types of features and activities, was offered by 66.7% of respondents, including a slightly higher percentage of high school students (67.3%) than college students (66.1%). Therefore, during this period the young people were interested in parish priests who worked in parishes and also in the academic ministry environment. In addition, 33.3% of respondents, including 32.7% of high school students and 33.9% of college students, did not answer this question, not giving reasons for their attitude.

Religious and secular characteristics and activities of priests preferred by respondents can be arranged in a rank ordering system, since the traits and activities of priests pointed out most oftenwere allocated positions from one to sixteen.

---

[19] See S. Dobrzanowski, "Młodzież o kapłaństwie i kapłanach" [The Youth on Priesthood and Priests], *Chrześcijanin w Świecie*, 1977, no. 2 (50), pp. 100–106.

The classification of attributes and behaviors of religious priests is presented as follows: 1 – living according to the principles of the Gospel: 81.1% total, including high school students 79.7% (3rd place) and college students 82.5% (1st place), 2 – having a genuine priestly vocation: 80.1%, including 84.5% (1) and 77.3% (2), 3 – deeply religious: 79.0%, including 80.8% (2) and 77.2% (3), 4 – being concerned about the faith of people: 74.7%, including 76.1% (6) and 74.7% (4), 5 – being concerned about the religiosity of adolescents: 75.5%, including 79.5% (4) and 71.9% (7), 6 – catechists by vocation: 75.1%, including 77.7% (5) and 72.5% (5), 7 – praying individually very often: 73.0%, including 75.2% (7) and 70.7% (8), 8 – being deeply religious and pious: 72.2%, including 72.0% (9) and 72.2% (6), 9 – being concerned about the parish: 69.0%, including 69.4% (10) and 68.7% (9), 10 – loving the Church: 68.5%, including 72.5% (8) and 64.5% (13), 11 – correctly preaching sermons and homilies: 68.3%, including 69.2% (11) and 67.5% (11), 12 – taking care of religious worship in the parish: 68.2%, including 68.8% (12) and 67.7% (10), 13 – caring for the maintenance and good appearance of the parish sanctuary: 65.7%, including 66.8% (13) and 64.6% (12), 14 – being obedient to the bishop: 58.8%, including 61.8% (15) and 55.7% (14), 15 – being concerned about the morality of their parishioners: 56.8%, including 63.9% (14) and 49.7% (15), 16 – being faithful to celibacy: 42.2%, including 43.4% (16) and 41.1% (16). In total, the religious characteristics and activities of priests were appreciated by 69.4% of respondents, including 71.4% of high school and 67.4% of college students. The importance of these qualities and activities of priests in the adopted period varied. Respondents valued some traits more than others, and this fluctuation significantly influenced their position on the model priest scale as designed by respondents.

The classification of attributes and behavior of secular priests identified by respondents is as follows: 1 – they should be tolerant: 82.4%, including 75.5% of high school 79.0% of college students, 2 – they should be apolitical: 79.0%, including 76.5% and 77.0%, 3 – they must be respected by the people: 77.5%, including 73.3% and 79.5%, 4 – they should be helpful and compassionate towards people: 74.9%, including 76.5% and 73.4%, 5 – approachable and courteous in dealing with people: 72.4%, including 75.3% and 69.5%, 6 – just: 72.3%, including 70.4% and 72.1%, 7 – they cannot have any bad habits or become addicted: 68.2%, including 66.9% and 69.5% 8 – they should be happy and rejoice: 67.2%, including 68.6% and 65.7%, 9 – they are honest in relationships with people: 67.1%, including 66.8% and 67.4%, 10 – they should be a well-educated labor force: 67.0%, including 59.1% and 74.9%, 11 – selfless and objective in dealing with people: 66.7%, including 64.5% and 68.9%, 12 – consistent in their proceedings: 66.4%, including 65.9% and

66.9%, 13 – understanding and gentle in dealing with people: 65.7%, including 66.5% and 64.9%, 14 – articulate and well-read in many fields of knowledge: 65.5%, including 60.1% and 70.8%, 15 – brave in decisions and beliefs: 65.3%, including 66.7% and 64.2%, 16 – considerate and cultural: 64.2%, including 66.6% and 61.9%, 17 – intelligent and possessing life wisdom: 64.1%, including 58.9% and 69.3%, 18 – should listen to people in matters of religion and the Church: 57.3%, including 60.3% and 54.3%, 19 – should be active in social work for the good of men: 53.7%, including 50.8% and 56.6%, 20 – should have a sense of humor and positive attitude towards life: 45.1%, including 45.8% and 44.5%, 21 – take care of their appearance and language aesthetics: 37.2%, including 38.4% and 36.1%, 22 – avoid gossip in the clergy environment and lay community: 36.8%, including 37.3% and 36.3%. These features and activities of secular priests were preferred by 64.0% of the respondents, including 63.2% of high school and 64.8% of college students.

During the study period, these features and activities, like the religious ones, were preferred by the respondents in both groups according to their dynamics and frequency – some gave them higher evaluations, and others were judged less important to the priestly or pastoral ministry model. A few of the characteristics and activities were identically approved of in the environmental structure of their priest model, but the views of secondary school and college students were clearly divided regarding the majority of these characteristics and secular actions.[20]

[20] Cf. M. R. Rewera, *Autorytet księży w świadomości młodzieży licealnej. Studium socjologiczne* [The Authority of Priests in the Awareness of High School Youth. A Sociological Study], Lublin 2006 (CUL typed doctoral dissertation work manuscript), pp. 276–277, cite from J. Mariański, *Emigracja z Kościoła. Religijność młodzieży polskiej w warunkach zmian społecznych* [Emigration from the Church. The Religiousness of Poland's Youth in Conditions of Social Change], Lublin 2008, pp. 443–444. [High school students from Sandomierz and Chobrzan interviewed in the years 2002–2004 by Miroslaw Rewera indicated the following characteristics of a priest's religious authority: a mediator between people and God (81.2%), concern for the Church and parish (82.4%), occupying a high position in the hierarchy (25.8%)]. See J. Baniak, *Między buntem a potrzebą akceptacji i zrozumienia. Świadomość religijna i moralna a kryzys tożsamości osobowej młodzieży gimnazjalnej. Studium socjologiczne* [Between Rebelion and the Need for Acceptance and Understanding. The Awareness of Religious and Moral a Crisis of personal Indentity in Junior High School Youth. A Sociological Study], Cracow 2008, p. 321, table 133. (Junior high students from schools in Kalisz pointed to the following necessary positive religious characteristics of a priest: the priestly vocation (77.4%), deep religious faith (71.0%), living according to the principles of the Gospel (70.8%), personal piety (71.0%), concern for the faith of parishioners (70.2%), concern for the faith and religiousness of youth (71.9%), love for the Church (67.4%), correctly preaching and delivering homilies (64.1%), concern for religious worship in the parish (60.7%), and properly conducting religious education classes (61.7%). Together, these features were indicated by 64.4% of respondents, including 65.2% of girls and 63.0% of boys, 67.8% of students from rural areas and 62.6% of students from the city.

Research shows that the model parish priest advocated by my respondents from Kalisz is characterized by significant coherence and complexity of religious and natural features that are mutually complementary and dependent. These features and activities are clearly dominant over secular traits and actions. In the conviction of most respondents, the model priest is clear and logical when both types and actions creating this model are mutually balanced, and in addition, religious features are supported by religious traits. Only in such a synthesis of traits and actions is the priest able to meet the wishes and expectations of the faithful, or the religious and spiritual needs of young people.

In the opinion of the majority of the surveyed high school (68.5%) and college students (63.4%), only a priest with these two types of features and activities, both religious (67.4% and 71.4%) and natural (64.8% and 63.2%) will cope with the demands of the priesthood, requirements of Church authority and expectations of the faithful in the parish, and as such experience a sense of satisfaction as a result of his priestly life and pastoral work. Such a priest, truly fulfilled by religion and life, in the evaluation of 81.4% of high school and 69.3% of college students, will interest religious boys (men) in the priesthood through his example, and encourage them to choose it as their personal way of life and career. In other words, the priest will show them the priesthood as an ideal value, which they can gain at the expense of other important values, such as the love to be experienced in marriage and with their own family. Priesthood authentically lived by priests may be attractive, and then be chosen by future candidates as a service to God and people in the structures of the Church, particularly in the parish and the community of religious life.[21]

In the priest model postulated by high school and college students from Kalisz, we noted trends that differed from tendencies established much earlier by Stefan Dobrzanowski among high school students. In that model, priests "[...] are strongly preferred for their natural features, which remain at the service of the religious characteristics of the priestly mission. [...] The young respondents usually put the religious values of the character traits of a priest

---

At the same time, respondents indicated the necessity for the following natural characteristics and activities of their model priest: tolerant (87.1%), non-political (77.1%), respect for people (72.5%), accessible to the parishioners (70.0%), merciful (76.3%), without bad habits (69.1%), articulate (64.9%), brave (54.0%), with a sense of humor (51.1%), cheerful and satisfied (47.4%), social (49.2%), aesthetic (41.9%). The average selection of these characteristics amounts to 62.2%, including 61.9% among girls and 62.7% among boys, and 65.6% among students of rural areas and 60.1% among urban students).

[21] See J. Baniak, *Ksiądz w oczach młodzieży. Obraz kapłana w świadomości młodzieży licealnej i akademickiej na przykładzie Kalisza. Studium socjologiczne* [The Priest in the Eyes of the Youth. The Image of the Priest in the Awareness of High School and College Youth in the Example of Kalisz. A Sociological Study], Poznan 1993, pp. 146–147.

in second place. Dominant are the demands requiring priests to have genuine faith and a spirit of prayer [...], and further on they place faithfulness to their vocation and commitment to the service of God. [...] Particularly striking is the disproportion between the natural and religious requirements addressed to priests, to the detriment of religious characteristics."[22] We also see a preference for natural features over the religious features in demands concerning the model parish priest in high school students surveyed by Janusz Mariański.[23]

Meanwhile, secondary school and academic youth, as well as junior high students from Kalisz, studied in the years 1983–1998–2008, clearly preferred religious and religious-institutional characteristics and activities associated directly with the Church and the parish, and only placed secular characteristics and activities – natural and humanistic – second as part of the personality of the modern priest. However, respondents in both groups often stressed the importance of combining both types of features and activities, to form a harmonious priestly personality in a particular priest. Preference for religious and Church traits and behavior in the proposed priest model does not imply recurrence to clerical tendencies in the religious lives of Polish youth, nor does it disregard the role of lay virtues in the personality of the priest. On the contrary, it may be a manifestation of a certain "nostalgia" in young Polish Catholics for genuine ministerial priesthood, at the core of which must be found very religious and ecclesiastical features, as opposed to priesthood based solely on power, which is, moreover, secularly interpreted.

Perhaps the youth seldom meet priests who are "soaked" or "filled" with the spirit of true faith and personal piety, living according to the spirit of Gospel principles, sincerely committed to the Church and the faithful in the parish. Maybe on their way to the Church they usually saw and met professional "officials" who might have been insensitive to the concerns and needs of the laity, or people excluded in various other ways, or over-ambitious in terms of their careers in the Church. Thus, youth want their priest model to show religious characteristics and activities resulting from deep spiritual faith, dominating the personality of the priest in the difficult present circumstances of secular and liberal morality. These religious features are to counteract these tendencies and offset the transition towards secular living. They are to be the guarantee of a truly ministerial priesthood, geared towards the religious, spiritual and moral needs of people. These expectations of the youth are of course hypothetical or wishful, but they cannot be ruled out, rather, they should be

[22] S. Dobrzanowski, "Młodzież o kapłaństwie i kapłanach" [The Youth on Priests and Priesthood], op. cit., pp. 100–103.

[23] See J. Mariański, *Emigracja z Kościoła...* [Emigration from the Church...], op. cit., pp. 441–443.

treated seriously, hoping that one day, sociologists of religion and sociologists of youth will verify this hypothesis.

These people also want modern priests to continually deepen their spiritual lives and unite it with personal piety and not "smother" amid secular values and their own instrumental goals. Otherwise, they will further the process of desacralization of the institutional priesthood, of which the young people are aware, especially in terms of its consequences on the religious and moral lives of priests and lay Catholics.

The priest today, as my respondents recognized, should, or rather must attract people, especially young people, to God and the Church, if he wants to genuinely fulfill the meaning and purpose of his vocation to the priesthood. He must do this through his own earnest and deep spiritual faith and religious life, based on the principles of the Gospel. Without this condition the priest will not fulfill his professional mission. On the contrary – he might repel many people from religion and the Church, impeding their way to God as their primary purpose in life. Such a goal must also lie in the consciousness of every priest, according to my respondents from Kalisz.

b) Personal and professional vices of priests identified by the respondents

According to the surveyed high school and college students, the negative traits and activities of priests and their personal and professional shortcomings, also play an important role in the model priest. These vices are familiar to the respondents from own experience and from encounters with "bad" priests, or stories told about them in families or the youth environment, such as religion lessons or other meetings. Perhaps these environmental "stories" about the immoral actions of priests contains a lot of stereotypical thinking, based on rumors or on slander, but we also cannot exclude the authenticity of many of them, even if they result from the personal experience of individuals with such a priest. If they are based on facts, discussion is unnecessary.

Władysław Piwowarski points out that criticism of the vices and bad behavior of parish priests, by Catholics and other lay people, is often justified, since it has a "tough basis" in specific life situations and circumstances, indicating at the same time the need to make important changes in the lives and behavior of priests. This criticism is often coupled with sincere concern for and forethought on the social prestige and rightful place of the priest in the local community. Lay Catholics, citing the numerous defects of parish priests, try to challenge the proposed model and type of priestly authority, which deviates from their own expectations and group feelings, that are different from their notions of a "real" priest.[24] It should be added that sociological studies inform us of the many and various personal and professional disadvantages of many parish priests and religious people, which adult[25] Catholics and young people[26] indicated.

The parish priest model advocated by my respondents also includes their perceptions and assessments concerning the "sins" of priests, meaning the catalog of their personal and professional shortcomings, inconsistent with secular principles of the Gospel proclaimed and the ethical guidelines of the Church, which are recommended for the priesthood. These vices are numerous and include both spheres of a priest's life – religious and secular. We will draw attention to these vices in further analysis of the phenomenon.

The research shows that respondents in both groups indicated as many as 41 vices in priests, which they noticed in various circumstances in contacts with priests, including 18 religious or Church vices and 23 vices of a secular type. Overall, both types of failings in priests were identified by 50.9% of respondents, including 47.8% of high school and 54.0% of college students, while the remaining respondents were unable to identify vices (42.3%) or refrained from answering the question concerning vices (6.8%). In the spheres of religion and the Church, a total of 47.1% of respondents made "accusations" towards priests, including 43.4% of high school and 50.7% of college students. In the secular sphere, 54.7% of respondents identified vices in priests, including 52.2% of high school and 57.3% of college students. Thus, secular failings in priests during the study period were noticed by a slightly higher percentage of respondents than religious and Church defects – a total of 13.0%, including 8.5% of high school students and 6.6% of college students.

In the sphere of religion and Church, respondents indicated 18 personal and professional shortcomings in priests, although the scale of their criticism varied greatly, comparing priests' performance to their model priest. According to the adopted scale, the ranks of vices are as follows: 1 – charging overly high fees for religious and sacramental services: 75.0%, including 82.6% of high school students and 77.7% of college students, 2 – infidelity to the rules of celibacy: 64.3% , including 59.5% and 69.1%, 3 – ignoring parishioners: 63.8%,

[24] See W. Piwowarski, "Tradycyjny autorytet księdza w procesie przemian" [The Traditional Authority of the Priest in the Process of Transformation), in idem, *Religijność ludowa – ciągłość i zmiana* [Folk Religiousness – Continuity and Change], Wroclaw 1983, pp. 121–131.

[25] See J. Baniak, *Obraz kapłana w świadomości katolików świeckich – na przykładzie Kalisza, Kotłowa i Przedborowa. Studium socjologiczne* [The Image of the Priest in the Awareness of Lay Catholics based on Kalisz, Kotłów and Przedborów. A Sociological Studies], Poznan 1994, pp. 150–159.

[26] See J. Baniak, *Ksiądz w oczach młodzieży...* [The Priest in the Eyes of the Youth...], op. cit., pp. 225–235.

including 60.2% and 67.3%, 4 – proceeding against the rules of the Gospel: 60.9%, including 54.6% and 67.1%, 5 – religious and worldview intolerance: 51.0%, including 45.0% and 57.1%, 6 – neglecting sermons and homilies: 49.5%, including 48.3% and 50.7%, 7 – neglect of personal prayer: 49.1%, including 46.1% and 52.1%, 8 – apparent personal piety: 48.9%, including 47.2%, and 50.6%, 9 – the lack of concern for the morality of their parishioners: 47.4%, including 45.9% and 48.9%, 10 – lack of concern for the faith of people: 44.4%, and 41.8%, and 47.1%, 11 – neglecting duty at school catechesis classes: 44.2%, including 41.1% and 47.4%, 12 – lack of faith in the Church: 43.2%, including 40.5% and 45.9% , 13 – poor management of the parish: 32.2%, including 30.3% and 34.2%, 14 – weak faith or lack of religious faith: 37.6%, including 34.2% and 40.9%, 15 – lack of concern for religious worship in the parish: 32.7%, including 27.6% and 37.7%, 16 – absence of a genuine vocation to the priesthood: 32.4%, including 26.4% and 38.3%; 17 – poorly managing parish funds: 32.2%, including 30.3% and 34.2%, 18 – causing strife in the rectory: 30.3%, including 27.3% and 33.3%. Together, these failings of priests were observed by 47.1% of respondents, including 43.4% of high school and 50.7% of college students. The significance of these vices either increased or decreased during the study period, which was determined by the specifics of the changes in successive subperiods, although higher proportions of respondents in both groups were more critical of them in 2008 than in 1983. The percentage of high school students in the group criticizing the shortcomings of priests during the whole period was 18.3%, and in the group of students it was even higher, amounting to 19.3%.

Disadvantages of priests of a secular nature can generally be placed into two groups: a) concerning their personality and professional activity and b) in regards to their relationships with the parish and local communities. The first group includes the following vices: 1 – practical materialism, valuing comfort and luxury, money, and a consumerist lifestyle: 69.4%, including 66.9% of high school students and 71.9% of college students, 2 – secular everyday lifestyle and mode: 71.0% (70.0% and 72.0%), 3 – ideologically and practically inconsistent: 56.9% (48.5% and 65.4%), 4 – alcohol abuse as a form of "treating" his own complexes: 50.6% (45.5% and 55.6%), 5 – obtrusive gambler: 50.0% (45.2% and 54.6%), 6 – abusing drugs: 40.5% (38.2% and 42.7%), 7 – arrogant and inaccessible to the laity in the parish: 68.8% (67.4% and 70.3%), 8 – religiously intolerant: 74.5% (72, 7% and 76.2%), 9 – poorly educated for his profession: 36.0% (35.2% and 36.8%), 10 – lacking sense of humor and joy: 41.4% (39.4% and 43.5%), 11 – tactless in dealing with people: 56.2% (51.9% and 60.5%), 12 – psychologically unstable and nervous: 25.2% (20.7% and 29.6%). All these defects were indicated by 53.6% of respondents, including 50.7% of high school and 56.5% of college students.

The second group (the public sphere) includes the following secular vices of priests: 1 – political involvement in state and local spheres: 68.0%, including 64.7% of high school and 71.3% of college students, 2 – belittling people in different circumstances: 66.6% (64.8% and 68.5%), 3 – unfair judgement of people: 36.5% (34.2% and 39.1%), 4 – gossip about priests and lay people: 35.9% (34.6% and 37.2%), 5 – egoism, disobliging to people: 68.4% (67.5% and 69.2%), 6 – asocial, ignoreing the needs of the local community: 64.0% (62.1% and 65.9%), 7 – backward and old-fashioned: 51.4% (47.8% and 55.1%), 8 – tolerating mediocrity, lack of ambition: 36.0% (35.2% and 36.9%), 9 – a rowdy troublemaker: 40.6% (38.9% and 42.3%), 10 – cheating people: 68.2% (65.8% and 70.5%). Altogether, 55.9% of respondents accused priests of these defects, including 53.7% of high school and 58.1% of college students who reported that all these defects lowered the authority of the parish priests at that time, undermining his credibility in the eyes of the people and their trust towards him in religious and moral matters.

Criticism of the laity towards priests' vices intensified in subsequent periods of research in both groups of respondents. The percentage of high school students criticizing priests for their vices increased during the whole period, from 40.3% in 1983 to 60.9% in 2008, an increase of 16.8%. The percentage of college students who criticized the faults of priests was also high, from 49.4% in 1983 up to 66.2% in 2008, an increase of 16.8%. The negative evaluation of these vices varied widely in both groups of respondents – some were more criticized by high school students, others by college students. High school students placed the following vices of priests in the first three places: 1 – intolerance: 72.7%, 2 – aloofness and arrogance: 70.0%, 3 – secular and consumerist lifestyles: 68.1%. Students indicated the same flaws, but invested them in other places: 1 – intolerance: 76.2%, 2 – love of a comfortable lifestyle: 73.4%; 3 – aloofness and arrogance: 70.5%.

The criticism of both types of vices in priests shows that the high school and college students, as young Polish Catholics, placed high religious, spiritual, ethical and humanistic demands on parish priests, expecting that their hopes would not be disappointed, since priests themselves would eliminate vices from their own lives and actions. Furthermore, the respondents declared in their statements that they still trust priests to be model persons and religious and moral authorities for young people finding their place in the Church and the parish, as well as in their adult lives. It is interesting that Fr. Czesław Podleski expressed a similar opinion 31 years earier, taking into account the expectations of contemporary Polish youth: "[...] young believers put great demands on priests, looking at them critically, but kindly. According to them, priests should represent a higher moral standard than the laity."[27]

My respondents referred to the religious and secular vices of priests in a similar way, knowing them from the life of the parish and from other contacts, chiefly catechism school classes and university ministry activities. Their criticism of these vices is constructive and logical, based on their kindness and positive attitude towards the role of priests in the Church, in the parish and the community, including their concern for the authenticity of their religious and moral life in the parish community, in school, youth, local and family environments. Respondents clearly indicated in the proposed priest model that they want today's priests to be able to meet the expectations and wishes of young people who are looking for their place in the Catholic Church, which means the requirements that are key components of the model priest. This criticism was not based on prejudice, hostility, resentment, contempt, distrust or social distance, since none of these were to be found in the respondents. Reliable and objective critique of one's attitudes and behavior is the basis for personal improvement in every man, including priests, and I perceived such concern for this development in a dominant percentage of high school (79.6%) and college students (81.4%) surveyed.

Continuing along the thought of Fr. Stefan Dobrzanowski, we can say that criticism of vices and praise of virtues in priests is an expression of care and concern – on the part of the respondents for every priest to properly achieve the ideal priesthood and correctly represent the institutional Church in its various structures in society.[28] The model postulated by my respondents is to a great extent in accord with the official model of the priest, which is required in the Catholic Church after Vatican II.[29] J. Mariański notes in this context that "[...] undoubtedly, honest criticism is necessary for the smooth management of the parish and may become an essential element of the devel-

[27] Cz. Podleski, "Model prezbitera diecezjalnego w opinii kleryków i księży" [The Model of the Diocesan Presbyter in the Opinion of Clerics and Priests], *Collectanea Theologica*, 1981, no. 51, pp. 132–154.

[28] See S. Dobrzanowski, "Młodzież o kapłaństwie i kapłanach" [The Youth on Priesthood and Priests], op. cit., 1977, no. 2 (50), pp. 105–106. (The author writes that "Young people want to see priests as intermediaries and stewards of the mysteries of God, who [...] through their personalities represent the ideal of harmony between natural and supernatural qualities. Also, criticism of blatant failings found in the clergy is an expression of young people's concern for the proper implementation of the priesthood and a decent representation of the Church").

[29] See M. Midali, "Crisi del sacerdozio e risporta dell Conzilio" [Christians on the Priesthood and the Voice of the Council], in *Il sacerdoti nelle spiriti del Vaticano II* [Priests in the Spirit of Vatican II], Torino 1968, pp. 307–345.

opment and improvement of priests."[30] This is precisely the concern shown by the high school, junior high and college student respondents I surveyed in Kalisz. In the opinion of the majority of the adolescents surveyed, the parish priest should be – in the words of Fr. Józef Majka – "[...] a man representing the inner uniformity of the spiritual man of prayer and action, confirming in their lives and activities natural and supernatural values, open to the needs of others and ready to sacrifice for their salvation [...]."[31]

4. Pope John Paul II as a personal model and model priest-pastor

The model of the parish priest postulated by my respondents in the face of the official model and priests' own visions of it, is largely wishful and environmental in nature. Teenagers are looking for priests who will meet their expectations and needs concerning religious, spiritual and ethical issues. At the same time, these priests are to meet the expectations of adult Catholics and the requirements of ecclesiastical authority concerning the model priest and pastor. The requirements of young people seem to be correct and accurate, and begs the question why they should have such demands at all in relation to priests and their professional activities. Perhaps presently there is a lack of such priests, at least in the youth environment. Maybe this lack is the reason why my respondents, as young people and young Catholics seeking good spiritual and religious guides at this stage of their religious and personal development, give such a report on priests.

We can place the concept of the priestly personality postulated by my respondents between the ideal, the desired and the actually received concept of a priest. On the one hand, the respondents indicate a lack of genuine priests, or at least that they are a small percentage of the total population, yet they earnestly seek priests to help in solving their existential problems and moral dilemmas. On the other hand, my respondents meet priests who are far from the expected ideal on a daily basis, even if they possess the main personal virtues and professional skills. The vices identified in the personalities of priests known to them, and failings or shortcomings in their professional activities concern and annoy young people. This calls for their removal and the restoration of values and methods arising from the general concept of the priesthood and their specific expectations of priests who work in parishes and academic environments for students.

---

30 J. Mariański, *Żyć parafią* [Living in the Parish], op. cit., pp. 12–15.

31 J. Majka, "Wpływ środowiska i przemian społecznych..." [Environmental Influence and Social Changes...], op. cit., p. 132.

The search for the perfect model personality of the priest, who is also a model pastor present in specific individuals and priests they know, has a real dimension, and indicates the existence of a problem in this regard. We may ask whether the surveyed secondary school and university students saw in Pope John Paul II the personality of a priest and model priest-pastor who met their expectations, the expectations of adults and the official model of a priest? I will present their answers to this question in further analysis of the issue.

a) John Paul II the personal priest model accepted in assessments of respondents

The empirical hypothesis assumed that the dominant proportion of high school and university students consider John Paul II as an authentic model for the priestly personality, which is essential to today's parish priests and the Church in search of Her place in modern society and aiming to fulfill Her religious mission within society's structures. The legitimacy of this hypothesis is confirmed by the respondents themselves.

The results allow for formulating the following three statements: firstly, they confirm the validity of the adopted empirical hypothesis, in which I assumed that the predominant majority of the survey respondents would consider Pope John Paul II as a priestly personality model for today's priests. This view was shared by 72.7% of the total respondents, including a higher percentage of high school students (75.8%) than college students (69.6%). The education level of respondents does not particularly affect these views, because less than 6.2% of all students stated differently. Every 14th respondent in both groups was not able to express an opinion on this subject. At the same time, 16.1% of respondents, including 15.5% of high school and 16.8% of college students rejected this view, declaring that Pope John Paul II is not, in their opinion, the priestly personality model for today's parish priests. Of many reasons given, the most frequent mentioned was: "This pope was a charismatic priest, rarely seen among today's clergy, gifted by God with exceptional qualities and therefore no ordinary priest can be compared to him, because he is not able to imitate the Pope" (a student, 20 years old).

Secondly, in subsequent periods of research, the dominant percentage of high school and college students fully agreed with this view, while a much smaller percentage rejected it as untrue. Thirdly, between the first (1983) and second (1998) periods of study, there was an increase in the percentage of respondents who saw John Paul II as a model priest – among high school students from 76.3% to 82.9% (or a 6.6% increase) and among college students from 68.8% to 79.2% (or a 10.4% increase). However, there was a drop in both groups between the second (1998) and third (2008) terms of studies. The percentage who approve of this view fell from 82.9% to 68.2% (or by 14.7%) among high school students and from 79.2% to 60.7% (or by 18.5%) among college students. These indicators are significant if we take into account the period of 10 years during which changes in the minds of young people on this subject occurred. During this period there was also an increase in the percentage of respondents who rejected this view – among high school students from 15.8% to 18.6% (or 2.8%) and among college students from 16.0% to 20.3% (or by 4.3%). The remaining respondents did not take a position on this issue (8.7% and 13.6%).

b) Characteristics of the priestly personality of John Paul II according to the respondents

What kind of priestly personality did Pope John Paul II present? What were the religious and secular characteristics that constituted his personality? I put these questions to the respondents during the three periods of research. They pointed to several specific features that distinguish John Paul II as a priest and pastor ("the pastor of the Catholic world") from previous popes and other priests. We will take note of the personality characteristics of the Pope in two areas that the surveyed high school and college students pointed out most decidedly during the period of study.

Studies indicate that the majority of respondents – a total of 70.1%, including 72.6% of high school and 67.7% of college students – considered Pope John Paul II as a personal model for contemporary priests as well as a model parish priest who meets the expectations and requirements of believers and a significant proportion of priests. In the description of the Pope's priestly personality, respondents pointed to his religious characteristics as well as natural and lay features, although the religious and ecclesiastical features and activities were appreciated most. The pope's religious features and activities were mentioned by a total of 72.3% of respondents, including a higher percentage of high school (75.8%) than college students (69.9%). The natural features and activities were appreciated by a total of 67.9% of respondents, including 72.6% of high school and 66.4% of college students. Although the religious and ecclesiastical characteristics were mentioned by a higher percentage in both groups, in numbers, they indicated more natural features (19) than religious features (14).

Respondents placed the following religious features in the top five places: 1 – he is a priest with a vocation: a total of 84.8%, including 87.8% of high school and 81.8% of college students, 2 – love of prayer, an example of a priest constantly praying to God: 82.7% (84.6% and 80.7%), 3 – deep and boundless trust in God: 81.8% (85.4% and 78.2%), 4 – lives according to the principles of the Gospel: 78.2% (85.3% and 72.9%), 5 – loves the Church without limits: 77.6% (82.5% and 72.7%). The remaining features and activities of the Pope in this area were generally evaluated in the range between 77.3% (a faithful priest of Jesus) to 60.1% (tolerant of other religions and denominations, and a charismatic leader of the Catholic Church), although these features were rated higher by other segments of the students. 67.7% of respondents indicated the Pope's concern for the faith and religious life of the youth, although it was placed 10th.

Among the 19 characteristics and lay activities in the next five positions, respondents preferred the following: 1 – polyglot, able to speak several languages easily: a total of 80.2%, including 78.9% of high school and 81.6% of college students, 2 – defender of human dignity and freedom: 76.8% (77.2% and 76.4%), 3 – a great scholar and philosopher: 76.2% (75.9% and 76.6%), 4 – just in evaluating people: 74.7% (76.8% and 72.5%), 5 – a master of experiencing pain and suffering: 72.2% (75.5% and 69.0%). Other natural features of the Pope were indicated by percentages ranging from 71.7% (honest and sincere in dealing with people) to 53.0% (appreciates dialogue and open to other ideas). These features were preferred by different percentages of high school and college students.

In both spheres – religious and secular – the Pope's moral and spiritual traits and his ethical activities emerge as distinct features that occupy an important and significant place in the preferences of the respondents. These features and activities were appreciated by 69.3% of high school and 58.6% of college students, a total of 64.0% of the surveyed. According to these respondents, Pope John Paul II was a man of courage, yet modest and humble. Furthermore, he was characterized by deep trust in people – he loved people and they loved and trusted him in return. Even people who stood at a distance from the Church and Christianity, or did not agree with some of his statements and opinions, trusted and respected him, because he was able to bring hope and appreciated dialogue with all those who approached conflicts between people in a similar way. My respondents judged that John Paul II devoted all his life and intellectual energy, as well as practical opportunities, to the struggle for rights, freedom and human dignity, and to the fullness of life – from conception to natural death, to truth and social and economic justice in the world, especially with regard to the difficult fate of people marginalized by the wealthy, to the struggle for peace in the world – between countries and peoples, between followers of different religions and churches in the ecumenical process, and he was also always concerned about marriage and the family. Young people also appreciate the Pope's concern for their needs, issues and problems in their environments, and consider him to be their friend and guide in life.[32]

Interest in the person of Pope John Paul II in both youth environments changed during the study period, in terms of both his religious and natural activities. In this regard, two distinct trends can be indicated: a positive one in the years 1983–1998, with an increased percentage of surveyed high school students (3.4%) and college students (5.6%) who appreciated the religious characteristics and actions of the Pope, while the percentages appreciating his secular traits and activities rose by 4.3% and 3.5%. There was a negative trend in 1998–2008, with the percentage of respondents in both groups who appreciate the charracteristics and actions of the Pope dropping: by 8.5% and 10.6% in the religious sphere and 13.4% and 13.3% in the secular sphere. However, during the whole period of 25 years, this decline amounted to 5.1% among high school and 9.8% among college students. Thus, though in the late eighties and early nineties of the twentieth century interest in the person of Pope John Paul II clearly intensified among my respondents, who saw him as a model priest personality and the role-model parish priest for other priests, in the late twentieth century and the first decade of the twenty-first century, this interest weakened considerably, with the result that almost every 10th respondent no longer saw in the priesthood of John Paul II a personality role-model for priests and model parish priest for the present and future.

In summary, it should be noted that in the analyses in this chapter, the model parish priest is seen as a "property" of the surveyed Kalisz high school, college and junior high school students. However, it seems that the features of this model can also be identified in similar environments of junior high, high school and college students in other regions of the country, and differences in their attitudes towards the model priest would be rather small. In this work, I only perform an environmental sociological analysis of the model priest as represented according to the ideas and postulates of my respondents, but I ignore its axiological characteristics and evaluation. This fully applies to the description of the personal and professional virtues and vices of priests considered by the respondents. On the other hand, my studies reveal a peculiar tension between their personal ideal priest and the daily reality in which real priests live and work. The surveyed youth indicate a dearth of "good" priests in the given period, and they are looking for these men earnestly, desiring to be under both their religious and moral care through pastoral advice. The respondents were familiar with "ordinary" priests in whom they saw many

---

[32] See J. Baniak, *Ksiądz w oczach młodzieży...* [The Priest in the Eyes of the Youth...], op. cit., pp. 163–165.

religious, spiritual, moral, intellectual and secular virtues, but also knew priests who were far from the ideal model of a priest, as expected today by the Catholic youth as well as adults.

The youth want to remove or replace the personal and professional vices in priests with values from their own conceptions of the ministerial priesthood and expectations of particular priests.[33] This conclusion corresponds quite closely to a similar conclusion by Janusz Marian on the topic, where he states that "[...] the obtained 'picture' of a priest based on the responses of the young people is quite critical, but less hostile towards the clergy. Specific objections are raised to manifestations of conspicuous consumption among some representatives of the Church and 'inhumane' ways of dealing with the faithful. Criticism of priests and bishops is expressed in social circles and in the public sphere. Criticism of the clergy does not mean there is a wider confrontation with the religious role of priests, fulfilled to the spirit of Evangelical authenticity, but rather that this is another way of fulfilment, which may indicate upcoming changes in the authority of priests and the model religious. [...] In the future, the mission of the Church and priests will focus on pastoral and specifically religious matters, but take into account the positive personal features of the priest ('a humane relationship with the faithful') more broadly."[34] Such a transformation in the priestly personality and pastoral activities of priests, which will determine the type of relationships with the lay faithful in the future, was called for by my respondents, and judged necessary in their own environmental model of the modern parish priest.

---

[33] See J. Baniak, "Papież Jan Paweł II jako wzór osobowy i model kapłana duszpasterza w świetle opinii i ocen młodzieży polskiej" [Pope John Paul II as a Personal Role-Model and Model Priest Minister in the Light of the Opinions and Evaluations of Polish Youth], *Ateneum Kapłańskie*, 1991, no. 2–3 (495–496), pp. 295–305.

[34] J. Mariański, *Emigracja z Kościoła...* [Emigration from the Church...], op. cit., p. 448.

Chapter VI

Mandatory celibacy of Catholic priests in the understanding and evaluation of the youth

Mandatory celibacy for priests in the Catholic Church is a continuously controversial phenomenon and complicated problem, generating various perspectives, those of clergy themselves. those of lay Catholics, and of course those of the Church hierarchy. In the Roman Catholic Church, celibacy comprises a basic condition for obtaining priestly ordination and for a priest to maintain the status of priesthood. This essentially means a priest's life-long commitment to being single and unmarried. A priest can not marry or start a family, and must abstain fully from any kind of relationship with a woman. The institutional priesthood is based on celibacy as a necessity due to a priest's undivided service to God and the Church.

A candidate for the priesthood, in choosing the priestly ministry, must at the same time decide on living in permanent celibacy, since the Roman Catholic Church does not allow him the option that does exist in Christian Churches and Old Catholic Church rites: free choice of lifestyle in the priesthood, as a celibate or in marriage with family. Theologians state that love for a woman, and sexual contact with her, especially in marriage and family, would cause difficulties for a priest fulfilling his priestly role in a parish or religious community and his fully engagement in increasing the glory of God.

Celibacy guarantees a priest's exclusive love for God and the Church, devoting himself undivided to serving the people in the parish. Awareness of the meaning of celibacy in service for the Church is binding for clerics during the time of their formation for the priesthood in the seminary, when celibacy is presented as a particular "gift" from God, closely related with their vocation to priestly ministry, and also a necessary condition for their entering into the clerical state. Questioning this condition makes it impossible for an alumnus to continue seminary formation and obtain priestly ordination.[1]

Józef Augustyn states that "[...] Education towards purity and priestly celibacy requires integrated formation, in which the human sphere has also been taken into account – the emotional and psychic, as well as the entire spiritual and religious dimension. Therefore, in discerning a vocation, including the vocation to celibacy, human problems should be skillfully joined with spiritual and religious problems. Only such a candidate to priesthood who in a conscious and involved way strives to become emotionally and spiritually mature can sacrifice his exclusive love for a woman and marriage without internal bitterness, in order to give new spiritual meaning to the desire for nuptial and parental love."[2]

This assumption does not present any illusions as to the essential need for celibacy in the life of a Catholic priest. However, achieving integrated formation, such which strives to create in the priest a feeling of personal resignation from marital love and fatherhood, still seems to be problematic for seminarians, since not all may have obtained the "gift" of a vocation to live without marriage. Crises in priestly vocations in many seminarians, and priestly identity crises in general, which may lead to a priest resigning from the priesthood, are often based on mandatory celibacy.

Some seminarians, even though they do not have the gift of living in celibacy, feel the vocation to priesthood and continue with seminary formation, obtain ordination, and are then sent by their bishop to pastoral parish ministry or to religious communities. Parish life, without seminary regulations and the control of educators, very quickly proves that these priests made a mistake in choosing priesthood and its life of mandatory celibacy. The only way to correct this error is to resign from the priesthood and return to life as a layman in marriage and family, since life without a woman, without sex, marriage and family is no longer acceptable to them. It is not uncommon that they become emotionally and sexually involved with a woman in the parish, in order to verify their personal attitude towards celibacy and at the same time make sure of their decision to leave the state of priesthood.

---

[1] Cf. J. Augustyn, *Wychowanie do czystości i celibatu kapłańskiego* [Educating to Purity and Priestly Celibacy], Cracow – Zabki 2000, pp. 133–180; S. Miecznikowski, "Praktyczne uwagi o wychowaniu w seminarium do celibatu" [Practical Remarks on Seminary Education to Celibacy], *Ateneum Kapłańskie*, 1967, no. 3–4, pp. 168–179; S. Olejnik, "Dlaczego Kościół podtrzymuje prawo celibatu kapłańskiego" [Why the Church Maintains the Right to Priestly Celibacy], *Homo Dei*, 1973, no. 2, pp. 133–144; B. Gardey, "Le célibat sacerdotal met en question notre culture" [Priestly Celibacy Questions Our Culture], *La Vie Spirituelle*, 1968, no. 21, pp. 222–244.

[2] J. Augustyn, *Wychowanie do czystości...* [Educating to Purity...], op. cit., p. 37.

As a consequence, they do not remain faithful to the religious vocation, which is not celibacy, but which led them, to the seminary and institutional priesthood. Unfortunately, celibacy was not for them, it turned out to be a condition beyond their capabilities, so they prefer to leave the priesthood than live in it burdened by their conscience and the conflictual morality of a cohabiting lifestyle in an illegal relationship with a woman. A deep feeling of love for the woman they chose, and often for their common offspring, makes it easier and quicker for many priests to decide to resign from celibacy and a priesthood based on it, and to return to the lay lifestyle.[3] A priest's leaving the priesthood is always a dramatic and complicated experience, which causes many difficulties and trials in his future life, including material (lack of employment and means for maintaining himself and his family), as well as deep moral and religious dilemmas (conflicting conscience), as well as family (resignation from the priesthood causes a priest to be rejected by his close family members and lack of acceptance from his wife and children), and frequently all this means change in their place of residence.

At this point, it should be noted that mandatory celibacy ensures discipline in Church structures, is a strong advantage in personnel policies of the institutional Church, and also guarantees the safety of her material goods, since priests do not have their own families who might participate in the distribution of Church property. This always played an essential role in the Church maintaining priestly celibacy, on top of religious and theological aspects.[4]

Lay Catholics are critical about the necessity for mandatory celibacy for priests, or at least argue for its being optional for priests who choose it, rather than enforced by Church hierarchy.[5]

---

[3] Cf. J. Baniak, *Wierność powołaniu a kryzys tożsamości kapłańskiej. Studium socjologiczne na przykładzie Kościoła w Polsce* [Faithfulness to Vocation and the Priestly Identity Crisis. A Sociological Study Based on the Church in Poland], Poznan 2000, pp. 93–134; idem, *Rezygnacja z kapłaństwa i wybór życia małżeńsko-rodzinnego przez księży rzymskokatolickich w Polsce. Studium socjologiczne* [Resignation from the Priesthood and Choice of Married and Family Life by Roman Catholic Priests in Poland. A Sociological Study], Cracow 2001, pp. 115–178.

[4] Cf. S. Heid, *Celibat w Kościele pierwotnym. Początek obowiązku wstrzemięźliwości dla duchownych na Wschodzie i na Zachodzie* [Celibacy in the Original Church. The Beginning of Mandatory Abstinence for Ministers in the East and West], transl. S. Stańczyk, Tuchow 2000; G. Ryś, *Celibat* [Celibacy], Cracow 2002, pp. 7–8.

[5] Cf. J. Baniak, *Ksiądz w oczach młodzieży. Obraz kapłana w świadomości młodzieży licealnej i akademickiej na przykładzie Kalisza. Studium socjologiczne* [The Priest in the Eyes of the Youth. The Image of the Priest in the Awareness of High School and College Youth in the Example of Kalisz. A Sociological Study], Poznan 1993, pp. 118–122. (Catholic adults in Kalisz, questioned about this need answered as follows: required for all clergy – 10.2%; voluntarily chosen – 17.4%, quite unnecessary – 45.7%, no opinion – 15.6%; lack of interest – 8.0%, no data – 3.1%. All together, only 27.6% of the 1,200 Catholics respondents surveyed accept celibacy for priests).

With this in mind, the question arises: what was the attitude of my young respondents towards mandatory celibacy for priests – which percentage of youth were for this form of celibacy and which against it? What where their reasons justifying their positions towards priestly celibacy – both in support and opposing?

1. The attitude of the respondents towards compulsory celibacy for parish priests

Given the critical attitude of adult Catholics towards mandatory celibacy for priests, I accepted the research assumption that the same critical attitude would be manifested in this period by the Polish youth in high school and university. I asked my respondents the following questions: does mandatory celibacy for priests violate their personal liberty, given that he has to accept it under pressure of not receiving ordination to priesthood? Should celibacy be a necessary condition for becoming a priest and required of all priests? Should priests be able to choose their personal lifestyle – in celibacy or in marriage and family – in the priesthood freely? Does mandatory celibacy cause many priests to live with a "dual" morality, resulting in their breaking the principles of the Gospel and the ordinances of the Church which shape the priestly ethos? Does mandatory priestly celibacy relate to the systematic quantitative decrease in priestly vocations in Poland? Does the celibacy of Roman Catholic priests hinder the effectiveness of the process of the unification of Christianity and the churches? Would the respondents themselves accept married priests who have their own families? I will present their replies to these questions in the following sections of this chapter.

a) Mandatory celibacy as a violation of a priest's personal liberty

Fr. Franciszek Mirek wrote that priestly celibacy should be seen as a priest's tool for getting to know his social personality better. Celibacy, in his opinion, helps him in the process of secondary socialization, making him priest a "stranger" in the world and excluding him from its frameworks. However, this exclusion does not mean isolation from the community, but it allows a priest to specify his relationship towards the community by means of a distinctly different lifestyle. This difference can sometimes create the sense of "exclusion" when among people living in normal human relationships, where the single life is not a normal feature of social life. This situation may also raise the issue of the violation of the personal freedom of the individual living in mandatory celibacy.[6] How did

[6] Cf. D. S. Malinowski, *Franciszka Mirka koncepcja socjologii humanistycznej* [Franciszek Mirek's Conception of Humanistic Sociology], Cracow 2005, pp. 116–118.

my respondents relate to this issue, and are they of the opinion that mandatory celibacy actually restricts the personal freedom and autonomy of a priest?

Research shows that a dominant percentage of respondents (50.4%) assess the influence of celibacy on the personal freedom of a priest negatively, stating that it fully (33.5%) or partially (16.9%) limits it. We see such an assessment among high school students (44.8%) and college students (56.0%), and both groups are dominated by people indicating a complete restriction of freedom for the priest due to mandatory celibacy – 29.3% and 37.8%. This negative impact of celibacy on a priest's freedom and autonomy intensified in the later periods of research, and also throughout the entire period of 25 years. The percentage of high school students agreeing with this position increased during this research time period: from 33.8% to 54.6% (by 20.8%), and the percentage of college students increased from 48.4% to 64.3% (by 12.9%). However, smaller percentages of respondents in both groups expressed a different opinion on this subject, arguing that celibacy in no way limits the personal freedom and autonomy of priests, and to speak of such a restriction is only an "invention" of either "confused" priests or laity with a "hostile" attitude towards celibacy, since celibacy is an objective value in the life of a priest. This opinion is expressed by 26.7% of respondents, including 30.7% of high school students and 22.7% of college students, and these percentages decreased from 36.7% to 24.8% and from 28.2% to 18.4% during the research period. The remaining respondents either failed to reply to this issue (14.0% and 10.4%), or indicated no connection between these issues (6.9% and 7.6%), or avoided answering this question (3.6% and 3.3%).

In fact, the dominant percentage of high school (44.8%) and college students (56.0%) surveyed saw a clear influence of mandatory celibacy in reducing the personal freedom and autonomy of a priest, compared to the percentage of those who questioned such an influence – 30.7% and 22.7%. This influence, according to these respondents, is the result of the arbitrary or mandatory nature of celibacy, since the freedom and autonomy of the individual requires a priest's free choice of lifestyle.

b) Celibacy as a necessary condition for obtaining and remaining in the priesthood

In the Roman Catholic Church, mandatory celibacy is both a basic prerequisite for alumna to obtain holy orders and an essential criterion of fidelity in their vocation and remaining in the priesthood. This condition is known to all seminarians and priests, although only a certain percentage of them persevere in their vocation to the priesthood. In light of this situation, is should be asked whether the surveyed high school and college students also accept this condition and see celibacy as a necessary condition for the alumna to obtain ordination and for a priest to stay in the priesthood?

Studies showed that the necessity of celibacy for obtaining priesthood by a deacon was voted for by a total of only 29.6% of respondents, including 31.9% of high school and 27.4% of college students. This group of respondents is dominated by those who believe that celibacy may be needed by only some priests, if they freely choose celibacy in the priesthood, especially priests in religious orders (71.3%), while the remaining respondents (28.7%) were convinced that celibacy should include all priests. By contrast, the dominant majority of respondents (58.4%) were of the opinion that celibacy cannot be a necessary condition for a deacon to obtain priestly ordination, and its uselessness is indisputable. Such opposition towards the necessity of celibacy for obtaining priesthood is evident in 57.0% of high school and 60.0% of college students. The remaining subjects in both groups either could not take a position on this issue (7.2% and 8.6%) or did not answer the question (3.9% and 4.0%).

An even smaller percentage of respondents showed attitudes critical of the need for celibacy in order for priests to remain in their vocation and the priesthood. If we compare the percentages of respondents who accept celibacy as a condition for obtaining priesthood (31.9% and 27.4%) with the percentage of those who accept it as a criterion for persistence of priests in their priestly vocation (27.9% and 25.2%), we see that their percentages decreased by 4.0% and 2.2%. At the same time, there was an increase in both groups of respondents who indicated a total redundancy of celibacy: among high school students it was from 57.0% to 60.2% and among college students from 60.0% to 61.5%.

During the entire period, percentages of respondents accepting the necessity of celibacy in both situations – for obtaining and persevering in the priesthood – decreased: in the group of high school students, these decreased from 36.8% to 28.5% and 32.6% to 22.8%, and in the group of college students these viewpoints decreased from 30.7% to 23.6% and 29.1% to 21.5%. At the same time, there was an increase in percentages of both groups of respondents who rejected the need for celibacy in both situations: among high school students from 57.3% to 63.7% and among college students from 58.4% to 64.6%. In addition, there was also an increase in the percentage of high school students (from 6.6% to 9.3%) and college students (from 8.0% to 10.4%) who did not comment on this issue.[7]

[7] Cf. J. Baniak, *Między buntem a potrzebą akceptacji i zrozumienia. Świadomość religijna i moralna a kryzys tożsamości osobowej młodzieży gimnazjalnej. Studium socjologiczne* [Between Rebelion and the Need for Acceptance and Understanding. The Awareness of Religious and Moral a Crisis of personal Indentity in Junior High School Youth. A Sociological Study], Cracow 2008, p. 342,

c) The impact of mandatory celibacy on the decrease in the number of candidates to the priesthood

In the first half of the twentieth century in Poland, the recruitment rates of candidates to the priesthood in diocesan and religious order seminaries beat all records. Such a situation had not occurred in any other Catholic country for many years. Over half of the students successfully finished their theological studies and obtained ordination. This situation changed radically in the second half of the 20th century, and continued to decline in this century: the number of applications for priesthood studies has dropped dramatically, due to many different reasons and motives. This decrease was evaluated by sociologists in the range from 26.7% to 44.6% on a national global scale, although in some dioceses and religious orders it was much higher, exceeding half the number of candidates recruited in the twentieth century. Currently, Church authorities are already talking about a clear quantitative and qualitative crisis of priestly vocations in Poland, and are searching the main reasons for this phenomenon. Most important is the quality crisis of priestly vocations, because it indicates an almost unique phenomenon, which is an increasing percentage of candidates to the clergy who reveal flaws in their emotional, psychological, sensual, sexual and social characteristics, in the spheres of faith, religion and morality. Many of them are totally unsuitable for the profession of a priest, but try to find their place within the structures of Church life.[8]

Sociologists of religion and other ecclesiastical authorities give different reasons underlying the crisis of vocations to the priesthood, and only some of these reasons are indicated by representatives of both environments. Results from the findings of sociologists show that priests, seminarians and lay Catholics believe that one of the main reasons for the decline in priestly vocations is mandatory celibacy for priests, which requires them to remain single and completely asexual. Many religious men, who are aware of their predisposition to serve in the profession of a priest, are not able to fulfill this requirement,

---

table 135. (Surveyed junior high school students need to obtain a celibate priesthood evaluated as follows: the total – 12.3%; as partial – 19.8%; as unnecessary – 57.8%; no rating – 5.9%; unknown – 4.2%. Contrast, the duration of the priests in the priestly vocation as: total – 8.7%; partial – 13.2%; redundand – 69.6%; no rating – 4.2%; no data – 4.3%).

[8] Cf. J. Baniak, *Dynamika powołań kapłańskich i zakonnych w Kościele rzymskokatolickim w Polsce w latach 1900–1994. Studium socjograficzne* [The Dynamics of Priestly and Religious Vocations in the Roman Catholic Church in Poland in the Years 1900–1994. A Socio-Graphics Study], Cracow 1997; K. Pawlina, *Kandydaci do kapłaństwa trzeciego tysiąclecia* [Candidates to the Priesthood in the Third Millenium], Warsaw 2002.

and for this reason, a significant percentage of priests leave the priesthood and returned to the secular life of marriage and family.[9]

In the light of these theories, we ought to ask whether the surveyed high school and college students perceive mandatory celibacy as the main cause of decline in vocations to the priesthood and whether they are familiar with cases of seminarians and priests who, because of celibacy, either opted out of trying to enter the priesthood, or abandoned priesthood for marriage and family.

Research shows that as many as 64.4% of respondents, including 63.9% of high school and 64.8% of college students, clearly stated that mandatory celibacy discourages many religious men from choosing the priestly profession. The dominant percentage of this group (44.4% and 50.2%) had no doubts in this regard, and 19.5% and 14.6% had certain objections: does every case of a priest struggling with celibacy discourage him from the profession of being a priest? The youth pointed to other reasons for this phenomenon, perhaps related to some degree with celibacy. On the other hand, during the research period, increased proportions of respondents in both groups openly stated that celibacy is a major factor "frightening religious men away" from the priesthood. Among high school students, this percentage increased from 37.5% to 53.3% (i.e. 15.8%) and among college students from 42.6% to 58.6% (or by 16.0%). The influence of celibacy on the decline in priestly vocations in Poland at that time was not noted by an overall 17.8% of respondents, including 18.5% of high school and 17.2% of college students. At the same time, this percentage decreased in both groups throughout the period: from 19.9% to 15.6% and from 18.5% to 15.6%. The remaining respondents were either unable to assess this impact (13.4% and 13.5%) or did not answer the question (4.5% and 4.4%).

The study also indicated that the respondents have knowledge on this subject from personal experience. Cases where either clerics or priests resigned from the priesthood because of celibacy were personally known to 41.4% of respondents, including 40.4% of high school and 42.4% of college students, and 19.6% (including 18.6% and 20.6%) had heard stories from colleagues or friends. Thus, up to 61.0% of respondents, including 59.0% of high school and 63.1% of college students were aware of circumstances, and personally knew the men who, because of mandatory celibacy, either abandoned their career aspirations of priesthood, or resigned from the profession of priesthood. The percentage of respondents who personally knew these men increased during

[9] Cf. J. Baniak, "Źródła i przyczyny kryzysu tożsamości kapłańskiej księży rzymskokatolickich w Polsce – studium socjologiczne" [Sources and Reasons for the Identity Crisis in Roman Catholic Priests in Poland – a Sociological Study], in M. Libiszowska-Żółtkowska (ed.), *Tożsamości religijne w społeczeństwie polskim. Socjologiczne studium przypadków* [Religious Identity in Polish Society. A Sociological Case Study], Warsaw 2009, pp. 67–107.

this period in both groups: among high school students from 30.4% to 48.4% (or by 18.0%) and among college students from 33.3% to 50.3% (an increase of 17.0%). On the other hand, 34.6% of respondents did not know of such cases, including 36.8% of high school and 32.4% of college students, and their percentage in this period decreased in both groups: from 44.3% to 30.6% (i.e. 13.7%) and from 36.8% to 28.8% (or by 8.0%). The remaining respondents (4.2% and 4.5%) did not respond to this question.

My respondents, therefore, included mandatory celibacy as one of the main factors responsible for the systematic decline in vocations to the priesthood and the priestly identity crisis among many diocesan priests and religious men during this period of 25 years. A large percentage of respondents knew personally, or from other communications, situations in which men either gave up their career aspirations of priesthood, or left the priesthood after already being ordained in a parish or religious community.[10] The negative role of mandatory celibacy in the crisis of priestly vocations and identity crises of many priests is not unknown to my respondents.

d) The influence of celibacy on the weakening of ecumenism between Roman Catholic and Christian churches

The process of ecumenism between the Roman Catholic and Christian Churches is encountering many different obstacles and barriers that slow the progress and implementation of already agreed-upon resolutions and mutual decisions. These obstacles are known to both clergy and lay Catholics and Christians, living in the structures of both types of churches. This does not mean that the churches indicate the same reasons and causes of the delay and hindrance of ecumenism. Christian and Old Catholic rite churches consider obligatory celibacy of Roman Catholic priests to be among the main obstacles to ecumenism. To them it does not apply to all priests, but only to religious men in some orders, and also sometimes to bishops. The Roman Catholic Church knows about this problem, but does not intend to give up on the celibacy of its priests because of ecumenism. In addition, the authorities of the Church are inconsistent on this issue, because on the one hand they continue to impose celibacy on priests, but on the other, they agree to marriage and family for Greek Catholic priests and priest-converts from other Christian churches, such as the Anglican or Old Catholic Church. Due to this, Roman Catholic

[10] Cf. Z. Jonaczyk, "Socjologiczne badania powołań kapłańskich w Polsce" [Sociological Studies of Priestly Vocations in Poland], *Colloquium Salutis. Wrocławskie Studia Teologiczne*, 1976, vol. 8, pp. 207–222; J. Baniak, *Ksiądz w oczach młodzieży*... [The Priest in the Eyes of the Youth...], op. cit., pp. 101–104.

priests, as they themselves state in research studies, experience a feeling of hurt and injustice, because they must observe celibacy and cannot enter into lawful marriage with a woman.

In the context of these observations, the question arises as to how my respondents feel about this matter. In their opinion, should the Roman Catholic Church resign from the celibacy of Her priests, in an attempt to accelerate the progress of inter-Christian and inter-confessional ecumenism?

Studies have shown that the dominant percentage of respondents – 71.5%, including 70.0% of high school and 73.1% of college students believed that the Roman Catholic Church must withdraw from the mandatory celibacy requirement of Her priests in order to accelerate the work of ecumenism, where the majority decidedly opted for such a solution to this problem. What is more, the percentage of respondents who share this view increased in both groups: among high school students from 58.4% to 67.9% (or by 9.5%) and among college students from 62.5% to 69.2% (or by 6.7%). By contrast, a total of 11.6%, including 12.4% of high school and 10.8% of college students felt that the current situation should remain unchanged, namely, that the Roman Catholic Church should not resign from the celibacy of priests for the benefit of inter-church and inter-confessional ecumenism, although it should continue to participate in the development of this process. However, this percentage decreased in both groups: among high school students from 17.6% to 9.2% (or 8.4%) and among college students from 13.4% to 8.4% (by 5.0%). The rest either abstained from an assessment on this issue (5.9% and 5.6%) or did not answer the question (2.9% and 2.5%).

For 77.2% of respondents, including 74.6% of high school and 79.9% of college students, inter-church ecumenism is a priority matter regarding celibate Roman Catholic priests, with an increased percentage in this period in both groups: among high school students from 70.5% to 81.4% (by 10.9%) and among college students from 76.8% to 82.6% (by 5.8%). 13.1% of respondents, including 15.7% of high school and 10.5% of college students, feel that celibacy for Roman Catholic priests is more important than inter-church ecumenism, and consequently the Church should not abandon celibacy for the sake of it. However, the percentage of respondents who share this view decreased in both groups: among high school students from 21.5% to 9.3% (by 12.2%) and among college students from 12.8% to 8.5% (by 4.3%).[11]

[11] Cf. J. Baniak, *Między buntem a potrzebą akceptacji i zrozumienia...* [Between Rebelion and the Need for Acceptance and Understanding...], op. cit., pp. 343–345, table 136. (Junior High School school students believe that the liberalization of the present status of the celibacy of Roman Catholic priests should be undertaken in order to accelerate ecumenism, and the classification of their replies is as follows: convinced – 48.8%; rather yes – 17.2%; should

Given the research results presented above, can we generally conclude that the mandatory celibacy of priests is now undoubtedly a controversial phenomenon and contentious issue, especially in the youth environment? The respondents' views on the celibacy of priests are diverse and depend on many factors, including gender, type of school, place of permanent residence, and above all on their level of faith and frequency of performing religious practices. Most of them are clearly against mandatory celibacy, seeing it as a factor that affects the limits of personal freedom and autonomy of a priest, causing a reduction in vocations to the priesthood, as well as hindering the process of unification of Christians into one Church. A small percentage of them advocate for celibacy freely chosen by priests, who are convinced that they feel they have the unique characteristics enabling them to live without marriage, and commit themselves to the exclusive service of God and the members of the Church. In other cases, they consider celibacy unnecessary and they want the Church to change its mandatory formula and give candidates to the priesthood a free choice of lifestyle in the priesthood, either celibate, or married with family. This raises the important question: will this ever be possible to achieve?

remain unchanged – 16.7%; it is the decision of priests – 8.1%; lack of evaluation – 6.1%; no data – 3.1%. A convinced position on this issue appeared more commonly among the boys – 49.8% than girls – 48.3%, more commonly among city students – 55.8% than among rural students – 37.7%).

Chapter VII

Religious and social correlates of the respondents' attitudes towards institutional priesthood and parish priests

In the previous chapters (II–VI), I broadly presented the image of the institutional priesthood and the parish priest in the religious and social awareness of high school and college students, and indirectly among junior high school students as well. This image is composed of their attitudes and views directly related to the institution of the priesthood and the priest – his personality, his role in the parish and community, his religious and moral authority and his prestige among other professionals, the model, his importance for the religiosity and morality of believers, as well as celibacy and its role in the lives of priests, in new vocations to the priesthood and the process of unifying Christian churches. This picture is concluded by discussing the behavior and actions of the respondents in direct or indirect association with parish clergy. Thus, this picture was presented in a multi-faceted way, although some of its features receive special focus. This picture is somewhat different among high school and university students, and even more different among junior high school students. Differences on these issues were shown up in all detail in subsequent chapters of this study, taking into account the typology of respondents, based on the type of school and level of academic knowledge acquired, as well as research deadlines during the given study period, from the years 1983 to 2008.

However, this analysis has some gaps, because it ignored the important issue of the relationship between other specific features of the respondents and their ideas, attitudes and evaluations towards the institutional priesthood and parish priests. I want to make up for this in this chapter, taking into account the relationship of gender, global attitudes towards faith, and religious practice attitudes from respondents' environmental image of the priesthood and the parish priest.[1] Taking the connection between these factors as independent variables, the views, attitudes, evaluations and actions of the respondents, with their image of the priesthood and the priest, it will be possible to extend and deepen the analysis of this issue and gain new insights beyond the scope of previous chapters.

The problems tackled in this study are quite extensive, bringing together many distinct and important specific cognitive issues. This complexity significantly affects the selection of issues included in further analysis, which depends on the adopted interfering variables. However, the extent of this study does not allow for the presentation and evaluation of the relationship between these variables with all the attitudes and views of the young people regarding the priesthood and priests. As a result, I will undertake a detailed analysis of 10 issues in this chapter, which together play a fundamental role and at the same time show the level of association between the independent variables. The issues here are addressed as follows: religious vocation as a basis for choosing the priesthood, the nature and structure of the institutional priesthood, the prestige of the priestly profession, celibacy of priests, the role of the priest in the parish, the desire to have a priest in the family, the desire for a personal relationship with a priest, a priest's religious mediation between people and God, the environmental model of a priest, and Pope John Paul II as a personality model and model priest and pastor.

The issues discussed in detail in the previous five chapters and those presented in this chapter already provide a much broader and clearer picture of the institution of the priesthood and the parish priest, firmly anchored in the religious and social awareness of young Poles at the turn of the 20th and 21st centuries, which consists of their views, attitudes and evaluations related to varying degrees with the institutional priesthood and parish priests.

---

[1] Cf. J. Baniak, *Postawy katolików Kalisza wobec wierzeń i praktyk religijnych* [Attitudes of Catholics in Kalisz towards Religious Beliefs and Practices], *Rocznik Kaliski*, 1989, vol. 22, pp. 173–224; J. Baniak, "Zaangażowanie religijne a postawy młodzieży wobec kapłaństwa i księży parafialnych" [Religious Involvement and Attitudes of Youth towards the Priesthood and Parish Priests], in J. Baniak, *Ksiądz w oczach młodzieży. Obraz kapłana w świadomości młodzieży licealnej i akademickiej na przykładzie Kalisza. Studium socjologiczne* [The Priest in the Eyes of the Youth. The Image of the Priest in the Awareness of High School and College Youth in the Example of Kalisz. A Sociological Study], Poznan 1993, pp. 167–188.

1. Gender structure of the respondents and their attitudes and views on the priesthood and parish priests

In the research assumptions, I assumed the hypothesis that women are more positively disposed than men towards the institutional priesthood and parish priests. As a result, they also criticize the vices of priests more gently than men, yet at the same time they expose priests' personal and professional virtues. The correlation between these two variables will appear in the following analysis.

The dominant percentage of respondents (58.5%) believed that a religious vocation is a necessary condition of selection and endurance of the priest in the priesthood, adding that God gives a priest his calling. This view is shared by more women (62.9%) more than men (49.1%). On the other hand, more men (30.1%) than women (21.9%) spoke of the uselessness of a religious calling for entering the priesthood. More men (15.4%) than women (11.2%) did not take a position on this issue. Thus, gender affected the viewpoint of the respondents towards the priesthood and priests significantly. This relationship between the two variables is confirmed by statistical indicators ($x^2 = 143.58$, $df = 4$, $p < 0.01$).

Gender also differentiates the views of respondents on the nature and structure of the institutional priesthood. Women more often (55.0%) than men (44.1%) see in the priesthood both a religious vocation and a common profession. They more commonly (11.3%) also treated priesthood exclusively as a vocation from God than men (9.5%). On the other hand, men were more likely (29.0%) than women (21.7%) to see the priesthood only as an ordinary profession and more often (12.7%) than women (8.2%) were unable to take a position on this issue. Statistical indicators put the correlation between these variables at the essential dependency level ($x^2 = 138.47$, $df = 4$, $p < 0.01$).

The specificity of professional priesthood, the importance of a priest's work in a parish and the scope of a priest's religious and moral competence are at the core of the long-term peak in the prestige of the priesthood and authority of priests in Poland. A similar assessment of the prestige of the priesthood was made by my respondents, since 53.8% were of the opinion that it was very high (34.4%) or high (19.4%), including 57.3% of women (38.3% and 19.0%) and 46.1% of men (26.0% and 20.1%). In addition, 12.4% of women and 9.6% of men rated priestly prestige as average. This high prestige of the priesthood was awarded by 69.7% of women, and 55.7% of men, a difference of 14.0%. More men rated this prestige as low (10.6%) and very low (9.0%), and indicated complete lack of prestige (20.6%), while women were less likely to give these evaluations (7.8%; 8.9%; 10.2%). The relationship between the two variables is significantly high ($x^2 = 174.45$, df = 6, $p < 0.001$).

The high authority of priests in Polish society and their similarly important role in the Church means that a large percentage of Catholics would like to have a priest in their family. A similar desire was expressed by 39.0% of my respondents, while 33.2% had no such desire. This desire is significantly dependent on the gender of the respondents, with women more commonly (40.4%) expressing it than men (36.2%), who, did not show such a desire in greater numbers (34.8%) than women (32.4%). Men are also more likely to remain neutral (15.0%) in this case, or not to be able to give their own opinion (10.4%). The relationship between these two variable statistical indicators shows an important medium level ($x^2 = 193.46$, df = 4, $p < 0.01$). The research hypothesis stated that the desire for having a priest in the family would be expressed by the majority of subjects. However, empirical indicators showed different results in this area, and moreover, gender differentiated only to a certain extent the attitude of the respondents towards the desire to have a priest in the family, women being slightly higher. Thus, the data only confirmed the accuracy of this hypothesis to an extent.

The role of the priest in the parish consists of a number of specific functions. The scope of this role is understood differently by Catholics and people outside the Church and non-believers. Catholics mostly perceive the role of the priest broadly and include in its structure religious-Church, moral, and secular elements. A significant percentage of my respondents describe it similarly. Women did so slightly less (56.7%) than men (64.9%), while men would rather (16.7%) than women (15.2%) deny priests any competence that would shape their role in the Church. However, gender only slightly differentiates the attitudes of respondents towards this question, as shown by statistical indicators ($x^2 = 154$, df = 6, $p < 0.97$). According to more or less equal percentages of men and women (a difference of 8.2%), the role of the priest in the Church is necessary, in particular with regard to the religious life of the Catholic laity, and in other cases, this role becomes redundant or rather marginal.

Catholic theology accepts the idea that the priest is a mediator between people and God and helps them obtain eternal salvation. Such powers in a priest are due to his priestly ordination and the very essence of the priestly office. This mediating role was accepted by the majority of Polish Catholics. A similar attitude was displayed by 50.2% of my respondents, including 53.0% of women and 44.4% of men (8.6% less). However, 38.2% had a different opinion and questioned priestly mediation, including more men (42.3%) than women (36.3%). Gender distinguishes their attitude towards the mediating role of the priest at an average level of significance ($x^2 = 127.56$, df = 4, $p < 0.01$).

People questioning this role, especially men, think that Catholics can connect with God and receive His mercy for salvation without the intercession of priests.

The surveyed high school and college students quite frequently expressed a personal desire to develop, maintain or keep personal contacts and relationships with parish priests, and some said they intend to make such contacts with priests in the near future. This desire was revealed by a total of 45.7% of the respondents, including more women (48.7%) than men (39.0%). In turn, more men (48.2%) than women (40.6%) wanted no such ties and did not have any. Gender quite significantly differentiates the attitude of respondents to this issue, which is confirmed by statistical indicators ($x^2 = 193.54$, df $= 4$, $p < 0.01$).

My respondents have their own parish priest model, partly in line with the official Church's model. In their model, there are both religious characteristics and natural features – the former were preferred by a total of 54.5% of the surveyed people and the latter by 45.5%. Gender quite significantly differentiates this preference, as woman were more likely (62.2%) than men (38.2%) to recognize the religious characteristics, while men more commonly (61.8%) indicated the natural features of the model priest than women (37.8%). Thus, in the evaluation of women (greater by 24.0%), religious characteristics play a greater role, while men rate the natural characteristics higher (23.6%). The influence of gender on the construction of a model priest is therefore very important, which is also confirmed by statistical indicators ($x^2 = 224.86$, df $= 2$, $p < 0.001$).

Priests in the Roman Catholic Church are subject to mandatory celibacy, which is a prerequisite for selection and persistence in the priesthood. The Catholic laity is quite critical of this form of celibacy. My respondents also showed their personal attitude towards the celibacy of priests, among whom 38.7% accept it, including 24.5% as voluntarily chosen by priests themselves, and 14.2% as a result of necessity and the arbitrary decision of the Church. The vast majority of respondents (50.6%) reject the necessity for celibacy in the life of priests, claiming it to be completely unnecessary. Gender influences the evaluation of the necessity and superfluity of celibacy at a medium level, because women accept it less frequently (37.5%) than men (40.9%), but they are more in favour of its voluntary choice (27.7%), while men more commonly favour mandatory celibacy (23.5%). On the other hand, women are more likely (54.5%) than men (42.6%) to consider celibacy redundant in the life of priests. The dependence of these statistical indicators are essential at a medium level ($x^2 = 184.58$, df $= 4$, $p < 0.01$).

The majority of respondents (66.3%) considered Pope John Paul II as a model priest personality and a model parish priest. Gender only marginally differentiated assessment of the role of the pope, since women were slightly more likely (68.9%) than men (60.6%) to recognize the role of the pope as fundamental. Similarly, they more rarely (20.0%) than men (26.5%) saw a model parish priest in the priest personality pattern of John Paul, at the same time claiming that this view is "greatly exaggerated" in public opinion in Poland. Statistical indicators capture the dependence between these variables as minimally essential and significant ($x^2 = 182.37$, df = 2, $p > 0.93$).

In summarizing this analysis, it is clear that gender acts inconsistently on the views and attitudes of the surveyed respondents concerning the priesthood and priests. However, women were more favorably disposed towards both phenomena than men, who often showed a "reserved" or indifferent attitude.

2. Global profession of faith and the religiosity of youth and their attitudes towards the priesthood and parish priests

Attitude towards the institutional priesthood and parish priests is one of the fundamental components of the religiousness of lay Catholics. Sociologists of religion, when examining such religiousness, claim that the attitudes of Catholics towards parish priests and the frequency and quality of contacts with priests are indicators of the religious vitality of individuals and religious groups.[2] These attitudes are dependent upon various factors which affect their dynamics and intensity. Practically speaking, the attitudes of Catholics towards parish priests and their views on the priesthood are not merely a kind of "interpretation" of their good will, but are also subject to external factors. These factors include the examined attitudes of young people towards religious faith. The empirical hypothesis assumed that the higher the level of religious faith of the respondents, the more positive their attitude towards parish priests would be, and the more correct their understanding of the essence and other characteristics of the institutional priesthood. However, weakness or loss of religious faith in the respondents causes increased criticism and negative attitudes towards priests and distortion of their views concerning the nature, structure and characteristics of the priesthood. How did the global attitudes of respondents influence their attitudes towards selected features of the priesthood and parish priests?

---

[2] Cf. J. Mariański, "Konsens im Glauben am Beispiel Polen," in K. Zapotoczky (ed.), *Ziwilisatorische Ursachen von Konflikten: Ergebnise d. 4, Polen – Asterreich. Soziologen Symposions 1980 in Lublin*, Linz 1986, pp. 235–248; D. Tułowiecki, *Kościół, parafia i duchowni w świadomości młodzieży ponadgimnazjalnej w małym mieście* [The Church, Parish and Clergy in the Consciousness of Secondary School Teenager in a Small Town], in J. Baniak (ed.), *Laikat i duchowieństwo w Kościele katolickim w Polsce. Problem dialogu i współistnienia* [The Laity and Clergy in the Catholic Church in Poland. The problem of dialogue and coexistence], Poznan 2010, pp. 349–368.

The need for religious vocations to the priesthood is mostly accepted by respondents who are deeply religious – 71.7%, including 79.7% of high school and 63.6% of college students, but least frequently by non-believers – 16.0% and 27.3%. Non-believers accepted this (necessary) condition five times less frequently than deeply religious people. Non-believers in both groups and the general population questioned the need for a religious vocation as a condition for choosing and persevering in the priesthood four times more frequently. The relationship between these variables is statistically quite significant ($x^2 = 128.36$, $df = 10$, $p < 0.001$). Among deeply religious people, a vocation was considered superfluous by only one in six respondents, including twice as many college students. Acceptance of the condition of vocation weakened gradually in the remaining categories of respondents: believers by 13.3%, and religiously neutral by 40.2%, while there were increasing percentages of people questioning it (8.6% and 27.3%). In these three groups of respondents, the percentage of people who did not take a clear position on this issue also increased, and it was greatest (10.2%) among non-believers.

Almost the same level of statistical dependence is evident in both groups between the level of faith in respondents and their interpretation of the nature and structure of the institutional priesthood ($x^2 = 136.54$, $df = 12$, $p < 0.001$). The specificity and the structure of the priesthood were properly interpreted by the greatest percentage of respondents who were deeply religious and standard believers (high school 61.6% and college students 64.0%). However, non-believers and religiously neutral people were most at fault here, understanding the priesthood differently from the Church definition. More than 3/5 of believers and deeply believing people perceived in the priesthood both a religious vocation and a profession, but this same structure was accepted by only 1/4 of non-believers and 1/3 of religiously neutral people. At the same time, more than half of non-believers and over 2/5 of religiously neutral people perceived priesthood as an ordinary profession, no different from other professions that young people choose. None of the non-believers in high school and college perceived the priesthood exclusively in its religious aspect (as a religious vocation). However, this interpretation is most frequently seen among respondents who are deeply religious (20.4%), including twice as many numbers of high school students. No opinion on this issue was most common among non-believers (14.4%), and least of among believers (6.3%).

Rating the prestige of priests in society strongly depends on the level of the religious beliefs of respondents, which the statistical indicators clearly show ($x^2 = 123.35$, $df = 12$, $p < 0.001$). This prestige was mostly valued by deeply religious respondents (58.4% of high school and 46.4% of college students), but this assessment rarely appeared among the other categories of respondents. An expression of these differences is the so-called optimal assessment level of prestige, which consists of the degrees "very high" and "high." The group of people who deeply believe in it came to a total of 74.9% and in the group of believers 69.1%, which is 2–4 times greater. At the same time, in both groups of believers, no one questioned this level of authority of priests, which was the case among every fifth non-believing respondent and one in seven of the religiously neutral respondents, slightly higher among college than high school students. Non-believers and those who are religiously indifferent are also more likely to judge the prestige of parish priests as very low and average than religious believers.

The nature and scope of the role of the priest in the Church and in society also significantly depend on the level of understanding religious faith, as indicated by statistics ($x^2 = 118.46$, $df = 8$, $p < 0.001$). Respondent non-believers (67.0%) and the religiously indifferent (63.2%) most frequently limited this role to only religious and Church matters, and a much lower percentage (14.5% and 12.9%) included religious and moral issues. On the other hand, none of the deeply religious and believing people in both groups questioned the role of the priest in the Church and in society. On the contrary, it is precisely these respondents who included the role of a priest in all matters – religious, Church, moral and typically lay. Secular matters were mostly added to the scope of a priest's role by deeply religious respondents (16.7%), but were completely neglected by non-believers, and among the religiously indifferent, only 8.5% of high school and 6.4% of college students took them into consideration.

Mediation of a priest in the salvation of people is quite a problematic issue in the environments of the youth. A fairly large percentage of high school (33.9%) and college students (40.1%) rejected it completely, stating that everyone can have a relationship with God and strive for their own salvation (37.0%). Acceptance of a priest's mediation in the salvation of people is also largely dependent on the level of religious belief of the respondents, as shown by statistical indicators ($x^2 = 118.53$, $df = 8$, $p < 0.001$). Consequently, this necessary mediation is accepted without reservation most by deeply religious people (74.6%), followed by those who believe (62.6%). The percentage of people who evaluate the role of the priest in this way declines radically among religiously neutral people (to 26.0%), and reaches the lowest acceptance rate among non-believers, up to 13 times less. Percentages conversely form among non-believing high school and college respondents who questioned a priest's mediation in people's salvation. We observe this attitude and evaluation mostly among non-believers (57.5%), especially among college students (7.9% more than those in high school), and in 2/5 of the religiously neutral. None of the deeply believing respondents rejected this role of the priest. On the other hand, less than a third of respondents, and a higher percentage of college students, did not take a position on this issue, including 21.5% of those with deep faith and 20.8% of believers.

The high prestige of the priestly profession in Poland and the various privileges granted to priests in society and in the Church have, for a long time, meant that a certain percentage of surveyed high school and university students expressed a personal desire to have a priest in their family. This desire is also significantly dependent on the level of faith of the respondents, as shown by statistical indicators ($x^2 = 114.34$, $df = 8$, $p < 0.001$). The desire to have a priest in the family was most often expressed by deeply religious respondents (74.6%) and believers (54.4%), a difference of 20.1%. This desire is a very rare phenomenon among the religiously neutral, manifested by only 30.2% of respondents, which is 44.4% less than among the deeply religious. Only non-believing respondents did not want someone in their family to become a priest. In addition, the matter was irrelevant to a third of non-believers and the religiously indifferent, and also to 10.5% of the deeply religious and 20.0% of believers.

There is low-level statistical dependence between the level of religious belief and the desire for respondents to have a personal relationship with their parish priests or priests at academic pastoral ministry centers ($x^2 = 106.37$, $df = 4$, $p < 0, 01$). A total of 30.7% of the respondents would like to have a relationship with priests, including mostly deeply religious people (43.5%), and the least religiously indifferent people (14.1%). On the other hand, we see that as many as 53.8% of respondents did not desire to have a relationship with priests, the most numerous being non-believers – 34.4%, which is less by as much as 41.1%, although we see a similar attitude among two-fifths of believers. In both groups of believers, up to 40% did not desire to have a relationship with priests, including 36.1% of high school students and 42.8% of university students. In addition, one in five respondents did not take a position on this issue, the largest percentage being the religiously indifferent (20.5%) and the lowest the deeply religious (18.3%).

The characteristics of the model parish priest have a significant impact on the level of religious faith of respondents. The relationship between these variables remained at a low level of significance, which is indicated by statistics ($x^2 = 96, 45$, $df = 2$, $p < 0.01$). Deeply religious people (69.4%) and believers (66.6%) preferred the religious features and activities in their personal model of a priest minister more often than those indifferent to religion (49.5%) and atheists (39.8%). The respondents who were non-believers (60.2%) and the religiously indifferent (50.5%) placed strong emphasis on the secular characteristics and actions of the priest in their model, thereby undermining the priority of religious features and activities.

Celibacy is a contentiously debated issue in both groups of young people, and its problematic nature clearly dominates the respondents' attitudes towards religious belief. The dependence between these variables is significant at an average level, which is indicated by statistics ($x^2 = 117.36$, df = 8, $p < 0.01$). Celibacy is accepted most often by deeply religious people (58.5%), and least often by non-believers (11.4%), but only when voluntarily chosen by the priest, not as formally imposed by ecclesiastical authorities. Consequently, non-believers (56.2%) and people indifferent to religion (49.8%) consider mandatory celibacy completely unnecessary in the life of priests, as a meaningless and authoritarian demand of the Church without theological justification. This view is also shared by 13.4% of the people with deep faith and 36.1% of believers.

The level of religious faith plays a central role in the attitudes of the surveyed high school and college students towards the personal characteristics of Pope John Paul II, who offers them a role-model priest personality and model parish priest, which is statistically confirmed ($x^2 = 137.26$, df = 4, $p < 0.001$). This view was most often accepted by deeply religious people (79.2%) and least often by non-believers (9.9%). The difference between these two percentages is very high (69.3%), meaning that up to eight times fewer non-believers agree with this view. A high percentage of respondent non-believers (70.2%), including 63.9% of high school and 74.5% of college student non-believers, questioned this view. In the remaining groups, the percentage who question this view are lower, and lowest among the deeply religious (8.7%) and slightly more among believers (19.0%). In addition, a total of 13.9% of respondents did not take a stance on this issue, mostly including the religiously indifferent (20.4%) and least of all the deeply faithful (7.8%).

That the level of religious belief is a factor that significantly differentiated the attitudes of high school and university student youth towards parish priests and their level of knowledge regarding the nature, structure and function of the institutional priesthood. An overwhelmingly positive attitude is discernible only in high school and college students who believe in God deeply, and it weakens significantly in people whose belief are at a more generally occuring level. However, non-believers and a large proportion of religiously indifferent people responded extremely critically towards the institution of the priesthood and parish priests or pastors in academic ministry. Strong believers represented the highest percentage, and a significant percentage of people who believe demonstrated a correct understanding of the priesthood and priests. Non-believers, and a large percentage of the religiously indifferent, were the most likely to explain the nature and structure of the priesthood and the role of the priest incorrectly and contrary to the teaching of the Church. Statistical indicators show this dependence to be at a high level of significance ($x^2 = 127.58$, df = 6, p < 0.001), indicating the importance of the level of religious belief in this matter.

Knowledge about priesthood and attitude towards priests were also significantly differentiated by the level of education of the respondents, displaying different levels of religious faith as well as indifference and unbelief, demonstrated by statistical indicators ($x^2 = 106.47$, $df = 4$, $p < 0.001$). This attitude is more positive and less critical among believing high school and university students.

3. Religious beliefs of the respondents and their attitudes towards priesthood and priests

Religious practices are the most prominent and basic components of traditionally understood religiousness. In Poland, they are still the only feature of folk piety and the Catholic Church,[3] because they were performed *en masse* in the eighties of the 20th century. However, now the frequency of participation in religious practices has decreased significantly, especially in cities. Religious practices have an individual and private as well as corporate and public character. Sociology of religion has divided practices into the so-called ritual behavior and instrumental behavior. In particular, ritual behavior focuses on how actions should be performed by the faithful, and less importance is placed on their purpose and motivation. However, instrumental behavior emphasizes purpose and motivation, and less importance is placed on implementation by an individual. Thus, they include the Church's cultural activities and are related to conveying their faith.[4] Religious practices are closely linked to the system, contents and purpose of religion. In this respect, the institutional Church has the right to demand that its members implement religious practices, punishable by the sanction of serious fault ("sub gravi").

There is certainly a close statistical relationship between religious practices and the internal religiousness of Catholics. This relationship occurs when there is a "continuum" of ritual practices, drawing on two different principles: a) when the individual believer fulfills a particular religious practice subject to the sanction of serious fault, in different circumstances and social environments, b) when an individual believer participates in several religious

---

[3] Cf. W. Piwowarski (ed.), *Religijność ludowa – ciągłość i zmiana* [Folk Religiousness – Continuity and Change], Wroclaw 1983, pp. 5–12; J. Baniak, "Specyfika religijności ludowej" [The Specifics of Folk Religiousness], *Tygodnik Polski*, 1984, no. 26, p. 7.

[4] Cf. E. Pin, *La paroisse catholique. Les formes variables d'un systeme social*, Roma 1968, pp. 99–100.

practices – obligatory and voluntary.[5] This approach to religious practices by a believer is a manifestation of deep involvement in ritual, a sign of the inner, spiritual depth of religiousness, of which these very practices are integral components.[6] Through religious cult, a religious group finds its own religious identity. Participation in religious practices, especially in those that are mandatory and repeated, means that Catholics belong and are bound to the universal and local Church – the diocese and parish.[7]

Religious practices, especially mandatory practices, both once-off and repeated, affect other areas of the religiousness of Catholics, including their perception of the institution of the priesthood and their personal attitudes towards priests. Does this situation also apply to the respondents?

In my empirical hypothesis, I assumed connections and interdependency between the frequency of fulfilling religious practices and the views, attitudes and evaluations of the young people in high school and college concerning the priesthood and priests. This hypothesis assumed that the greater (more regular) the frequency of participation in religious practices by the respondents, particularly those mandatorily repeated, the greater their knowledge of the institutional priesthood and the more positive their attitude towards parish priests and academic ministers. This hypothesis was positively verified by the results of my research.

A religious vocation is necessary in choosing the priesthood and remaining in it, especially in the assessment of regularly practicing respondents. They accepted this without reservations most often (65.0%), and stated that without a vocation, a man, even if he is deeply believing and religious, should not choose a priestly profession. As a rule, priests entering into the priesthood without the call of God, in their opinion, cannot meet the requirements of the priesthood, and later abandon it for the secular life. This view is shared by 71.4% of high school and 58.6% of college students regularly practicing their religious faith services. Only 13% of respondents who did not regularly perform religious practices accepted the necessity of a religious vocation to the priesthood, including 14.5% of high school and 11.5% of college students.

---

[5] Cf. J. Mariański, "Motywy wiary w świetle badań socjologicznych" [Faith Motives in the Light of Sociological Research], *Collectanea Theologica*, 1975, vol. 3, pp. 137–150; J. Baniak, "Motywy wiary i niewiary katolików miejskich (cz. 1)" [Faith Motives and Unbelief of Urban Catholics (part 1)], 1990, *W drodze*, no. 8, pp. 85– 93; idem, "Motywy wiary i niewiary katolików miejskich (cz. 2)" [Faith Motives and Unbelief of Urban Catholics (part 2)], *W drodze,* 1990, no. 9, pp. 86–92.

[6] Cf. J. Baniak, "Praktyki religijne katolików XX wieku – analiza socjologiczna" [Religious Practices of 20th Century Catholics – A Sociological Analysis], *Studia Gnesnensia*, 2002, vol. 16, pp. 277–318.

[7] Cf. G. Le Bras, *L'Église et le village*, Paris 1976, pp. 167–168.

However, the necessity of being called was denied most by non-practicing respondents (66.9%), mostly by college students (70.5%) and less by high school students (63.3%). The necessity of vocation was most approved of by those regularly practicing their faith – 20.9%, including 15.1% of high school students and 26.7% of college students (a difference of 11.6%). The statistical relationship between these two variables is significantly high ($x^2 = 123.45$, $df = 10$, $p < 0.001$) and indicates the significant impact of the frequency of religious practice on the respondents' attitudes towards the role of God in calling a man to the institutional priesthood. Respondents systematically practicing their faith were 5 times more likely to accept and appreciate this role of vocation than non-practicing respondents, who were 6 times more likely to question the role of a priestly vocation.

The frequency of participation in religious practices also influenced, to a lesser extent, understanding of the structure of the priesthood. We see the correct terminology (the priesthood as a vocation and profession) used by the majority of respondents in both groups, most of all by those who regularly practice their faith, and second by those who do not practice regularly. Those who are not involved in religious practice could define the structure of priesthood properly half as much as those who are. They were also four times more likely (57.8% vs. 16.0%) to perceive the priesthood as an ordinary profession, which was needed at a specific time. Some practitioners saw only a vocation from God in the priesthood – 21.4% of high school and 16.5% of college students, while non-practicing respondents did not perceive the priesthood as such. The relationship between these variables, described as essential on the average level ($x^2 = 116.28$, $df = 8$, $p < 0.01$) is demonstrated by statistical indicators.

Regular participation in religious worship creates the opportunity for young people to get to know priests better, and at the same time assist them in assessing their prestige in the parish, school and university environments. The highest prestige was granted to priests by high school (72.0%) and college students (58.5%) regularly practicing and maintaining close contacts with the parish rectory, in the catechetic classroom and at pastoral ministry academic centers. These respondents were the most likely to recognize the prestige of priests as very high (45.8%) and high (19.5%), and none of them denied the authority of priests. Non-practicing respondents (25.0%) were most likely to deny the authority of priests, and assessed it as average (19.4%), low (17.9%) and very low (15.8%), with only 4.7% thinking that priests deserve authority and social recognition. Thus, people who practice their faith regularly were almost ten times more likely (46.0%) than those not practicing (4.7%) to judge the authority of the clergy as very high, taking into account the parochial and academic environment. Correlation indicators of the relationship between these variables show a high level of significance ($x^2 = 127.48$, df = 10, $p < 0.001$), and indicate that the higher the level of participation in religious worship, the greater the possibility of granting priests authority of a very high and high level. Thus, a low participation rate or neglecting religious worship practice contributes to underrating or denying the authority of priests.

We see the same situation in the respondents' assessments of the role of the priest. Respondents who consistently observed religious practices most often described the role of a priest very broadly, recognizing his competence in pastoral skills both in religious and ecclesiastical matters (51.5%), as well as secular matters, those related to religion (16.8%) and moral issues (21.2%). None of them questioned the role of the priest in the Church and in society. A different position was taken on this matter by some non-practicing high school (15.3%) and college students (18.1%), who denied priests competence in every case. They also most often (66.5% and 71.4%) reduced the scope of the role of the priest to only religious and Church matters (69.0%), completely excluding secular matters. Correlation indicators of the relationship between these variables are classified as essential at a significantly high level ($x^2 = 107.48$, df = 8, $p < 0.001$), and indicate that the higher the frequency of religious practice, the more broadly is the role of the priest understood by the surveyed high school and college students.

Mediation of the priest between people and God is accepted most often by regularly practicing (66.6%) and least often by non-practicing respondents (5.5%), who were also the most likely (60.5%) to consider this role superfluous in people's religiosity. However, none of the respondents who regularly partake in religious cult stated this, and they maintain that the help of priests is necessary for the salvation of people. These respondents were twelve times more likely than non-practicing respondents to consider priestly mediation as necessary for salvation, three times more likely than occasionally practicing respondents, and 10.8% more than those who practice irregularly. The relationship between these correlation indicator variables is significant to a high degree ($x^2 = 112.53$, df = 8, $p < 0.001$), and indicate that the higher the frequency of participation in religious services, the more positive the respondents acceptance of the mediating role of a priest in matters of salvation.

The frequency of religious practice also influences the personal statements of respondents concerning their willingness to have a priest in their family. Systematically practicing respondents most frequently declared such a desire (66.5%). Among the high school students it was 74.5%, and among college students 58.4%, but such a desire was not declared by non-practicing respondents (65.9%). Those who practice were positively disposed towards priests, and the possibility to have a priest in their family was considered an honor in the local parish and community. Correlation indicators of the relationship between these variables are essential at a significantly high level ($x^2 = 108.42$, $df = 8$, $p < 0.001$) and indicate that regular participation in religious worship has a positive influence on the desire to have a priest in the family.

Participating in religious practices contributes significantly to forming and maintaining ties between the respondents and their parish and academic ministry priests. Systematically practicing respondents expressed a desire for this relationship most often (32.8%), those who neglect these practices least often (12.7%) and the non-practicing never. The correlation dependence between these variables is represented by high-level important indicators ($x^2 = 114.36$, $df = 8$, $p < 0.001$), and indicate that the higher the frequency of participation in religious practices, the deeper the desire for a personal relationship with a priest.

Respondents consistently participating in religious practices most often favored the religious and Church characteristics of the model priest (67.0%), and less frequently appreciated natural features. Non-practicing respondents answered opposingly, emphasizing only the importance of natural features in this model. To them, most of all, it is primarily important that every priest be a "decent" man, and only then that he be a professional priest carrying out his career tasks (60.4%). This view is shared by only 27.4% of respondents who regularly practice their faith. The relationship between these variable correlation indicators can be classified as significant at a high level ($x^2 = 125.58$, $df = 8$, $p < 0.001$). This indicates that the higher the frequency of religious practice, the more likely the respondents were to value the religious characteristics in their model priest and spiritual minister higher.

Participation in religious practices also affected the attitudes of respondents towards the celibacy of priests. Among those opposed to mandatory celibacy of priests are both systematically practicing respondents (24.0%), irregular practitioners (40.3%) and those practicing religion occasionally (51.4%), although the largest percentage belong to the group of the non-practicing (79.5%). The relationship between these variable correlation indicators is at a significantly high level ($x^2 = 126.43$, $df = 10$, $p < 0.001$), and indicates that higher frequency of religious practice relates directly to acceptance of the celibacy of priests, whereas decreasing religious practices relates to rejection of priestly celibacy.

Religious piety, evident in the systematic fulfillment of religious duties, also influences the perception of Pope John Paul II as a role-model for the priestly personality and model parish pastoral minister. Respondents who practice their faith regularly most often saw in the Pope these two options (73.8%), including 78.3% of high school students and 69.4% of college students. Those who do not practice perceived these options the least (8.7%) – eight times less frequently (65.1%). They were most likely (66.4%) to question this view and not to see in John Paul II a role-model for the priestly personality and model parish pastor. Among those practicing regularly, this number is only 11.0%. Statistical indicators of the dependence between these variables appear as very significant at a high level ($x^2 = 98.46$, df = 6, $p < 0.001$), and indicate that deep devotion helps the respondents to perceive John Paul II as a personality role-model for priests and model parish pastor.

In this chapter, I presented and explained the correlations that exist between the respondents' views, attitudes and evaluations concerning the priesthood and priests and gender composition, declarations of religious faith and the frequency of religious practice religion as independent variables. These studies showed the significant impact of these characteristics on the attitudes of my respondents towards the institutional priesthood, parish and academic ministry priests. Statistical indicators confirm the accuracy of the adopted empirical hypothesis and the real impact of these factors on the priestly awareness of the surveyed high school and college students.

Conclusion

In this study, I present the comprehensive knowledge, various viewpoints, attitudes and evaluations of the Polish youth studying in high school and college in Kalisz, towards the institutional priesthood and priests working in parishes and academic pastoral ministry centers. The attitude of the young people towards the priesthood and priests depends on many different independent variables, including the type and specificity of the school environment, gender, social background, level of academic achievement and the level of their faith and religious practices, which plays a fundamental role. An important factor in the attitudes and assessments of respondents concerning the priesthood and priests is the time period in which these studies were carried out. I carried out sociological research on this topic in the years 1983, 1998 and 2008. The main question motivating this study was whether and to what extent the views, attitudes and evaluation of high school and college students concerning the institutional priesthood and priests have changed during these 25 years, and in which direction these changes have taken place.

This study addressed the following issues and problems:

1) the theoretical and hermeneutical concepts of the hierarchical priesthood, referring to the methodological assumptions of other sociologists of religion and scholars of this phenomenon, which represents a theological-pastoral, psychological-religious and social-religious orientation. At the conclusion, I tried to take a position concerning the area of analysis;

2) determining the methodological procedures of my empirical studies, in which the main role is played by empirical and theoretical hypotheses, creating a framework for the issues analyzed here;

3) analysing the indicator values of selected elements of the religious life of the youth – their attitudes towards religious beliefs, religious and sacramental practices, which I took as independent variables conditioning their beliefs, attitudes and assessments of the priesthood and priests;

4) selected demographic-social features of the respondents that determine their views on the priesthood and attitudes towards priests;

5) respondents' knowledge of the broader issues of the institutional priesthood: its nature and structure, the religious-social role of the parish priest, the authority of the priest in the parish, local community and global society, the professional prestige of the priesthood in Poland, the model of the priesthood operating in Poland's youth environment, and the mandatory celibacy of Roman Catholic priests;

6) the direction in which views, attitudes and evaluations of the respondents concerning the priesthood and priests have changed over the period of 25 years in Poland, under the influence of various factors, including changes in the religious awareness of high school and college students.

The results of this research and analysis allow us to make generalizations about the issues presented surrounding the priesthood and the life of priests.

1. The institutional priesthood and its specific perceptions according to the theoretical understanding and the ideas of the youth:

a) The hierarchical priesthood is a multidimensional, structurally complex phenomenon. In this study, I present it in three dimensions: the theological, as a religious vocation; the psychological, as a defined and specific way of life for a priest; and the sociological, as a religious profession and specific existential value, preferred in the Catholic Church. The sociological dimension places institutional priesthood in specific social, cultural, economic, educational, business, family, and schoolconditions. It is perceived as a social fact, as a profession with a religious profile which is in demand in the Catholic community. In this dimension of the priesthood, the supernatural does not matter, whereas it acquires the characteristics of a socially useful profession in a secular dimension. The idea of the priesthood and its reality ("materialization") is found in the person of the priest, who tries to implement the theological assumptions of the concept of priesthood. This concept assumes that the foundation of priesthood is a unique kind of religious vocation, ensuring the relevance of the choice of priesthood and a priest's perseverance. The necessity of this vocation to the priesthood was judged necessary by 63.8% of high school and 47.0% of college student respondents, while 21.3% and 26.9% denied this necessity. During the study period of 25 years, the percentage of high school (32.6%) and college students (23.0%) who accepted the necessity of priestly vocation declined systematically, and during the same time the percentage of people questioning the need for choosing the priestly profession increased by 7.2% and 14.5%;

b) The majority of high school students (63.1%) and college students (57.3%) saw in the institutional priesthood both a religious vocation and a profession, and small percentages saw only a religious vocation (10.7% and 10.3%) or ordinary profession (22.3% and 27.1%). Over the entire period of 25 years, lower percentages of high school (15.8%) and college students (19.2%) perceived the priesthood objectively, including both the religious and secular dimensions at the same time;

c) The religious dimension of the priesthood is fulfilled in practice by a priest performing a variety of functions that drew the attention of the respondents. These functions are rated as follows: religious-cultic (indicated by 44.2% of high school students and 43.6% of college students), Church (26.7% and 30.7%), secular (9.0% and 8.0%), the personal life of the priest (9.4% and 7.1%) and being a priest in all circumstances (7.0% and 6.5%). Thus, religious-Church functions clearly dominated, as a total of 70.9% of high school and 74.3% of college students indicated. The importance of these functions increased over the given period, as indicated by higher percentages of respondents in both groups;

d) Respondents evaluated the professional prestige of priests in Poland in the years 1983–2008 according to the following scale: very high – 43.0% of high school students and 40.4% of university students, high – 16.8% and 10.0%, average – 9.6% and 9.2%, low – 9.5% and 12.0%, very low – 9.1% and 10.8%, none – 10.8% and 15.0%. During this period, the percentages of high school students (12.8%) and college students (18.1%) who indicated very high prestige for priests in Poland decreased, while there was an increased percentage of 7.6% and 6.4% of those who refused to grant priests social recognition;

e) The high school and college students, assessing the current position of the priesthood among 25 different professions, rated the profession of priest seventh – as suggested by 74.5% of respondents, including 82.3% of high school students and 67.5% of college students. Higher positions were given to the following professions: medical doctor, university professor, judge, prosecutor, lawyer and businessman. Respondents were guided by four criteria in their rating of these professions: income, difficulty in getting and keeping the position, job stability, and attractiveness for young people. The profession of priest, according to these criteria, gained considerable prestige: a) personal revenue – 66.7% of high school students (8th), with college students at 72.5% (6th), b) the difficulty of mastering the profession – 71.4% (2nd) and 63.2% (8th), c) stability – 67.6% (3rd) and 74.3% (2nd), d) attractiveness – 63.8% (8th) and 61.5% (9th). These positions have changed over the study period in both groups of respondents;

f) Professional advancement in the priesthood, as measured on the scale of importance from very high to none at all, has changed significantly over the research period. The percentage of respondents indicating a decline in priestly promotion in each category rating increased systematically, by the following percentages: very high – 9.4% of high school students and 5.1% of college students, high – 7.7% and 3.7%, average – 4.7% and 10.1%. At the same time, the percentage of those who indicated a clear decline in the social significance of the priesthood increased: by 13.1% among high school students and 7.4% among college students. Respondents were critical of the current prestige of the priestly profession, and the following percentages judged it to be redundant: 20.2% of high school students and 11.2% of college students. At the same time, percentages of respondents confirming the need for priests decreased, the "very high" rating dropped by 21.9% and 13.6% and "high" by 5.1% and 1.9%;

g) Not all respondents expressed a desire to have a priest in their family. Moreover, their declining percentages represent a regular decrease during the study period in both groups. In the first study period (1983) this desire was expressed by 51.1% of high school and 44.3% of college students, during the second study period (1998) this had dropped by 7.5% and 3.8%, while in the third study period (2008), the percentage further decreased by 11.0% and 6.2%. At the same time, there was a constant increase in the percentage of those who definitely did not want to have a priest in their family – by 14.4% and 11.0%. 21.3% of high school students and 19.4% of college students were completely indifferent to this question.

2. Respondents also assessed the role of the priest in parishioners' religiosity and in their personal religious lives, indicating his necessity or redundancy:

a) In the opinion of 59.5% of the respondents, including 64.6% of high school and 54.4% of college students, the religious role of the priest in the pursuit of salvation is necessary. However, throughout the period of 25 years, there were decreases in the percentages of respondents confirming this role of the priest: among high school students by 20.5% and college students by 15.7%. Over the same period the percentage who consider this role to be quite unnecessary in people's religious lives grew by 15.7% and 11.9%. However, in relation to their own religiosity, initially 46.6% of high school and 35.3% of college students rated the role of the priest as necessary, but this percentage decreased by 13.0% and 5.0% over the entire period, and those confirming the redundancy of this role in their religiosity increased;

b) The role of the priest in the parish encompasses many different issues and problems. Respondents felt that within the framework of his role, the priest performs the following actions: stabilizes people's belief in God – 19.8% of high school and 22.2% of college students (during the entire period there was an increase of people claiming so of 3.8% and 11.6%), celebrates the Mass – 37.1% and 36.4% (an increase of 11.6% and 10.3%), administers the sacraments – 26.4% and 19.4% (a decrease of 3.3% and 11.0%), shapes people's morality – 12.9% and 17.2% (a decrease of 0.2% and an increase of 0.9%), directs the parish – 24.6% and 25.9% (an increase of 15.8% and 18.5%); ensures pastoral care for parishioners' matters – 14.4% and 10.0% (a decrease of 7.7% and 3.0%). Therefore, the role of the priest includes different aspects of human life, which respondents rate as follows: a) exclusively religious – 53.4% and 56.6% (during the period, this increased by 19.9% and 20.9%), b) exclusively secular – 7.6% and 8.7% (down by 4.2% and 2.8%), c) ethical and moral – 18.8% and 13.0% (a decrease of 10.2% and 11.2%), d) nothing indicated – 11.0% and 11.6% (an increase of 5.0% and 3.2%);

c) Many respondents expressed a desire for personal contact and relationships with priests – 46.8%, including 50.0% of high school students and 44.1% of college students. However, over the research period, there was a decrease of 11.9% and 9.7% in the proportion of those who want this relationship and also an increase (of 9.8% and 12.6%) in those who did not want any contact with priests. Situations which facilitated respondents establishing and maintaining relationships with priests include: religious practices – 25.0% (including 27.2% of high school students and 26.1% of college students), catechesis and pastoral academic ministry – 22.8% (27.2% and 18.4%), personal problems and needs – 16.2% (13.3% and 19.1%), trips and pilgrimages to shrines – 13.9% (14.2% and 13.5%), difficulties in life and moral dilemmas – 11.5% (10.3% and 12.7%);

d) During the 25 years study period, Polish priests were personally involved in the political affairs of the nation and local governments. Personal conviction of politicization was expressed by 63.9% of the respondents, including 61.3% of high school and 66.6% of college students, while 36.5% and 41.2% spoke of "excessive" politicization in Poland's parish clergy. The percentages of those who see political commitment in priests increased during this period by 7.0% and 4.6%, and those confirming no political involvement of parish priests decreased by 12.2% and 10.0%. Politicized priests instructed the faithful during parliamentary, presidential and local elections as to which candidates the people should vote for, as stated by 73.5% of respondents, including 71.9% of high school and 77.0% of college students. Over the study period, there was an increase of 10.1% and 9.2% of respondents confirming such political briefings by priests, presented to the faithful during religious services (31.8% and 37.8%) and during times of special campaigning (14.5% and 13.3%);

e) The respondents assessed the authority of priests according to the following scale: very high – high school students 44.5% and college students 32.1%, high – 13.3% and 12.6%, average – 11.2% and 12.0%, low – 13.6% and

15.0%, very low – 9.0% and 10.2%, no authority – 8.0% and 11.0%. During the given period, the percentage of those judging the authority of priests to be very high decreased by 20.3% and 23.3%, and by 5.1% and 5.9% in the "high" category, whereas there was an increase of 9.2% and 11.6% of respondents indicating a complete lack of authority granted to priests. The dominant percentage of high school students (86.8%) and college students (72.4%) limited the authority of priests to religious and Church matters, including the religious education of children and youth (74.6% and 70.3%), religious belief formation in people (55.6% and 58.4%), and only 34.5% of high school and 18.6% of college students included priests in secular affairs. In addition, 35.4% and 41.4% of respondents in both groups did not grant priests any advisory competence. 45.7% of high school students and 51.4% of college students stated that priests have no influence on their consciences, and over the study period, this percentage increased by 9.8% and 10.5%. Those accepting the authority of priests in moral issues most frequently benefited from the assistance of confessors, so they would entrust priests with problems in their consciences – as did 70.5% of high school and 56.3% of college students, but this percentage decreased by 16.2% and 18.6% during the study period;

f) The studied youth also spoke in terms of their confidence in the institutional Church and parish priests. A total of 54.6% of the respondents trusted the Church, including 59.3% of high school and 49.9% of college students, although this confidence declined during the study period: among high school students by 18.5% and college students by 19.7%, while there was an increase of 17.4% and 19.5% of those who did not trust the Church. Overall, 34.2% of respondents did not trust the Church, including 31.1% of high school students and 38.8% of college students. The parish pastor was trusted by 59.0% of respondents, including 63.6% of high school students and 54.3% of college students, but these percentages decreased by 16.5% and 14.8% over the study period, and there was an increase of 14.3% and 17.0% of those not fully trusting their parish priest.

3. The surveyed youth have their own environmental model of a parish priest, and they placed the features and actions of priests into a religious and secular profile. Religious features and activities were judged positively by 69.4% of respondents, including 71.4% of high school and 67.4% of college students, while the secular features were approved of by 64.0% of respondents, including 63.2% and 64.8% in both groups. 65.5% of respondents, including 68.5% of high school students and 63.4% of college students, claimed that only a priest "equipped with" these two types of traits and talents – religious and secular – will cope with the demands of the clerical state and the ecclesiastical authorities as well as the expectations of the faithful in the parish, as

a result of which he himself will ultimately be satisfied with his vocation, life and work as a priest. In the model priest, respondents also added personal and professional vices of a religious and secular nature. Vices in the religious sphere were criticized by a total of 47.1% of respondents, including 43.4% of high school and 50.7% of college students, while secular vices were criticized by 54.7%, including 52.2% and 57.3% in both groups. Over the study period there was an increases of 16.1% and 16.8% in the percentage of respondents criticizing the vices of priests.

4. My respondents, seeking a personality type and model parish priest suitable for today's priests, found such a priest in the person of Pope John Paul II and his style of pastoral work. The Pope was perceived in this way by 72.7% of respondents, including 75.8% of high school and 69.6% of college students. Over the study period, these percentages dropped by 8.1% and 8.5%. However, according to 16.1% of respondents, including 15.5% of high school students and 16.8% of college students, Pope John Paul II cannot be a role-model for priests and the priest model for today's priests, because they would not be able to match his charism and exceptional talents (Statements such as "This pope cannot be duplicated," "The pope cannot be copied in any way," "Pope Wojtyła was an extremely original and charismatic priest, so trying to follow his person and actions is not realistic" justified the concern of some respondents, who did not see the Pope as a personal role-model and the model for priests).

5. Respondents also took a position on mandatory celibacy for Roman Catholic priests. The majority defined celibacy from the secular point of view (78.6%), while only 16.5% saw it in its religious aspect, in accordance with the teachings of the Church. Among the secular views, 82.3% of respondents, including 78.4% of high school and 86.3% of college students saw a celibate priest as deprived of his natural tendency to get married and set up his own marriage and family, and celibacy asr an absolute and fanciful prohibition imposed on priests for a few unimportant and artificially motivated reasons – 84.1%, including 79.7% and 88.5% in both groups. However, among the religious perspectives, the dominant proportion of respondents interpreted celibacy as a priest's total dedication to the exclusive service of God and the people in the Church – 17.9%, including 21.3% and 14.5%, or as full and undivided love for God and the Church, without sharing their love with a wife and children – 15.6%, including 18.4% and 12.8%. On the other hand, 50.4% of respondents, including 44.8% of high school students and 56.0% of college students, recognized that celibacy restricts the personal freedom and autonomy of a priest, and the majority of them claimed that this is a total restriction – 35.5%, with 29.3% and 37.8% in the respective groups. The percentage of

people appreciating the impact of celibacy on the life of a priest grew during the study period by 16.9%, among high school students by 20.8% and college students by 12.9%.

By contrast, only 26.7% of respondents, including 30.7% of high school students and 22.7% of college students, claimed that celibacy in the current form does not affect the personal freedom and autonomy of a priest, but rather teaches him to make proper use of it for religious purposes. During the study period, there was a 10.9% decrease, including 17.9% of high school and 9.8% of college students, in the percentage of those who shared this opinion. In the opinion of 58.4% of respondents, including 57.0% of high school and 60.0% of college students, celibacy is not a necessary condition for entering and remaining in the priesthood, and over the study period there was an increase (6.0% and 7.1%) in the percentages who stressed the redundancy of celibacy in the lives of priests. However, the necessity of celibacy was expressed by 29.6% of respondents, including 31.9% of high school and 27.4% of college students, but this percentage decreased by 8.3% and 7.1% over the period of 25 years. The dominant percentage of the surveyed – a total of 64.2%, including 59.2% of high school and 69.4% of college students – declared that they knew of priests who left the priesthood because of celibacy and were married to women they met while performing their professional duties. This percentage increased during the study period by 10.4% and 8.9%. However, 31.4% did not know of such priests, a number which declined by 10.9% and 11.3%. In the opinion of 57.2% of respondents, including 55.3% of high school and 59.5% of college students, imposed celibacy promotes immoral behavior in a number of priests, and this percentage increased by 10.8% and 9.9%. A different view on the subject was expressed by 29.3% of high school and 23.6% of college students, who claimed that celibacy contributes to a drop in the number of vocations to the priesthood, of which 63.9% of high school and 64.8% of college students were convinced. This percentage increased by 4.8% and 8.7% over the research period. The opposing view was stated by 18.5% of high school and 17.2% of college students, and this proportion decreased by 4.3% and 2.9% during the period. In the opinion of 74.6% of high school students and 79.9% of college students, the unifying of all Christians into one Church is something more important than the celibacy of priests, and the Roman Catholic Church should change its present form of celibacy for priests for this purpose. The percentages of respondents sharing this view increased by 10.9% and 5.8% during the research period. A different opinion was expressed by only 15.7% of high school students and 10.5% of college students, and this percentage decreased by 12.2% and 4.3%.

6. Studies have shown the existence of correlations between the accepted independent variables – gender, level of academic achievement, level of religious faith, frequency of performing religious practices, the time-frame of the research – and the attitudes of respondents towards priests and their views on the institutional priesthood. These factors are influenced to varying degrees by the image of the priesthood and priests operating in the religious and social awareness of the surveyed Polish high school and college students. This image is to a large extent consistent with the theological concepts and teachings of the Catholic Church on the institutional priesthood and the life of priests, and their role and authority in the parish and in the local community. The results verified the validity of the empirical hypotheses adopted in the methodological assumptions.

The research presented in this study is a continuation of an empirical sociological project of the eighties and nineties of the twentieth century, which increased the empirical knowledge of the Catholic Church and its structures in Poland, including the institutional priesthood and priests, the central issue in the internal and external Church discourse. These studies represent a voice in the ongoing discussion on the changes in the perception of the priesthood and priests in Polish society, especially in high school and university students' environments. In this discussion, there are also critical remarks about the personal qualities and professional activities of parish priests. Many hypotheses accepted and verified in this research must wait for confirmation in further sociological studies involving national samples.

Achieving these results was essentially dependent on the good will and the willingness of my respondents – junior high school, high school and university students – during all periods of research and surveying. Their willingness to take part and their seriousness towards the research issue was instrumental in the success of this study. Therefore, at this point I express my heartfelt gratitude to all of them. We would also like to thank the organizations and individuals who contributed to the publication of this academic research study and made it available to readers.

Bibliography

Audet J. P., "Priester in der christlichen Gemeinde," in *Das priesterliche Dienst*, Freiburg – Basel – Wien 1970, pp. 116–175.

Augustyn J., *Wychowanie do czystości i celibatu kapłańskiego* [Educationing to Purity and Priestly Celibacy], Cracow – Zabki 2000.

Babbie E., *Badania społeczne w praktyce* [Social Research in Practics], transl. W. Betkiewicz, Warsaw 2007.

Badora B., "Młodzież o polityce i demokracji" [The Youth on Politics and Democracy], in *Młodzież 2003. Opinie i diagnozy nr 2. CBOS* [The Youth 2003. Opinion and Diagnostics no. 2. CBOS], Warsaw 2004, p. 49–60.

Bachl G., "Das Gottesbilds und die Entschiedenheit christlicher Berufung," in *Priesterbild im Wandel*, Linz 1976, pp. 147–164.

Balthasar H. U. von, "Das priesterliche Amt," *Civitas*, 1968, no. 23, pp. 784–826.

Balthasar H. U. von, "Die Gegenwart des Jesus Christus in der Einheit der Kirche", in *In der Nachfolge Jesu Christi*, Mainz 1976, pp. 38–54.

Balthasar H. U. von, "Der Priester in der Kirche," *Lebendige Seelsorge*, 1972, no. 23, pp. 11–25.

Balthasar H. U. von, "Priesterliche Existenz," in *Sponsa Verb*, Einsiedeln 1961, pp. 387–408.

Baniak J., "Aksjologiczny wymiar zawodu księdza" [Axiological Dimensions of the Priest's Profession], *Studia Socjologiczne*, 1989, no. 4, pp. 215–232.

Baniak J., "Autorytet i rola kapłana w społeczności religijnej" [The Authority and Rolle of a Priest in the Religious Comminity], in idem, *Religijność miejska w warunkach uprzemysłowienia i ruralizacji na przykładzie Kalisza* [Urban Religiousness in Industrialized and Rural Conditions based on the Example of Kalisz], Cracow 1990, pp. 199–208.

Baniak J., "Autorytet księży parafialnych (cz. 1)" [Authority of Parish Priests (part 1)], *Przegląd Powszechny*, 1998, no. 2, pp. 150–163.

Baniak J., "Autorytet księży parafialnych" (cz. 2)," [Authority of Parish Priests (part 2)], *Przegląd Powszechny*, 1998, no. 3, pp. 325–337.

Baniak J., "Bibliografia ważniejszych prac w języku polskim na temat powołań duchownych, kapłaństwa i życia zakonnego w latach 1945–1994" [Bibliography of Important Works in Polish on the Topic of Clerical Vocations, Priesthood and Religious Life from 1945–1994], in J. Baniak, *Dynamika powołań kapłańskich i zakonnych w Kościele rzymskokatolickim w Polsce w latach 1900–1994. Studium socjograficzne* [The Dynamics of Priestly and

Religious Vocations in the Roman Catholic Church in Poland in the Years 1900–1994. A Socio-Graphics Study], Cracow 1997, pp. 193–248.

Baniak J., "Czynniki kryzysu tożsamości kapłańskiej wśród księży rzymskokatolickich w Polsce. Studium socjologiczne" [Factors of Priestly Identity Crisis among Roman Catholic Priest in Poland. A Sociological Study], *Teologia Praktyczna*, 2007, vol. 8, pp. 209–264.

Baniak J., *Desakralizacja kultu religijnego i świąt religijnych w Polsce. Studium socjologiczne* [The Desacralization of Religious Cult and the Religious World in Poland. A Sociological Study], Cracow 2007.

Baniak J., "Deternimants of Social Origin and Evolution of Sacerdotal Vocations in Poland, in W. Cross (ed.), *Percevided Influences on the Career of Polish Priest*, Illinois 1990, pp. 12–47.

Baniak J., "Dlaczego księża w Polsce rezygnują z kapłaństwa?" [Why do Priests in Poland Resign from the Priesthood?], *Przegląd Powszechny*, 2000, no. 5, pp. 158–176 and no. 6, pp. 317–324.

Baniak J., *Dynamika powołań kapłańskich i zakonnych w Kościele rzymskokatolickim w Polsce w latach 1900–1994. Studium socjograficzne* [The Dynamics of Priestly and Religious Vocations in the Roman Catholic Church in Poland in the Years 1900–1994. A Socio-Graphics Study], Cracow 1997.

Baniak J., "Kapłan jako typ roli społecznej" [Priest as a Type of Social Role], in I. Borowik, W. Zdaniewicz (ed.), *Od Kościoła ludu do Kościoła wyboru. Religia a przemiany społeczne w Polsce* [From the Church of the People to the Church of Choice. Religion and Social Change in Poland], Cracow 1996, pp. 148–175.

Baniak J., "Kapłan w oczach wiernych" [The priest in the eyes of the faithful], *W drodze*, 1992, no. 9 (229), pp. 90–95.

Baniak J., "Kapłani i kapłaństwo w świetle badań socjologicznych i postulatów Vaticanum II" [Priests and Priesthood in the Light of Sociological Research and Postulates of Vatican II], *Prace Naukowe Wyższej Szkoły Pedagogicznej w Częstochowie*, 1987, no. 1, pp. 81–102.

Baniak J., "Kapłaństwo hierarchiczne w świadomości licealistów i studentów – analiza socjologiczna" [The Hierarchical Priesthood in the Awareness of High School and College Studensts – A Sociological Analysis], *Studia Gnesnensia*, 2000, vol. 14, pp. 285-304.

Baniak J., "Katolicki etos małżeńsko-rodzinny w świadomości »byłych« księży" [The Catholic Ethos of Mariiage and Family in the Awareness of "Former" Priets], *Problemy Rodziny*, 2000, no. 6, pp. 23–30.

Baniak J., "Katolicy niewierzący i praktykujący? Między wiarą i ateizmem" [Practicing Catholics and Non-Believers? Between Faitf and Atheism], *Homo Dei*, 2007, no. 1 (282), pp. 23–42.

Baniak J., *Ksiądz w oczach młodzieży. Obraz kapłana w świadomości młodzieży licealnej i akademickiej na przykładzie Kalisza. Studium socjologiczne* [The Priest in the Eyes of the Youth. The Image of the Priest in the Awareness of High School and College Youth in the Example of Kalisz. A Sociological Study], Poznan 1993.

Baniak J., "Losy powołań kapłańskich w Polsce w latach 1945-2010. Studium socjograficzne" [Priestly Vocation in Poland in years 1945–2010. A Socio-Graphics Study], *Ateneum Kapłańskie*, 2012, no. 2 (621), vol. 159, pp. 211–239.

Baniak J., *Między buntem a potrzebą akceptacji i zrozumienia. Świadomość religijna i moralna a kryzys tożsamości osobowej młodzieży gimnazjalnej. Studium socjologiczne* [Between Rebelion and the Need for Acceptance and Understanding. The Awareness of Religious and Moral a Crisis of personal Indentity in Junior High School Youth. A Sociological Study], Cracow 2008.

Baniak J., "Model kapłana diecezjalnego w Kościele katolickim. Analiza socjologiczna i teologiczna" [The Diocesan Priest Model in the Catholic Church. A Sociological and Theological Analysis], *Człowiek i Światopogląd*, 1987, no. 8, pp. 72–86.

Baniak J., "Motywy wiary i niewiary katolików miejskich (cz. 1)" [Faith Motives and Unbelief of Urban Catholic (part. 1)], *W drodze*, 1990, no. 8, pp. 85–93.

Baniak J., "Motywy wiary i niewiary katolików miejskich (cz. 2)" [Faith Motives and Unbelief of Urban Catholic (part. 2)], *W drodze*, 1990, no. 9, pp. 86–92.

Baniak J., "Niedziela jako dzień święty w wyobrażeniach i ocenach katolików polskich" [Sunday as a Holy Day in the Ideas and Evaluations of Polish Catholics], *Teologia Praktyczna*, 2004, vol. 5, pp. 245–260.

Baniak J., *Obraz kapłana w świadomości katolików świeckich – na przykładzie Kalisza, Kotłowa i Przedborowa. Studium socjologiczne* [The Image of the Priest in the Awareness of Lay Catholics based on Kalisz, Kotłów and Przedborów. A Sociological Studies], Poznan 1994.

Baniak J., "Obraz kapłana w świadomości świeckich" [The Image od a Priest in the Awareness of the Laity], *W drodze*, 1990, no. 12, pp. 84-92.

Baniak J., "Obraz kapłana w świadomości współczesnych katolików polskich" [The Image of a Priest in the Awareness of Contemporary Catholic in Poland], *Colloquium Salutis. Wrocławskie Studia Teologiczne*, 1988, vol. 20, pp. 221-251.

Baniak J., "Papież Jan Paweł II jako wzór osobowy i model kapłana duszpasterza w świetle opinii i ocen młodzieży polskiej" [Pope John Paul II as a Personal Role-Model and Model Priest-Minister in the Light of the Opinion and Evaluation of Polish Youth], *Ateneum Kapłańskie*, 1991, no. 2–3 (495–496), pp. 295–305.

Baniak J., "Postawy katolików Kalisza wobec wierzeń i praktyk religijnych" [Attitudes of Catholics in Kalisz towards Religious Beliefs and Practices], *Rocznik Kaliski*, 1989, vol. 22, pp. 173–224.

Baniak J., *Powołania do kapłaństwa i do życia zakonnego w Polsce w latach 1900–2010. Studium socjologiczne* [Vocations to the Priesthood and Religious Consecration in Poland in years 1900–2010. A Sociological Study], Poznan 2010.

Baniak J., "Powołania zakonne w Polsce – analiza socjologiczna" [Religious Life Vocations in Poland – A Sociological Analysis], *Ruch Prawniczy, Ekonomiczny i Socjologiczny*, 1986, no. 1, pp. 279–300.

Baniak J., "Praktyki religijne katolików XX wieku – analiza socjologiczna" [Religious Practices of 20th Century Catholics – A Sociological Analysis], *Studia Gnesnensia,* 2002, vol. 16, pp. 277–318.

Baniak J., "Prestiż Kościoła instytucjonalnego i księży w Polsce a zmiana społeczna. Studium socjologiczne" [The Prestige of the Institutional Church and Priests in Poland and Social Change. A Sociological Study], *Poznańskie Studia Teologiczne*, 2002, vol. 13, pp. 153–195.

Baniak J., "Problem roli społecznej kapłana" [The Problem of the Priest's Social Rolle], *Teologia Praktyczna*, 2002, vol. 3, pp. 251–274.

Baniak J., "Problem z politycznym zaangażowaniem Kościoła instytucjonalnego w Polsce" [The Problem with Political Involvement of the InstitutionalChurch in Poland], *Społeczeństwo i Kościół*, 2007, vol. 7, pp. 7–13.

Baniak J., *Rezygnacja z kapłaństwa i wybór życia małżeńsko-rodzinnego przez księży rzymskokatolickich w Polsce. Studium socjologiczne* [Resignation from the Priesthood and Choice of Life in Marriage and Family by Roman Catholic Priest in Poland. A Sociological Study], Cracow 2001.

Baniak J., *Socjologia religii i religijności. Bibliografia prac polskich i przekładów obcych za lata 1929–1979* [Sociology of Religion and Religiosity. Bibliography of Polish Work and Foreign Translations from 1929–1979], Warsaw 1981.

Baniak J., "Specyfika religijności ludowej" [The Specifics of Folk Religiousness], *Tygodnik Polski*, 1984, no. 26, pp. 6–7.

Baniak J., "Vocation for the ministry in Poland during the pontificate of John Paul II (1978–1987)," *Christian Life in Poland*, 1989, no. 264, pp. 16–24.

Baniak J., *Wierność powołaniu a kryzys tożsamości kapłańskiej. Studium socjologiczne na przykładzie Kościoła w Polsce* [Faithfulness to a Vocation and Priestly Identity Crisis. A Sociological Study Based on the Church in Poland], Poznan 2000.

Baniak J., "Zaangażowanie religijne a postawy młodzieży wobec kapłaństwa i księży parafialnych" [Religious Involvement and Attitudes of Youth towards the Priesthood and Parish Priest], in idem, *Ksiądz w oczach młodzieży* [The Priest in the Eyes of the Youth], Poznan 1993, pp. 167–188.

Baniak J., "Zaangażowanie społeczne i polityczne Kościoła i księży w Polsce w wyobrażeniach katolików" [Social and Political Involwement of the Church and Priests in Poland in the Perception of Catholics], *Społeczeństwo i Kościół*, 2005, vol. 2, pp. 107–154.

Baniak J., *Zaufanie młodzieży gimnazjalnej w Polsce do Kościoła instytucjonalnego, "Społeczeństwo i Kościół"* [Confidence in the Institutional Church among School Children in Poland, "Society and the Church"] 2009, vol. 6, pp. 89–144.

Baniak J., "Źródła i przyczyny kryzysu tożsamości kapłańskiej księży rzymskokatolickich w Polsce. Studium socjologiczne" [Sources and Reasons for the Roman Catholic Priestly Identity Crisis in Poland. A Sociological Study], in M. Libiszowska-Żółtkowska (ed.), *Tożsamości religijne w społeczeństwie polskim. Socjologiczne studium przypadków* [Religious Identity in Polish Society. A Sociological Case Study], Warsaw 2009, pp. 67–107.

Bartoszek A., "Zaufanie jako czynnik aktywności obywatelskiej na lokalnej scenie politycznej" [Trust as Factor in Civil Activity on the Lokal Political Scene), in E. Nycz (ed.), *Budowa lokalnego społeczeństwa obywatelskiego w perspektywie integracji europejskiej* [Construction of the Local Civil Society in the Perspective of European Integration], Opole 2003, pp. 47–66.

Bednarski F., *Wychowanie młodzieży dorastającej* [Educating Adolescent Youth], Warsaw 2000.

Berger P., "Człowiek Zachodu: wyzwolenie i samotność" [Western Man: Liberation and Loneliness], *Aneks. Kwartalnik Polityczny*, 1986, no. 43, pp. 6–11.

Berger P., "Etyka społeczna w postsocjalistycznym świecie" [Social Ethics in the Post-Socialist World], *Teraźniejszość. Człowiek. Twórczość. Kwartalnik Myśli Społeczno-Pedagogicznej*, 2000, no. 3, pp. 12–24.

Blalock H. M., *Statystyka dla socjologów* [Statistics for Sociologists], transl. M. Tablin and others, Warsaw 1977.

Boff L., *Die Neuentdeckung der Kirche*, Mainz 1980.

Carrier H., *Sociologie du Christianisme. Bibliographie Internationale*, Roma 1975.

Chałasiński J., *Młode pokolenie chłopów* [The Young Generation of Peasants], vol. 1–4, Warsaw 1958.

Ciupak E., "Kapłaństwo – powołanie i zawód" [Priesthood – Vocation and Profession], in idem, *Kult religijny i jego społeczne podłoże* [Religious Cult and its Social Foundation], Warsaw 1965, pp. 391–414.

Congar Y., *Die Lehre von Kirche*, Freiburg – Basel – Wien 1971.

Danielou J., "Der priesterliche Dienst bei den griechischen Kirchenvätern," in *Das apostolische Amt*, Mainz 1961.

Davie E., *Illicit Celibacy and the Deposit of Faith*, Nashville 2007.

Deschwanden L. von, "Die Rolle des Gemeindepriesters zwischen Kirche und Gesellschaft," in J. Wossner (ed.), *Religion in Umbruch*, Stuttgart 1972, pp. 374–412.

Deschwanden L. von, "Eine Rollenanalyse des katholischen Pfarreipriester," *Internationales Jahrbuch fur Religionssoziologie*, t. IV: *Beitrage zur religionssoziologischen Forschung*, Köln – Opladen 1968, pp. 125–135.

Dingemans L., "Przyczynek do socjologii powołań" [Contribution to the Sociology-of Vocations], in F. Houtart (ed.), *Socjologia religii* [Sociology of Religion], transl. Z. Skórzyńska, Warsaw 1962, pp. 145–165.

Dobrowolski K., "Przeobrażenia świadomości społecznej ludności chłopskiej w południowej Małopolsce po drugiej wojnie światowej" [The Transformation of Social Consciousnes in the Peasant Population in Southem Lesser Poland after World War II], in A. Sarapata (ed.), *Przemiany społeczne w Polsce Ludowej* [Social Transformations in the People's Republik of Poland], Warsaw 1965, pp. 426–437.

Dobrzanowski S., "Młodzież o kapłaństwie i kapłanach" [The Youth on Priesthood and Priests], *Chrześcijanin w Świecie*, 1977, no. 2 (50), pp. 95–110.

Durkheim E., *L'education morale*, Paris 1922.

Frankfort-Nachmias Ch., Nachmias D., *Metody badawcze w naukach społecznych* [Research Methods in Social Teaching], transl. E. Homowska, Poznan 2011.

Gardey B., "Le célibat sacerdotal met en question notre culture" [Priestly Celibacy Questions Our Culture], *La Vie Spirituelle*, 1968, no. 21, pp. 222–244.

Głowa P., "Kapłaństwo według myśli Soboru" [The Priesthood according to Conciliar Thinking], in *Kościół w świetle Soboru* [The Church in the Light of the Concil], Poznan 1968, pp. 186–204.

Goddijn W., "Rola kapłana w Kościele i w społeczeństwie," *Znak*, 1966, no. 139–140, pp. 6–21.

Gostkowski Z., *Podstawowe metody statystyczne w psychologii i pedagogice* [Principle Statistical Methods in Psychology and Pedagogy], Warsaw 1964.

Granat W., *Sakramenty święte. Cz. 1* [The Holy Sacraments. Part 1], Lublin 1961.

Greshake G., *Być kapłanem – teologia i duchowość urzędu kapłańskiego* [Being a Priest – the Theology and Spirituality of Priestly Office], transl. K. Wójtowicz, Wroclaw 1983.

Grotowska S., *Religijność subiektywna. Studium socjologiczne na podstawie wywiadów narracyjnych* [Subiective Religiousness. A Sociological Study Based on Narrative Interviews], Cracow 1999.

Grzesik A., *Między kryzysem a odrodzeniem moralności. Wartości moralne w świadomości studentów* [Between a Crisis and the Re-birth of Morality. Moral Values in the Awareness of Studensts], Rzeszow 2002.

Gy P. M., "La théologie des prières anciennes pour l'ordination des évêques et des prêtres," *Revue des Sciences Philosophiques et Theologiques*, 1974, no. 58, pp. 586–612.

Haarsma F., "Einige pastoraltheologische Thesen uber den Priester," in *Der Priester in einer sekularisierten Welt*, Maastricht 1968, pp. 85–112.

Hahn F., "Neutestamentliche Grundlagen für eine Lehre vom kirchlichen Amt," in *Dienst und Amt*, Regensburg 1973, pp. 32–47.

Heid P., *Celibat w Kościele pierwotnym. Początek obowiązku wstrzemięźliwości dla duchownych na Wschodzie i na Zachodzie* [Celibacy in the Original Church. The Beginning of Mandatory Abstinence for Ministers in the East and West], transl. S. Stańczyk, Tuchow 2000.

Hoffman H., *Repräsentation. Studium zur Wort Und Begriffsgeschichte von der Antike bis 19. Jahrhundert*, Berlin 1974

Holbock F., *Der eucharistlische Und mystische Leib Christi*, Rom 1961.

Holly R., "Badania nad przywództwem nieformalnym w małych grupach" [Studies on Non-Leaderships in Small Groups], *Przegląd Psychologiczny*, 1979, no. 3, pp. 457–478.

Holly R., "Funkcjonalne teorie przywództwa. Typologia przywództwa [Functioning Theories of Leadership], *Studia Socjologiczne*, 1981, no. 2, pp. 43–61.

Jonaczyk Z., "Socjologiczne badania powołań kapłańskich w Polsce" [Sociological Studies of Priestly Vocations in Poland], *Colloquium Salutis. Wrocławskie Studia Teologiczne*, 1976, vol. 8, pp. 207–222.

Katz D., "Badania terenowe" [Field Studies], in *Metody badań socjologicznych* [Metods of Sociological Research], Warsaw 1968.

Kasper W., "Sein und Sendung des Priesters, Geist und Leben," *Zeitschrift fur Askese und Mystik*, 1978, no. 51, pp. 184–214.

Kilmartin E. J., "Apostolic Office: Sacrament of Christ," *Theologii Studien*, 1975, no. 36, pp. 243–264.

Klaus G., Ebner H., *Podstawowe statystyki dla psychologów, socjologów i pedagogów* [Basics of Statistics for Psychologists, Sociologists and Pedagogues], Warsaw 1972.

Klosterman F., *Gemeinde ohne Priester?*, Mainz 1981.

Kłoskowska A., "Modele społeczne i kultura masowa" [Social Models and Mass Culture], *Przegląd Socjologiczny*, 1959, no. 2, pp. 49–56.

Kłoskowska A., Wzory i modele w socjologicznych badaniach rodziny" [Patterns and Models in Sociological Family Studies], *Studia Socjologiczne*, 1962, no. 2, pp. 35–48.

Kotarbiński T., *Sprawy sumienia* [Matters of Conscience], Warsaw 1956.

Kowalewski M., *Mały słownik teologiczny*, Poznan 1960.

Królikowska A., *Współczesna katolickość – w kierunku enklawy. Przypadek Polski* [Contemporary Catholicism – Towards an Enclave. The Polish Example], in L. Gołdyka, I. Machaj (ed.), *Enklawy życia społecznego. Kontynuacje* [Enclaves a Social Life. A Follw-up), Szczecin 2009, pp. 323–342.

Krucina J., "Przenikanie się powszechnego i lokalnego wymiaru Kościoła według społecznej zasady pomocniczości" [Penetrations of the Universal and Lokal Church According to the Social Dimension oft the Subsidiarity Principle], *Colloquium Salutis. Wrocławskie Studia Teologiczne*, 1972, vol. 4, pp. 38–56.

Kuczyńska A., *Wzory modne w życiu codziennym* [Popular Patterns in Daily Life], Warsaw 1983.

Kurpas J., "Charakterystyka dekretu [Characteristics oft he Decree] »De presbyterorum ministerio et Vita«," *Ateneum Kapłańskie*, 1966, no. 69, pp. 193–203.

Kurzępa J., "Zagrożona niewinność. Zakłócenia rozwoju seksualności współczesnej młodzieży" [Threatened Innocence. Disruption of the Development of Contemporary Youth Sexuality], Cracow 2007.

Küng H., *Wozu Priester?*, Zurich – Einsiedeln – Köln 1971.

Kwiatkowski M., "Zaufanie i nieufność w Kościele. Perspektywa socjologiczna" [Trust and Distrust in the Church. A Sociological Perspective], in J. Baniak (ed.), *Katolicyzm polski na przełomie wieków: teologiczny, instytucjonalny i wspólnotowy wymiar Kościoła* [Polish Catholicism at the Turn of the Century: Theology, Institutional and Community Aspects of the the Church], Poznan 2002, pp. 95–110.

Kwiatkowski S., "Stosunek do religii a orientacje polityczne Polaków" [The Attitude of Religion and the Political Orientation of Poles], *Edukacja Polityczna*, 1989, no. 10, pp. 314–326.

Kwiatkowski S., Kościerza-Jaworska E., "Polacy o religii i miejscu Kościoła w życiu kraju" [Poles in Religion and the Place Church in the Life of the Counrty], *Nowe Drogi*, 1989, no. 2, pp. 96–117.

Le Bras G., *L'Église et le village*, Paris 1976.

Legrande H., "La presidence de l'eucharistie selon la tradition ancienne," *Spiritus*, 1977, no. 69, pp. 409–431.

Lisowski G., "Praktyczne problemy związane z doborem próby do badań" [Practical Problems Related with Selecting a Research Test Group], in *Metody statystyczne w socjologii* [Statistical Methodes in Sociology], Warsaw 1986.

Lofhink G., "Paulinische Theologie in der Rezeption der Pastoralbriefe," in *Paulus in des neutestamentlichen Spatschriften*, Freiburg – Basel – Wien 1981.

Lubowicka G., *Sumienie jako poświadczenie. Idea podmiotowości w filozofii Paula Ricoeura* [Conscience as a Credential. The Idea of Subjectivity in the Philosophy of Paul Ricoeur], Wrocław 2000.

Majka J., "Socjologiczna analiza duszpasterskiej roli proboszcza" [A Sociological Analysis of the Role of the Parish Priest], in idem, *Socjologia parafii. Zarys zagadnienia* [Parish Sociology. An Outline oft he Topic], Lublin 1971, pp. 176–183.

Majka J., "Wpływ środowiska i przemian społecznych na kształtowanie się modelu kapłana duszpasterza" [Environmental Influence and Social Changes on the Model Priest-Minister], in idem, *Osobowość kapłańska* [The Priestly Personality], Wroclaw 1976, pp. 105–132.

Majka J. (ed.), *Osobowość kapłańska* [Priestly Personality], Wroclaw 1976.

Malinowski D. S., *Franciszka Mirka koncepcja socjologii humanistycznej* [Franciszek Mirek's Conception of Humanistic Sociology], Cracow 2005.

Mariański J., "Autorytet księdza – aspekty socjologiczne" [The Priest's Authority – Sociological Aspect], *Chrześcijanin w Świecie*, 1977, no. 50, pp. 74–94.

Mariański J., *Emigracja z Kościoła. Religijność młodzieży polskiej w warunkach zmian społecznych* [Emigration form the Church. The Religiousness of Poland's Youth in Conditions of Social Change], Lublin 2008.

Mariański J., *Etos pracy bezrobotnych. Raport z badań empirycznych* [The Ethos of Work by the Unemployed. Empirical Studies Raport], Lublin 1994.

Mariański J., "Konsens im Glauben am Beispiel Polen," in: *Ziwilisatorische Ursachen von Konflikten: Ergebnise d. 4, Polen – Asterreich. Soziologen Symposions 1980 in Lublin*, K. Zapotoczky (ed.), Linz 1986, pp. 235–248.

Mariański J., *Kościół katolicki w Polsce a życie społeczne. Studium socjologiczno-pastoralne* [The Catholic Church in Poland and the Social Life. A Sociological and Pastoral Study], Lublin 2005.

Mariański J., "Kościół ludowy w poszukiwaniu nowej tożsamości społecznej" [The Folk Church in Search of a New Social Identity], *Znak*, 1997, no. 1, pp. 42–57.

Mariański J., *Moralność w procesie przemian. Szkice socjologiczne* [Morality in the Process of Change. Sociological Sketches], Warsaw 1990.

Mariański J., "Motywy wiary w świetle badań socjologicznych" [Faith Motives in the Light of Sociological Research], *Collectanea Theologica*, 1975, vol. 3, pp. 137–150.

Mariański J., "Postawy młodzież wobec duchowieństwa parafialnego" [The Attitudes of Youth Towards Parish Clergy], in idem, *Emigracja z Kościoła. Religijność młodzieży polskiej w warunkach zmian społecznych* [Emigration form the Church. The Religiousness of Poland's Youth in Conditions of Social Change], Lublin 2008, pp. 430–447.

Mariański J., "Patologia kierownictwa parafialnego" [Pathologies in Directiong a Parish], in idem, *Żyć parafią* [Living with the Parish], Wroclaw 1984, pp. 185–223.

Mariański J., *Religijność społeczeństwa polskiego w perspektywie europejskiej. Próba syntezy socjologicznej* [Religiousness of Polish Society in the European Perspective. An Attempt a Sociological Synthesis], Cracow 2004.

Mariański J., *"Struktury grzechu" w ocenie społecznego nauczania Kościoła* ["The Structure of Sin" in the Evaluation of the Church's Social Teaching], Plock 1998.

Mariański J., "Zakres władzy przyznawanej osobom duchownym" [The Scope of Authority Granted to Religious], in idem, *Żyć parafią* [Living with the Parish], Wroclaw 1984, pp. 114–121.

Mariański J., *Żyć parafią* [Living with the Parish], Wroclaw 1984.

Marliangeas B.-D., *Clès pour une théologie du ministère*, Paris 1978.

Mayntz R., Holm K., Hubner P., *Wprowadzenie do metod socjologii empirycznej* [Introduction to Empirical Sociological Methods], transl. W. Lipnik, Warsaw 1985.

McKinney J. C., "Methodology, Procedures and Techniques in Sociology," in *Modern Sociological Theory in Continuity and Change*, New York 1975, pp. 176–193.

Midali M., "Crisi del sacerdozio e risporta dell Conzilio" [Christians on the Priesthood and the Voice of the Council], in *Il sacerdoti nelle spiriti del Vaticano II* [Priests in the Spirit of Vatican II], Torino 1968, pp. 307–345.

Miecznikowski S., "Praktyczne uwagi o wychowaniu w seminarium do celibatu" [Practical Remarks on Seminary Education to Celibacy], *Ateneum Kapłańskie*, 1967, no. 3–4, pp. 168–179.

Nowak S., *Metodologia badań socjologicznych* [Methodology of Sociological Research], Warsaw 1970.

Nowak S., *Metodologia badań społecznych* [Methodology of Social Research], Warsaw 1985.

Olejnik S., "Dlaczego Kościół podtrzymuje prawo celibatu kapłańskiego?" [Why Church Maintains the Right to Priestly Celibacy?], *Homo Dei*, 1973, no. 2, pp. 133–144.

Opinie Polaków o Kościele. Komunikat z badań OBOP [Poles' Opinions about the Church. OBOP Research Communique], July 2004, Warsaw.

Ossowska M., *Social Determinants of Moral Ideals*, London 1970.

Pacholski T., *Statystyka. Wykład zagadnień podstawowych* [Statistics. Contribution of Basic Issues], Warsaw 1978.

Pawlik W., *Grzech. Studium z socjologii moralności* [Sin. A Moral Sociology], Cracow 2007.

Pawlina K., *Kandydaci do kapłaństwa trzeciego tysiąclecia* [Candidates to the Priesrhood in the Third Millenium], Warsaw 2002.

Pin E., *La paroisse catholique. Les formes variables d'un système social*, Roma 1968.

Piwowarski W., "Księża w opinii parafian wiejskich" [Priests in the Opinion of Countryside Parishoners], *Homo Dei*, 1963, no. 2, pp. 97–121.

Piwowarski W., "Moralność jako sprawdzian żywotności religijnej katolików Południowej Warmii" [Morality a Test of the Religion Life of Catholices Southem Warmia], *Studia Warmińskie*, 1966, vol. 3, pp. 95–183.

Piwowarski W. (ed.), *Religijność ludowa – ciągłość i zmiana* [Folk Religiousness – Continuity and Change], Wroclaw 1983.

Piwowarski W., *Religijność miejska w rejonie uprzemysłowionym. Studium socjologiczne* [Urban Spirituality in an Industrialized Region. A Sociological Study], Warsaw 1977.

Piwowarski W., "Religijność miejska w warunkach uprzemysłowienia – na przykładzie Puław" [Urban Religiousness with Industrialization Conditions – the Situation in Puławy], *Studia Warmińskie*, 1973, vol. 10, pp. 426–443.

Piwowarski W., "Tradycyjny autorytet księdza w procesie przemian" [The Traditional Authority of the Priest in the Process of Transformation), in idem, *Religijność ludowa – ciągłość i zmiana* [Folk Religiousness – Continuity and Change], Wroclaw 1983.

Piwowarski W., "Więź z przywódcami religijnymi" [The Bond with Religious Learders], in idem, *Religijność wiejska w warunkach urbanizacji* [Rural Religiosity in the Conditions of Urbanization], Warsaw 1971, pp. 272–296.

Podleski Cz., "Model prezbitera diecezjalnego w opinii kleryków i księży" [The Model of the Diocesan Presbyter in the Opinion of Clerics and Priest], *Collectanea Theologica*, 1981, no. 51, pp. 132–154.

Pollack D., "Religios–kirchlicher Wandel im Mittel- und Osteuropa – ein Uberblick" [Religious-Church Changes in Central-Eastern Europe – an Overview], *Ost–West. Europäische Perspektiven*, 2000, no. 2.

Postawa A., *Powołania kapłańskie w Towarzystwie Salezjańskim w Polsce. Studium socjologicznopastoralne* [The Priestly Vocation in the Salesian Society in Poland. A Sociological-Pastoral Study], Cracow 2005.

Pottmeyer H.J., "Der Papst, Zeuge Jesu Christ in der Nachfolge Petri," in *In der Nachfolge Jesu Christi*, Wurzburg 1976.

Przybecki A., *Urzeczywistnianie się Kościoła w środowisku akademickim* [The Church Coming to Life in Academic Student Centers], Poznan 1986.

Przybylski B., "Wprowadzenie do dekretu »O posłudze i życiu kapłanów«" [Introduction to the Decree »Service in the Life of a Priest«"], in *Sobór Watykański II: Konstytucje, dekrety, deklaracje* [The Second Vatican Council: Constitutions, Decres, Declarations], Poznan 1969, pp. 474–286.

Przybyłowski J., *Znaczenie nowej ewangelizacji dla duszpasterstwa młodzieży. Studium pastoralne* [The Meaning of New Evangelization for Student Youth Ministry. A Pastoral Study], Lublin 2001.

Putnam R. D., *Demokracja w działaniu. Tradycje obywatelskie we współczesnych Włoszech* [Democracy in Action. Civic Traditions in Modern Italy], transl. J. Szacki, Warsaw 1995.

Pytkowski W., *Organizacja badań i ocena prac naukowych* [Organization ofd the Evaluation of Research and the Evaluation of Academic Work], Warsaw 1985.

Rahner K., *Knechte Christi*, Freiburg 1967.

Rahner K., "Theologische Reflexionen zum Priesterbild von heute und morgen," *Schriften zur Theology*, 1970, no. 9, pp. 375–387.

Rankin R. P., "Professionalization of the Calling: Functional Implication," *Social Compass*, 1963, no. 2, pp. 112–124.

Religion. Polish Survey. Codebook, Warsaw 1992,

Rewera M. R., *Autorytet księży w świadomości młodzieży licealnej. Studium socjologiczne* [The Authority of Priests in the Awareness of High School Youth. A Sociological Study], Lublin 2006 [Catholic University in Lublin (CUL) typed doctoral dissertation work manuscript].

Roguska B., *Stabilizacja opinii o wpływie Kościoła na życie kraju. Komunikat z badań CBOS* [Stabilization of Opinions aboutthe Church's Influence on the Life in the Country. Comminique from CBOS Research], BS/79/2004, Warsaw 2004.

Ryś G., *Celibat* [Celibacy], Cracow 2002.

Sadowski W., *Teoria podejmowania decyzji. Wstęp do badań operacyjnych* [The Theory of Decision-making. Introduction to Operational Research Studies], Warsaw 1964.

Sarapata A., "Zawód jako wyznacznik miejsca w społeczeństwie" [Profession as a Place Indicator in Society], in A. Sarapata, *Socjologia zawodów* [Sociology of Professions], Warsaw 1972, pp. 142–168.

Sarapata A., "Z badań nad prestiżem zawodów w Polsce" [From Studies on Profesional Prestige in Poland], in idem (ed.), *Przemiany struktury społecznej w Polsce i w ZSRR* [Change in the Social Strukture in Poland and in USSR], Warsaw 1965, pp. 126–134.

Schreuder O., "Le caractère Professionnel du sacerdoce," *Social Compass*, 1965, no. 1–2, pp. 5–15.

Sieg J., "Praca zawodowa jako wyraz wiary chrześcijanina obecnego w świecie" [Work Experience as an Expression of Christian Faith Present in the World], *Śląskie Studia Historyczno-Teologiczne*, 1973, vol. 6, pp. 33–41.

Słowiński G., "Ksiądz wczoraj i dziś. Społeczne konstruowanie powołania do kapłaństwa" [The Priest Yesterday and Today. Social Construction of the Vocation to Priesthood], in M. Libiszowska-Żółtkowska, S. Grotowska (ed.), *Religijność i duchowość – dawne i obecne formy* [Religiosity and Spirituality – Past and Present Forms], Cracow 2010, pp. 408–424.

Smarzyński H., "Problem zagrożenia moralnego współczesnej młodzieży" [The Problem of the Morald Hazard of Modern Youth], *Ruch Pedagogiczny*, 1974, no. 1, pp. 35–50.

Sowa K. Z., *Wstęp do socjologicznej teorii zrzeszeń* [Introduction to the Sociological Theory Associations], Warsaw 1988.

Spencer H., *Instytucje religijne* [Religious Institutions], Warsaw 1981.

Stachowski P., "Dylematy zaangażowania. Kościół katolicki wobec wyborów parlamentarnych i prezydenckich w Polsce: 1989–2001" [The Dilemma of Getting Involved. The Catholic Church towards Parlamentary and Presidental Elections in Poland: 1989–2001], *Przegląd Polityczny* 2003, no. 1, pp. 73–88.

Szewczuk W., *Sumienie. Studium psychologiczne* [The Conscience. A Psychological Study], Warsaw 1988.

Szlendak T., *Supermarketyzacja. Religia i obyczaje seksualne młodzieży w kulturze konsumpcyjnej* [Supermarketization. Religion and Sexual Mores of Young People in Consumer Culture], Wroclaw 2008.

Szostkiewicz P., *Procedury i techniki badań socjologicznych* [Procedures and Techniques in Sociological Research], Warsaw 1964.

Sztompka P., "Kulturowe imponderabilia szybkich zmian społecznych: zaufanie, lojalność, solidarność" [Cultural Imponderables of Rapid Social Change: Trust, Loyaly, Solidarity], in idem, *Imponderabilia wielkiej zmiany: mentalność, wartości i więzi społeczne czasów transformacji* [Imponderables of Great: Attitudes, Values and Social Bond's of Transformation Times], Warsaw 1999, pp. 95–110.

Sztumski J., *Wstęp do metod i technik badań społecznych* [Introduction to the Metods and Techniques of Sociological Research Studies], Katowice 1999.

Szulc P., *Metody statystyczne* [Statistical Methods], Warsaw 1968.

Świątkiewicz W., "Portret księdza" [Portrait of the Priest], in W. Zdaniewicz, S. H. Zaręba (ed.), *Kościół katolicki na początku trzeciego tysiąclecia w opinii Polaków* [The Catholic Church at the Beginning of the Third Millenium in the Opinion of Polish People], Warsaw 2004, pp. 107–120.

Taras P., "Problem modelu kapłana w Kościele katolickim" [The Problem with the Model Priest in the Catholic Church], *Znak*, 1968, no. 20, pp. 1120–1127.

Taras P., *Społeczne uwarunkowania i motywy wstąpienia do zakonnego seminarium duchownego* [Social Conditions and Motivations for Entering the Religious Order Seminary], Poznan – Warsaw 1972.

Tomczyk B., "Model kapłana w świetle dokumentów Soboru Watykańskiego II" [The Priest Model in the Light of the Documents of the Second Vaticans Council], *Studia Warmińskie*, 1975, vol. 12, pp. 304–324.

Tułowiecki D., "Kościół, parafia i duchowni w świadomości młodzieży ponadgimnazjalnej w małym mieście" [The Church, Parish and Clergy in the Consciousness of Secondary School Teenager in a Small Town], in J. Baniak (ed.), *Laikat i duchowieństwo w Kościele katolickim w Polsce. Problem dialogu i współistnienia* [The Laity and Clergy in the Catholic Church in Poland. The problem of dialogue and coexistence], Poznan 2010, pp. 349–368.

Wciórka B., *Kościół w III Rzczypospolitej. Komunikat z badań Centrum Badania Opinii Społecznej* [The Church in the III Republik of Poland. Communique from Studies of Center of Social Opinion (CBOS)], BS/79/1999, Warsaw 1999.

Wciórka B., "Opinie o roli Kościoła w Polskiej Rzeczypospolitej Ludowej" (PRL) [Opinions ebaut the Role of the Church in the People's Republik of Poland], *Zestaw Materiałów CBOS* [Set of CBOS Material's], Warsaw 1998, no. 3, p. 7.

Weber M., *Wirtschaft Und Gesellschaft. Grundgriß der verstehenden Soziologie*, ed. J. Winckelmann, Köln – Berlin 1964.

Witek S., *Duszpasterstwo w konfesjonale* [Pastoral Ministry in the Confessional], Poznan 1988.

Venetz H. J., *So fing es mit der Kirche an*, Zurich – Einsiedeln – Köln 1981.

Znaniecki F., *Chłop polski w Europie i Ameryce* [The Polish Peasant in Europe and America], vol. 1–5, Warsaw 1985.

Index of persons

[*] References to footnotes are in italics.